J. E Carlyle

South Africa and its Mission Fields

J. E Carlyle

South Africa and its Mission Fields

ISBN/EAN: 9783744757348

Printed in Europe, USA, Canada, Australia, Japan

Cover: Foto ©ninafisch / pixelio.de

More available books at **www.hansebooks.com**

SOUTH AFRICA

AND ITS

MISSION FIELDS.

BY THE

REV. J. E. CARLYLE,

LATE PRESBYTERIAN MINISTER AND CHAPLAIN, NATAL.

LONDON:
JAMES NISBET & CO., 21 BERNERS' STREET.
1878.

PREFACE.

IN this prefatory note I may explain the circumstances which led me to write this sketch of South Africa and its Mission Fields. At the meeting of the General Presbyterian Council, held in July last year at Edinburgh, there was a considerable gathering of members and associates specially interested in South African Mission work. The cause was represented by such men as Dr. Wangemann of the Berlin Mission; Dr Fabri, of the Rhenish Mission; M. Fisch, of the "Société des Missions Évangéliques;" Dr. Andrew Murray, of the Dutch Reformed Church of South Africa; Dr. Macgill, of the United Presbyterian Church; Dr. Murray Mitchell and James Stevenson, Esq., of the Free Church, with other South African brethren. There being so many men of high Christian position and influence thus present, it seemed a suitable occasion to hold a conference on the subject of combined action on the part of the Churches and Missions of South Africa represented in the Council. Mr. James Stevenson, well-known as a warm and liberal supporter of Missions—especially, I may add, of

Livingstonia, in Central Africa—took the initiative on the occasion, and the Committee of the General Council agreed to intimate that such a meeting of South African members would be held. These accordingly met. One of the resolutions submitted at their Meeting was " That a motion should be proposed in the Council, recognising the importance of combined action on the part of the Churches and Missions represented." The following motion was accordingly " submitted to the General Council by Mr. Stevenson, seconded by Dr. Murray Mitchell, and unanimously adopted " :—

" That as Southern and Central Africa are now wonderfully open to the preaching of the Gospel, and as it is eminently desirable that mutual understanding and co-operation be secured among the Churches labouring in that region, this Council earnestly hopes that the Churches represented in this Council will steadily aim at brotherly co-operation and combined action in all their Missionary operations."

I may add that in addition to the adhesion of those present, the other South African Societies not represented at this meeting, but belonging to the Council, have since heartily concurred in the proposal; and in several of the Annual Mission Reports it has been referred to with much satisfaction.

Another resolution passed at the meeting of South African Members and Associates, was the following :—" That statistical and other information should be collected—the members present proposing to send documents to the Rev. J. E. Carlyle, who agreed to receive and put such information into shape."

I, for my part, cordially accepted this honourable commission. I scarcely, however, anticipated that to collect such information would lead me into so large a field of inquiry. My ultimate conclusion on the subject was, that before the churches and the friends generally of South African Missions could be expected to take practical steps for extended co-operation and combined action, it would be well to have before them no mere statistical information, but some general survey of the whole progress of work in the South African Mission fields. I have thus attempted in the pages that follow to give to the reader some general idea of the life, action, and progress of South African Missions, and I have sought to dwell on the importance of the field thus occupied as a basis of Central African evangelisation. No one can be more conscious than I am how imperfectly this work has been accomplished.

In treating of the subject I may say I have allowed myself considerable latitude. I have not limited myself to Mission information, but have sought to glance, at least, over the wide field of educational, social, and other vitally important South African questions. For the opinions and judgments I express, and for the statistics I furnish, I am alone responsible. I have been indebted for them, to a very limited extent indeed, to any private communications; my chief information has been derived from published official statements. At the same time I trust that, while I am alone to blame for any deficiencies, which may be met with, it will still be found that what I have written is in harmony with the fine Christian tone of this General Presbyterian Council, which was not more marked by its adhesion to the early orthodox councils of the Church, and to the great principles of evangelical doctrine embodied in the Confessions of the Reformation, than by that catholic, brotherly, evangelistic spirit which may be said especially to mark the living Christianity of the Nineteenth Century.

J. E. CARLYLE.

London, 34 Eastbourne Terrace, Hyde Park,
5th October, 1878.

CONTENTS.

CHAP.		PAGE
I.	Introductory, ...	1
II.	Geographical Outline of South African Mission Fields, ...	8
III.	The South African Coasts and their Mission Fields, ...	14
IV.	Inner South Africa and its Mission Fields,	26
V.	The Native Races of South Africa, . . .	36
VI.	The Hottentots, ...	41
VII.	The Kaffir or Bantu Tribes, ...	46
VIII.	Outlines of Kaffir History, ...	58
IX.	The Zulus, ...	66
X.	British Colonial Government of Zulus in Natal,	72
XI.	Outlines of the South African Missions, . .	80
XII.	The Rhenish Mission, ...	87
XIII.	Missions of the Church of the United Brethren,	110
XIV.	The London Missionary Society, . . .	126
XV.	The Dutch Church of South Africa, . .	145
XVI.	Wesleyan Missions in South Africa, . .	152
XVII.	The Society for the Propagation of the Gospel,	161

CONTENTS.

CHAP.		PAGE
XVIII.	The Scottish Presbyterian Missions of South Africa,	180
XIX.	The French Missions in Basutoland,	198
XX.	The American Board of Missions in Natal,	226
XXI.	The Hermannsburg Mission,	237
XXII.	The Norwegian Mission,	249
XXIII.	The Berlin Mission,	260
XXIV.	The Roman Catholic Missions in South Africa,	288
XXV.	The Mission of the Free Church of the Canton de Vaud,	282
XXVI.	South African Evangelisation in Central Africa,	290
XXVII.	Statistical Résumé,	307
XXVIII.	Conclusion,	314

ERRATUM.

Page 179, sixth line from foot, *for* "50,000" *read* "20,000."

ERRATA.

In the unavoidable hurry of publishing this edition, some Errata have occurred :—

Page 32, line 6, for "appears" read "appear."
,, 37, ,, 3, for "Du Chailly" read "Du Chaillu."
,, 45, ,, 8, for "Kaffir origin" read "Hottentot origin."
,, 56, ,, 15, for "holocaust" read "hecatombs."
,, 69, ,, 20, for "Moselekatzes" read "Matabeles."
,, 95, ,, 14, for "is fitted" read "are fitted."
,, 110, ,, 13, for "Zugenbalg" read "Ziegenbalg."
,, 154, ,, 14, insert "it."
,, 162, ,, 3, for "50,000" read "55,000."
,, 164, ,, 1, for "those" read "that."
,, 164, ,, 19, for "probably more numerous" read "nearly as numerous."
,, 179, ,, 17, for "50,000" read "35,000."
,, 179, ,, 18, for "16,000" read "20,000."
,, 190, ,, 9, for "has" read "have."
,, 202, ,, 11, "The Basutos, I find, have occupied Basutoland for four generations."

SOUTH AFRICA AND ITS MISSION FIELDS.

CHAPTER I.

INTRODUCTORY.

It is some seventy years ago when, as the British flag was hoisted on the Dutch Fort of the Cape, Henry Martyn, the noble missionary, being present, offered up the following prayer: "I prayed that the capture of the Cape might be ordered to the advancement of Christ's kingdom, and that England, while she sent the thunder of her arms to the distant regions of the globe, might not remain proud and ungodly at home, but might show herself great indeed by sending forth the ministry of her Church to diffuse the Gospel of Peace." That prayer has been surely heard and answered. Great Britain and other lands have sent forth a long array of faithful missionaries of the Cross to South Africa, and the triumphs of the gospel have been widely extended from the wide deserts and Karroos of the West across to the more fertile regions of the East, from Cape Agulhas and the Antarctic Ocean on to the North, to the Zambesi and the Portuguese territories of the West. And even now the missionary march is advancing on still further to Central Africa. Already the Lake Nyassa is occupied, and the Lake Tanganyika will soon also have its mission pioneers. The triumphs of the Gospel in South Africa have been thus almost as extensive as in India: while the agencies have been far less richly equipped. The native races of the West which seemed utterly degraded, as the Namaquas, the Damaras, the Hereros, the Orlams, have been wonderfully elevated. A great work of Divine grace has been accomplished among the Bechuanas and Basutos of the Central Plateaux, while on the East an open door has been found among the Bantu tribes, the Kaffirs, the Zulus, and other races. Native flourishing Churches have been formed; a native ministry is being educated and trained, Christian education in all its departments, higher and lower, has been introduced, and important Christian industrial institutions have been established, the results of which have been the elevation and civilisation of thousands of the native population. It is not very long ago since South African missions were regarded by some with despondency. A worthy writer on missions in his excellent Mission History* observes, "To no part of the world, with the exception of India, have mission societies directed so much attention as to South Africa. It would be natural to conclude from this that South Africa formed one of the finest fields for missions in the world; and yet we scarcely know a single recommendation which it possesses. The population is at once small,

* The Rev. Dr. W. Brown.

scattered, uncivilised, often wandering, poor, desolate, degraded." In the Providence of God, the choice of South Africa has been, since this was written, wonderfully vindicated. Under a Higher Hand and Builder, the foundation has been laid in silence of a great and glorious work of the future. The discoveries and Mission enterprise of Livingstone and others have shown that there is an open door from South Africa to the Central Tribes. We may venture to say of South Africa that it is the key of the position by which the vast populations of Central Africa are in all likelihood to be won to the Cross. I quote here the testimony of a distinguished German missionary, given nearly at the expiry of seventy years from the visit of Henry Martyn, and looking widely over the field at the positions gained by Christianity in South Africa. "We see in South Africa," he says, "the citadel from which a great part of the Continent will yet be converted to Christianity. Egypt, destined to high importance through its Nile channels, is in the hands of the Mahommedans. Only a stolid Islamism can propagate from this. Algiers is in the hands of Europeans, to whom it has cost in gold and men what can scarcely be reckoned; and yet it is separated from the interior by the Sahara, and on this account can win little influence. On the east and west coasts of the Continent, where attempts have been made to establish European Colonies these undertakings have to contend with the most unhealthy and deadly climates. In South Africa, the relations are entirely different."*

* Merensky's Beiträge, &c.

There is here one of the most salubrious climates in the world where colonisation may yet extend almost as widely as in the United States. And we may add that colonisation has not been in South Africa, as elsewhere, unfavourable to the existence and growth of the native races. On the contrary, it has rather tended to the extension of the native population, as indeed is seen in a very wonderful degree in Natal.* Besides, the South African Colonies have, by their organisation and fixed laws, consolidated, we believe to a considerable extent, the work of missions. I may refer, as an instance of this, to the admirable success of the French Basuto mission, since Basutoland has been accepted under British protection. Even the ruder government of the Boers in the Transvaal, in the judgment of the Rev. Mr. Merensky, a most competent judge, has contributed to the stability of Mission work. And then in South Africa, we have also happily new native churches, not only possessed of evangelical life, but marked by evangelistic zeal, ready to press onward.† It is an interesting fact to which our study of South African Missions has led us, that there is scarcely one which is not eager to move onward toward the North to Central Africa. Among the Bechuana tribes we believe there is still a usage handed down by venerable tradition, that the dead should be buried looking to the north-east, the land probably

---

* By natural increase and by an immense tide of black immigration, the Zulu population of Natal in the last half century has probably grown from 20,000 to nearly half a million.

† The Hon. Cecil Ashley in an important letter to Sir Bartle Frere refers to this. See *African Blue Book*.

of their fathers; and South African living Christianity, looking not to the past but to the future, has its noblest hopes and aspirations directed to those vast and gloomy regions, now the abodes of horrid cruelty, but one day to be flooded with Christian light and love.

South Africa has been of late years by no means overlooked in our British Literature; Travels, Journals of Residence, Reviews, the Press, the Blue Book, even the learned historian and the brilliant novelist, have made their contributions for our information. The scenery of South Africa, its colonial life, its wild sports, its various tribes, its rich diamond fields, its frontier wars, our British policy, our annexations, our treatment of the Aborigines, have all excited and continue to excite deep interest. Far less, however, is known regarding our South African mission fields, where we have no hesitation in saying, the noblest work has been achieved by long continued, laborious, and in some instances what may be called heroic, efforts. It is these Christian Missions which are the sheet-anchor of all stable peace and rest in South Africa, and which afford the highest guarantee to the Christian philanthropist that the native races will not be crushed and exterminated, by our advancing civilisation, but so assimilated and elevated as yet to form loyal subjects, strengthening the power of the Empire, and as Christian communities affording a bright hope as to the civilisation and christianisation of Africa.

We adopt in this sketch a somewhat extended idea of South Africa and its Mission fields. We regard them as embracing all those vast regions—some great wildernesses or Karroos; some lofty mountains, some regions rich in fertility, and in mineral resources; some, immense extended elevated plateaux stretching from the South to the Zambesi, and East and West from the Atlantic to the Indian Ocean. My reasons for embracing so wide a range, are these—The Missions of South Africa have gone on so widely enlarging as to embrace nearly all these regions—some at the very North. The London Missionary Society, for instance, occupies Inyati, a station far beyond the Colonies among the warlike Matabeles. The French Evangelistic Basuto Mission has also reached this point, and proposes to labour among the Banyai, if Lobengula, the Matabele king, will allow them. The trade and commerce of South Africa are rapidly stretching northwards, the ox-waggon of the traders, the Boer treker, the hunter of the wild, the gold-digger, the traveller and discoverer are all making, with every year that passes we may say, the path more familiar and frequented that lead to the Zambesi. And then the recent annexation of the Transvaal by the British Government points in the same direction. Sir Theophilus Shepstone, its experienced and sagacious administrator, is acquainted with the character of the Kaffir or Bantu tribes as perhaps few others. He has long had diplomatic relations, not only with Zululand and its savage chief, Cetywayo, but with those barbarous yet powerful tribes lying to the north of our recent annexation, as for instance, Umzila's kingdom. There can be little doubt that British power will speedily thus become predominant to the Zambesi on the East. On the West, again, thanks to a large extent to the noble work achieved by the Rhenish Mission, negotiations have been lately conducted by Mr. Palgrave with the Hereros, Namaquas, and Orlams, securing to us the rich copper mines of the West, the suzerainty of the native tribes, and a territory which may be said to reach from Table Bay to Cuanene the Portuguese frontier. An experienced German traveller, Mohr, has observed, " In my opinion, the whole of South Africa from the Zambesi to the Cape, will one day belong to the same great power which already possesses such important parts of it." The Zambesi is thus likely at no distant day to be the boundary of British territory, and thus, we may trust that all South Africa may yet obtain quiet and rest for all its scattered tribes, and Missions, and Colonies beneath the broad shield of British protection.

CHAPTER II.

GEOGRAPHICAL OUTLINE OF THE SOUTH AFRICAN MISSION FIELDS.

As our wish is to bring as vividly as we can before our readers the state and progress of the many missions scattered over South Africa, we think it may help this if we take as it were a bird's-eye view of the wide field, indicating, as we pass on in our geographical sketch, the various scenes of mission labour. In point of fact it will be found that the physical features of South Africa are not only associated with the character and condition of its native tribes, and with its colonial development, but also with the distribution of its missions. Some of these have indeed their stations widely scattered over South Africa, but nearly all of them, we may say, have their special centre of influence and power where they occupy the most prominent position in mission work. It is so with the Moravian Brethren, the London Missionary Society, the Wesleyans and Presbyterians, and with the Rhenish, Berlin, Hermansburg, and Norwegian missions. Perhaps the Society for the Propagation of the Gospel, while as widely extended as any, can scarcely be said to have any such marked centre of operation, unless it be in the West Cape Colony.

The most marked geographical feature of South Africa is perhaps, on the one hand, the vast and lofty plateau of the centre, and, on the other hand, its coast lines, which, while varied in aspect, are in most parts rapidly descending. It has been compared in this with some general accuracy to an inverted saucer. South Africa has in this aspect some analogy to India, only it is on a larger scale. When you arrive, for instance, at Bombay, you have the low-lying coast of the Concan near you, but beyond, at no great distance, there is the Deccan, a vast elevated plateau some 1500 or 2000 feet in height. In South Africa you have the same division. The coasts are either low-lying, or hilly as in parts of the Cape Colony and Kaffraria, or with gentle slopes, as in Natal, but beyond, generally at no great distance from the Indian Ocean on the east and the Atlantic on the west, you observe, not isolated peaks nor limited ranges, but vast mountain chains, which are also the mighty ramparts of that immense plateau of the interior, ranging in height from 3000 to 6000 feet, and averaging perhaps from 4000 to 5000 feet. We may say that this geographical feature determines very much the material conditions of South Africa. As, for instance, it gives a special character to its river systems. In general, the rivers of South Africa flow on in no gentle course, but rush, as mountain torrents, impetuously to the sea; the beds of many in the west in the season of drought quite dried up. Hence, to develop the resources of South Africa, a well-planned and extensive system of irrigation is perhaps more needed, and would probably be more profitable, than even in India. We may add here, as regards this physical conformation of South Africa, that the slope of the great elevated plateau is generally from east to west. The rivers in South Africa that flow eastwards are generally short and rapid in their course. Almost the only exception is the Limpopo, a river in the south running nearly parallel to the Zambesi, and forming the northern boundary of the Transvaal and of colonial South Africa. The great rivers of South Africa, the Orange and the Vaal, rise on the western slopes of these great eastern highlands. We may extend this geographical feature as belonging to Africa generally. Its great highlands lie near its east coasts, although there are lofty mountain ranges sweeping on round the west, up even to the Gulf of Guinea. The result is that beyond the Limpopo the only other great river of Africa that flows eastward is the Zambesi. The Nile and the Congo or Livingstone River flow differently, the one toward the north, the other pouring its mighty waters westwards. In this aspect Africa may be said to resemble South America, only that the Andes lie on the west, while these ranges extend along the eastern side of the continent. These eastern highlands of Africa may be said to stretch so far north as to Gebel Attaka, which the traveller on his way to India may remember opposite Suez. He will recall those red and lofty cliffs which looked down in all likelihood on Moses and Aaron and Egypt's embattled hosts. Further south these mountain ramparts more than rival in height, if not in grandeur, the Alps. Still further south in equa-

torial Africa there are Mounts Kilia and Kilimandj-
aro, the latter still more lofty, nearly 20,000 feet
in height. Beyond again there is the Livingstone
range, a mountain wall bounding Lake Nyassa on
the eastern side, rising to a height of 12,000 to
14,000 feet, and extending at a lower elevation to
Lake Tanganyika on the east and the Zambesi on
the south. Then at Tete you have these heights
broken through by the Zambesi, but on the southern
side still stretching onward. The knowledge of the
extent of these great eastern highlands we owe to
Grant and Speke and Cameron and Stanley, but in
largest measure to Dr. Livingstone. They have
opened up to us a view of Africa almost as wonderful as the discovery of America by Columbus. The
existence of these highlands is interesting as regards
South Africa, for it was in all probability by this
mountain-wall the bushmen, the Hottentots, and the
Kaffirs emigrated to the south, and by which we may
trust they shall again return bearing to Central Africa
the blessings of civilisation and Christianity. As
regards the future too, they open up to South African colonial enterprise a magnificent field, if not for
colonies, which cannot well be planted in tropical
countries, yet for colonial plantations, such as we are
now developing in India, only these may be
here on a more extensive scale. May we not hope
also that colonial planters and Christian natives
from the south established in these higher and
more salubrious grounds may yet be in most
favourable circumstances for aiding in the suppression of slavery and the extension of Chris-

tianity to the far west along the shores of the mighty Congo.

There is only one other observation we would make here, from the intimate relation which climate has had in the distribution of the South African races. The prevailing winds of South Africa are from the south-east. This naturally arises from the vast currents of cold moist vapour absorbed from the Antarctic and Indian Oceans rushing in towards the heated centre of the African continent. The result is that the east coasts of South Africa are well watered. But when these watery clouds reach the eastern slopes of the mountains much of their moisture is deposited. Then in passing over the great inner plateau the ascending heat gives to the clouds a greater capacity for retaining moisture, and thus they sweep on until they reach the Atlantic. The winds as they pass thus to the west are ever drier, as in the Orange State and Bechuanaland, until the climate of the Great Kalihari Desert is among the driest regions in the world.* It is true there are also on the Atlantic side northwestern breezes, but these scarcely reach beyond the coast. A north-westerly wind is in most of the interior of Africa and in the east almost as trying and enfeebling as the sirocco in Italy. The result of this difference of climates has been, as we have said, most important. The more vigorous Kaffir races have gradually driven out the inferior tribes of the Hotten-

---

* The value of this climate as regards asthmatic and pulmonary complaints is now generally recognised. Dr. Livingstone was the first, we believe, to bring it under public attention, but medical opinion has since strongly confirmed the opinion.

tots and Bushmen from all the more fertile and well-watered regions of the east. But for the Dutch and English colonists they would in all likelihood now have occupied also the southern coasts. The Hottentots have thus been gradually forced to the west, and the last home and fatherland of the poor Bushman is now the great sterile Kalihari Desert.

CHAPTER III.

THE SOUTH AFRICAN COASTS AND THEIR MISSION FIELDS.

ADOPTING the general division of coast and interior which we have noticed, we begin with a sketch of the South African coasts with their Mission Fields. Thanks to steam navigation, that lengthy circumnavigation of Africa in ancient times described by Herodotus, if it be not indeed a fable, can now be accomplished in some eighty or ninety days. Availing ourselves of this modern means of communication, let us glance around the coasts of South Africa, beginning on the east side at the Zambesi. This coast is at first, as we proceed downwards, low, swampy, and insalubrious, plagued with the tzetze fly and dangerous for fevers. The outer rim of the coast is held by the Portuguese, but a little farther inland is the kingdom of Umzila, a chief himself of Zulu origin, while the tribes over which he rules are of different Kaffir races. He may be said also to exercise suzerain rights over the Portuguese in some parts of their territory, as they are said to pay tribute to the Landeens who are subject to him. There are as yet no Christian Missions established here, but we doubt not that they will soon be formed, as both the American and Berlin and Swiss missionaries have their eyes turned in this direction. This coast has a deep religious interest, for here is Sofala, which recent discoveries warrant us in believing was the ancient Ophir of Solomon. Great ruins were found here recently by Mauch, the distinguished German traveller at Zimbabye which are certainly not of native origin, nor do they seem Arabic. Mr. Merensky, the able superintendent of the Berlin Mission, has attempted with much ingenuity and learning to establish that here is the ancient Ophir. My limits do not permit me to enter into the question, but I think the reasoning conclusive.* The argument is strengthened by the fact that gold was found by the Portuguese to a considerable extent in these districts, and that gold regions have been, and are being widely discovered of late in this part of Africa, as for instance, in the Transvaal, and also in Matabele land.

But we pass now southward to the estuary of the Limpopo and to Delagoa, a noble harbour, but with a dangerous climate. Here we bid farewell with no little satisfaction, as we advance onwards, to the last of those Portuguese settlements which have in the past done such dishonour to the Christian name, and rivetted so strongly the fetters of the slave. We have now reached Zululand, the home once of Chaka, the great South African conqueror of half a century ago. The country is still inhabited by the Zulus, the bravest, perhaps, of all the Kaffir tribes. Cetywayo, the lineal successor of Chaka, now rules there, whose attitude causes so

* See his "Beiträge zur Kenntniss sud. Afrikas Das Ophir Salomos," &c.

deep disquietude to our South African colonists and statesmen. Here we begin to find Mission fields, as of the Society for the Propagation of the Gospel, the Hermannsburg and the Norwegian Missions; but dark clouds at present gather over these. There have been Christian martyrdoms, and their relations with Cetywayo are daily more trying, and are becoming quite untenable. But we shall have subsequent occasion to refer to this more at large. Leaving Zululand again, you skirt the beautiful coasts of Natal with its quiet slopes, and its rich sugar cultivation, passing on your way Durban, its commercial capital, with its picturesque surroundings. Ascending in a series of terraces not unlike the ancient Cyrene, the voyager who lands here would reach, at the distance of about a hundred miles, the lofty precipitous Drachenberg range, rising the highest of all the South African mountains, a part of the great wall that bounds the vast interior plateau. In Natal there is already, although it is little more than forty years old, an important British Colony. There are many missions vigorously at work as the Americans on the coast, the Wesleyans, the Berlin and Hermannsburg Missions, the Society for the Propagation of the Gospel, the Free Church, with the Gordon Mission instituted by the Aberdeen family and entrusted to its care. Still skirting the coast to the South you now reach Kaffirland, the home of those rude yet warlike tribes, who have cost Britain so much both in men and money. Its wild lofty coasts may recall at times to the voyager the western Highlands of Scotland. Its many rapid rivers, as the Umzimvubo, the Umtata, the Umbashee, the Kei, have all their origin at no very great distance in the Drachenberg range. Here was but recently the home of Kreli, the paramount chief of the Kaffir clans, although his own tribe was neither the most numerous nor powerful. Here, too, scattered among these tribes are many excellent missions, as the Wesleyan, Bishop Callaway of the Propagation Society,* the Free and United Presbyterian Churches. Further away in the distance on the slopes of the Drachenberg, the Moravian brethren who have done so much for the christianisation of South Africa, have recently established a Mission. And now moving onward to the south, we have reached the eastern frontier of the great Cape Colony, stretching broadly across from the Indian to the Atlantic Ocean. We pass New London, with its sea roads more hazardous as yet to the voyager who would land there, than even those of Madras; and the Cape Province, which was recently called British Kaffraria. We have here also a large Kaffir population, such as the Gaikas for instance, who have recently given us so much trouble. The country is a rich and advancing one, and when its port has been improved and its railway system completed, with the interior and with the Orange Free State, it is certain to have a great future before it. The scenery of its river courses, of the Amatolas, and of other of its mountain ranges, is very fine, and will certainly attract to it in time the enterprising tourist. Here the United Presbyterian and the

* Society for the Propagation of the Gospel. For abbreviation's sake we shall write it thus—or S.P.G.

B

Free Churches have their principal stations in South Africa. Lovedale belongs to the latter, well known as the most successful Industrial and Educational Mission Institute in South Africa. The Wesleyans have also an excellent Mission College at Healdtown, and the S.P.G. at Grahamstown. The London Missionary Society, the S.P.G. and the Wesleyans, have many stations. Sailing still onward to the South, we pass Port Alfred and reach Algoa Bay, where the anchorage is by no means very safe, as it is exposed to the prevailing south-eastern gales, yet we find many ships, and often quite a fleet of magnificent steamers. Port Elizabeth situated there is the commercial metropolis of South Africa, and the great centre of British enterprise. Seen from the bay, Port Elizabeth has no very imposing appearance, but when you land, there are many marks of wealth and commercial energy. In the eastern districts of the Cape Colony there are various valuable Missions established, but it may, we think, be justly said, that both as regards Colonial Christianity and Mission work here, the Wesleyans occupy the first place. It is little more than half a century since British colonisation moved in this direction ; it has now taken firm root, almost outrivalling the progress of the Dutch Boers in more than two centuries. The Wesleyans were early in the field, and thanks under God to their able and sagacious Missionaries, such as their Shaws and Shepstones, and many more, a great work of evangelisation has been accomplished of which they are now gathering the rich fruits.

And now having passed Cape Recife at the

extremity of Algoa Bay, our course lies westward, for we have reached the great Antarctic Ocean, with its sweeping currents, its boisterous gales, and its tumultuous billows. We shall not attempt at any length to describe the Southern coasts of Africa. They are bold and striking with the great Agulhas bank with its Cape and lofty lighthouse, projecting broadly out, the most southerly point of Africa. The mountain ranges are not unlike those of Morocco and Algiers in North Africa, rising to the height of 3,000 or 4,000 feet, alternating with valleys and plains; and at one point the Knysna there are magnificent primeval forests where the elephant still roams. There are many towns and hamlets scattered over these coasts, extensive corn fields, rich vineyards, and sheep and cattle pastures. The distance from the Southern Coast to that great inner rampart we have described walling in its lofty plateau, is more considerable than on the East and West Coasts, extending to some 200 miles. Beyond the more southerly coast range of hills and mountains there follows another some 40 or 50 miles distant, higher still, averaging some 5,000 feet. And passing these again there are those great Karroos which form so striking a feature of South Africa, and occupy more than half of its surface. These in the dry season seem sterile as the desert, and are intolerably hot, notwithstanding their elevation above the sea; but during the rains they become a vast garden of gorgeous flowers, yielding most fragrant odours, and rich in succulent herbage for sheep and cattle. Their value to the Cape Colony is appreciated ever more highly, and here lies probably much of its future wealth. With irrigation, which, as we have noticed, is one of the greatest wants of South Africa, the seeming desert would speedily rejoice and blossom as the rose. We have only thus sketched the outlines of the South. Besides these we should add picturesque detached mountains, and groups of hill often of the tabular form, sometimes with fantastic peaks serrated and conical.

It is in this southern part that the Hottentot element first comes into prominence and that bushmen may be found, if but rarely. Driven by the Kaffirs from the richer pastures of the East, the Hottentot gradually settled in the South and West, from which indeed, at least from the South, the Kaffirs would, in all likelihood, long since have expelled them, but for the arrival of the Dutch, and later of the English. It may be questioned, indeed, if the former would have been able to resist Kaffir aggression. In this southern part of South Africa we may add that the Boer begins to occupy an influential place, and the Dutch Church holds colonially the first position as to numbers. The Boer in the Cape is not, after all, a bad Colonist. He is industrious, he has a considerable sense of the value of religion, and rarely neglects his Church, or even family worship. His worst side is his treatment of the natives. The Dutch Church, we may say, is higher than the Boer. It aspires to educate him, and not without success. Its ministry is earnest, and its leaders are able evangelical men.

We may add that it is on these southern coasts and partly also on the west, that we find still the great centre of South African missions represented by such societies as the London, the S. P. G., the Wesleyan, the Rhenish, the Berlin, and the South African Dutch Missions. But all of these will, we think, concede a first place here to those venerable Moravian missions founded so much earlier than any others, and the happy fruits of whose labours did so much to animate and inspire in the beginning of this century all the evangelical churches of Christendom. We may add here that Genadenthal, one of the earliest Moravian mission stations, is still the largest in South Africa.

Having passed Cape Agulhas, you now turn to the north-west. You pass Capetown with its noble bay and its picturesque Table Mountain. The latter does not form a part of those mountain ranges we have described as bounding the centre. Rather standing out on its peninsula, it is as it were a giant sentinel of the land. It is in this like Gibraltar, only on a grander scale. It seems somewhat strange that the name of so great a region as South Africa should be derived from this small extremity on the south-west.* At the same time the Cape Colony and its Table Mountain must always have their prominence as among the most striking features of South Africa. Table Mountain, flanked on the south by

* A well-informed writer in the *Cologne Gazette* observes of South Africa, in the large sense we have described as extending to Cuanene, the western Portuguese boundary, and the Zambesi on the east. "The circumference thus embraced is somewhat like that of Germany, Austria, and France united, or we might add to fill up the included space Holland, Belgium, Switzerland, and Denmark."

the remarkable Lion's Head and on the other side by the picturesque Devil's Peak, bears a certain resemblance to Arthur's Seat overhanging Edinburgh with its reposing lion and Salisbury Crags, only the proportions are grander. We must fancy Ben Lomond or Ben Nevis overhanging Edinburgh. Sometimes the mountain is overspread with what is called its table-cloth, the wind during the south-easterly gales rising charged with vapours from the ocean in masses of white fleecy clouds, covering the summit with a dense veil, while at times the vapour rolls down the side of the mountain like a mighty cataract, " a Niagara of vapour ;" or again, in the wondrously cloudless and bright nights of South Africa nothing can be more striking than to see the full moon as it pours its beams downwards on that massive mountain wall with its sharp-angled bastions in its grim lion-like repose, stern rocks around it and beyond, the breakers of the mighty Southern Ocean. The Cape was the first we may say in South Africa to receive the gospel. Its first governor, Van Riebeck, seems to have carried with him his Dutch religious faith. For a time the colony had but a catechist, only after some years an ordained minister arrived. Then later came the Huguenot refugees enriching South Africa as they did all Protestant Europe with their industry and skill, and blessing it with their piety. They introduced the culture of the vine into South Africa. The rich vineyards of Constantia are memorials of their enterprise. The districts allotted to them are still among the most rich and beautiful in the colony, and their blood still runs in the veins of the majority, we believe, of the Dutch gospel ministry.*

When we pass the Cape northwards we have still for a time districts belonging to the old Cape Settlements, and in many parts well cultivated. We pass Saldanha Bay, the securest harbour in South Africa, where the fleets of the world might ride, but wanting sadly a supply of fresh water. Gradually, we reach more sterile regions, the scenery is dull and uninteresting, as a rule there is a broad belt of sand towards the sea; beyond this is long scrubby bush swelling into hills, and in the distant background there are mountains rugged yet picturesque, forming, as regards Great Bushmansland, the margin of a vast plateau some 3000 feet in height. As the winter north-westerly rains do not extend further inland than some 100 miles, it is a land often of drought and barrenness. Its pastoral tribes are necessarily often migratory, passing from one place to another in search of water springs. Over the whole scene there hangs during the day the sultry haze caused by an almost tropical sun, but the nights are beautiful and clear, as only South Africa or Arabia has them. The dry climate is not unhealthy too, as, for instance, the moister heat of India in the Sunderbunds of Bengal. While the coast is thus unattractive, it possesses at the same time much mineral wealth; its copper mines are probably the richest in the world. These employ already considerable labour, and are promoting the

---

* It would be no uninteresting chapter of history the record of their arrivals, their difficulties, and their success. Some missionary of the French Basuto Mission might contribute this.

civilisation of the country. The voyager on the west now crosses outside the bar of the great Orange River, the course of which from the east is estimated at some 1200 miles, and which drains some 400,000 square miles. Yet, strange to say, while higher up a magnificent stream, as is also the Vaal, its tributary, its mouth is blocked up with hopeless sandbanks. Navigation is thus an impossibility. The country here is, on both sides of the river, "singularly dismal, savage and barren." Further north the coast is still as unattractive, or, rather we may say, Great Namaqualand is still more destitute of rain. It is a cheerless land with rugged peaks and sandy hills. The only relieving point is Walvisch Bay, some 400 miles further north. This is a position of value, from its secure anchorage, and its ready approach from the Cape. It is probably, also, the safest and easiest way by a short sea voyage, in place of a tedious land journey to reach the Zambesi and Central Africa. Beyond the bay again, some 100 or 120 miles in the interior, there are lofty table lands, such as the Herero and Damara country, rising to the height of some 6000 feet. "The barren and rugged range loses itself to the north, in the high and fertile plains of Ovampoland, growing large crops of maize and Kaffir corn, while on the east they sink into the elevated plateau of the Kalihari desert."*

On these western shores, we find the ruder tribes of South Africa, the Namaquas, the wild Bushmen, in some parts, the Damaras, the Orlams, and the

*We quote here from Silver's South Africa, a valuable compendium. Mr. Trollope has expressed his obligations to it.

Hereros, the last are the only tribes akin to the Kaffir race. Various Missions have been engaged in this field, as the Wesleyan, the London Missionary Society, and the S.P.G., but the first place is undoubtedly to be assigned to the Rhenish Mission. It alone now occupies Namaqua and Damaraland. It is much to its honour that it has so long devoted itself with so great energy, and so disinterested Christian beneficence, to the elevation of these inferior races. For a time the success of its efforts seemed doubtful often, among these wandering Nomads, but it is now reaping a rich harvest from its Mission toils, and its efforts have nobly paved the way along these sterile shores, for the progress of civilisation, colonisation and Christianity. But when we come to write of this Mission, we shall refer to this more at large.*

* "The Rhenish Church, whose admirable Institutions have contributed much to the civilisation and improvement of the native races." This is the testimony of the late Mr. Noble, a highly competent witness on the subject.

CHAPTER IV.

THE INNER SOUTH AFRICAN MISSION FIELDS.

WE pass here from the outer coasts of South Africa to the inner mission fields. A mere rapid outline will here, we think, suffice. We have noticed that this elevated inner region stretches widely across from east to west. When we cross, for instance, the Zambesi, we find the same girdle of mountains, the same eastern highlands, as further north. We discover them in the lofty ranges of the Mashona and Matoppo lands, in the Hooge Veldt of the Transvaal; and in the Drachenberg Mountains further south; there is the same giant range also in the Stormberg of the Cape Colony some 8000 feet high. Then the mountains trend westwards in the Sneeuwbergen, the Neeuwgveld, and the Roggeveld mountains. The last bends to the north-west. You pass the Great Kamiesberg and the Koperbergen, and across the Orange River similar ranges stretch on far beyond the confines of Southern Africa.

We look here first to the great northern zone beyond our colonial occupations, stretching from the Limpopo to the Zambesi. Here, on the eastern spurs of these inner mountain ranges, we have Umzila's Kraal, but, as we have already noticed, in his domains as yet there are no Christian missions.

Further west are the wide regions of the Matabeles, where Lobengula is suzerain, with the subject Mashonas, Makalakas, and Banyai. Those who have read Dr. Moffat's interesting mission travels will recall Moselikatze, the father of Lobengula, the savage yet intrepid and sagacious chief who obtained for his tribe half a century ago this wide rule, and over whom Dr. Moffat gained so great and happy an influence. Not, indeed, that he ever became a sincere Christian, as Africanor did, but that to the last he cherished for Christianity and its missions deep respect. It is to this we owe the interesting mission establishment at Inyati, the capital and centre of the Matabele power. This has been lately strengthened. The French Basuto Mission has also missionaries there now, but whose object is more the Banyai or subject tribe. Mashonaland is a fine country. Travellers say that it is as salubrious as the Transvaal, and it too has its gold. Were these countries colonised and christianised, as doubtless they soon will be, what a noble basis they would form for mission work in Central Africa. No Portuguese intrigues could hinder their advance. Now, this country, still but scantily occupied, is the great hunting-ground of South Africa. If Africa is not so rich botanically, we may say, as other lands, save perhaps in ferns, it is remarkable zoologically. It is crowded with giant mammalia, as the journals of the traveller and missionary will tell. The elephant, the rhinoceros, the giraffe, the hippopotamus, the lion, the wild African buffalo,* here have their

* Herr Merensky, in his interesting "Beiträge," has attempted, with much ingenuity and success, to show that the unicorn of the

homes, and in no part of the world are found so many varieties of the antelope, as the eland, the koodoo, the gemsbok, the springbok, and so many more. In an hour the traveller has reckoned that some 50,000 of these latter game must have passed, scouring the plains and rushing on to escape their deadly enemy the lion.

If we pass again westwards from these tribes, we reach the lake Ngami, and the northern confines of the vast desert of Kalihari extending in area some 200,000 square miles. These belong to the western plateau, and the lake Ngami is itself reckoned some 3700 feet above the sea. It is a region of red sand, and covered with a dense low bush. It has no running streams, but the Bushmen can discover here and there water. When the scanty rains descend it has, like the Karroos, its rich prairies, with herds of antelopes, ostriches, and giraffes, where the Bushman, the cunning hunter of the wild, finds a home and sustenance. Then again, when the arid season comes, there is the lone, desolate, waterless, uninhabited waste. We are interested to notice that the London Missionary Society proposes to occupy now this district of the Lake Ngami. Its discovery is owing to Livingstone and Oswell in 1849. The chief Moremi has cordially invited them, and another pioneer station to the north has been thus established.

Bible may be the South African buffalo. The bos caffir, exterminated in the east, its last refuge, has its home here. The fearful rage, the swiftness, strength, and formidable horns of the South African buffalo make him dangerous as the lion : the natives say indeed more so. The horns at their base so grow into one that one may speak of them as one horn with two points.

Passing from this northern zone of the inner mission fields to the south, you have, on the eastern side, the Transvaal, a magnificent hill country some 5000 to 7000 feet high above the level of the sea, well watered and the best wooded in South Africa, of which it is often described as the garden. It is a picturesque country with its Hooge Veldt, an extension northwards of the great Drachenberg range, and farther west the Magaliesberg, where there is some of the most beautiful and picturesque scenery in South Africa. The Transvaal is a fine grazing country for cattle, and in the future will be probably, as a wheat-growing country, one of the great granaries of the world. In its northern parts it is also admirably fitted for the growth of many semi-tropical products, such as cotton, coffee, sugar, and tobacco ; it is rich also in minerals, such as copper, silver, nickel, iron, and gold. There is one region, the Magnet Hoogte, so marked by its magnetic attraction—the magnetic sand so clinging to the wheels of the waggon as to impede the progress of the traveller. Here we find various missions, as the South African Dutch Church, the S.P.G., the Swiss of the Canton de Vaud, the Hermannsburg, but the society which from its extent and success comes chiefly into prominence is the admirable Berlin Mission—it too has had its martyrs, the story of whom is not so well known as it merits. One of its stations, Botshabelo with its 1300 adherents, and its many admirable Institutions may be named beside Lovedale or Genadenthal in the Cape Colony. To the west again in this zone of the great plateau we have most interesting Mission fields. We are in

Bechuanaland with its various tribes, akin in origin to the Kaffir or Bantu tribes—the classic scene we may almost call it of the labours of Moffat, Campbell, Livingstone, and so many more. Bechuanaland is a pastoral and salubrious, though arid country, which cannot be compared in wealth with the Transvaal. The London Missionary Society has achieved a noble work here for the present, and the issues of which in the future are likely even to be greater as regards the evangelisation and christianisation of Central Africa. Livingstone has heroically pioneered the way for this. Without undervaluing other missions in South Africa, we venture to say that by its various Christian enterprise the London Missionary Society has, in South Africa, won the golden medal.

And now we pass to the most southerly zone of this great inner plateau. We have on the north here, the Vaal, a noble river rising in the Eastern Highlands of the Transvaal, recalling, in the rainy season as it flows onward, to the German Missionary the Rhine at Cologne, pouring its stream at last beyond the Diamond Fields into the Orange River. On the south again there is the great Orange River discharging its mighty flood with the Vaal into the Atlantic, rising in the Eastern Drachenberg range; and beyond it in the south there is the great mountain wall of the Cape Colony. The eastern boundary of this region is again the Drachenberg Mountains. The view from these is striking and romantic. On the east side lies spread before the eye Natal, "a vast succession of hill and valley, table topped mountains, gleaming river, all green with grass, dew freshened, and silent."* On the western side again lies Basutoland with its innumerable table mountains, "a sight filled with a sense of freshness and pleasure." Basutoland may be called, from its picturesqueness, the Switzerland of South Africa. Its striking ranges have recalled to the Swiss missionary the noble panorama of the Righi. Here lies the country of Moshesh, the able and sagacious Basuto chief, who once worsted the British forces, even under a Sir George Cathcart; but who had the good policy to humble himself for his victory, and to be ever afterwards received as the good ally of the British. The fortunate result of this for him and his tribe was, that afterwards, when hard pressed by the Boers of the Orange State, he was received under the British Protectorate. His people are now with the Fingoes, perhaps the most prosperous, advanced and civilised, of all the South African tribes. These beautiful and romantic valleys are the interesting scene of the laborious and most successful French Missionaries, of the "Missions evangeliques de Paris."

Going further West than Basutoland you have the still elevated plateau of the Orange or Free State, now the alone remaining Dutch or Boer Republic. It was in 1854 that this colony was thrown off by the British Colonial government, an act of unwise policy, which was even then condemned by the ablest Colonial politicians and by the Missionaries; and which must now be deeply regretted as adverse to that federation of South

* We quote from a pleasing sketch of South Africa in "Good Words" by Major Butler.

Africa which is so much needed. The "Orange State," one traveller writes, "is a desert"—"It is richer than any part of Australia" writes another. "The flats of the Free State are characteristic features of the country. Wide stretches of grass land appears to be without bound, but the distant horizon. Occasionally there are undulations, and in some parts conical hills, the sides of which are covered with large and rounded stones. Very little wood or bush appears anywhere, except along the winding river lines. Great herds of deer graze upon the unfenced lands, and are at certain parts of the year to be seen close to every road."* Here there are again various missions at work: the Wesleyan, as at Thaba Nchu, where it has won a noble success. The Station is one of the most extensive and important in South Africa. Then there is Bishop Webb whose high ritualism and somewhat hostile relations to other missions as the French Basuto, has gained for him in South Africa a certain notoriety. The Dutch Cape Church and the Roman Catholics have also their Missions here.

If we travel westwards again we have, not far from the confluence of the Vaal and Orange rivers, the well-known diamond fields, where the diluvial torrent seems to have swept down the siliceous crags of the Drachenberg Mountains with their wonderfully rich deposits. The region is uninviting, yet healthy. The ten millions sterling worth of jewels discovered in its soil has told much on the colonial progress and prosperity of South Africa; and we

* Silver's South Africa, page 449.

doubt not also in the end on the extension of South African Missions. Kimberley, its capital, and the centre of its wealth, is situated in an angle formed by the Orange and Vaal Rivers, about 80 miles from their junction. "It is in the midst of a great plain, a plain so vast that its hills and undulations, its trap eruptions, Ropies and salt pans are all merged by distance into a uniform scene of level. Here is seen an immense assemblage of huts and houses, tents and flagstaffs. High above roof or flag-pole a huge irregular mound of earth rises from the centre of the city in the plain; and as the traveller approaches it he sees that it is built around the base of this great mound of twelve acres in artificial extent." "Around the edge of the pit rise, tier over tier, three rows of wooden platforms, from which wheels, and pulleys, and iron ropes run downward into the yawning pit below, in some parts 200 feet deep. Thick as black men can swarm on these platforms, stand nearly naked men working wheel and pulley, bucket and rope. Such a scene must the great tower by the Babylonian stream have presented, but assuredly nowhere else could the eye have taken in at a single glance such a vast accumulation of labour."* The diamond fields, we have no hesitation in saying, even in opposition to such an authority as M. Froude, belonged by right to the Griquas. The Boers may have had claims on certain farms which the British Government has lately, with considerable magnanimity, conceded; but their whole method of purchase from the natives

* Major Butler, Good Words, 1876.

was too frequently one that that cannot be in justice defended. It is an interesting fact we may notice here that the Western Griquas of the Diamond Field District and the Eastern of what was lately called Nomansland on the confines of Natal, owe their existence and their progress very much to the labours of the London Missionary Society, especially of its intrepid and venerable representative, Dr. Moffat. Waterboer, its able Christian chief, was at one time a teacher in one of the Mission Schools, and it was, we believe, the influence of Dr. Moffat which placed him at the head of a tribe which he ruled wisely and well. The Cape Colony found in him a firm and useful ally, and it would scarcely have been consistent with British honour to have left the Griquas at the mercy of the Boers. When the independence of the Orange State was recognised, this was entirely an act of British generosity, as the battle of Boomplats in 1848 placed them entirely at the mercy of the British forces. Express stipulations were made regarding the Griquas by the Colonial Government which justified their intervention as to the Diamond Fields.

We have nearly exhausted the Southern zone. Further west than Griqualand there is the Great Bushmanland with its wide Karroos, where there are comparatively few Missions. The Roman Catholics seem anxious to establish themselves here so as to penetrate Namaqualand, but their success has yet been limited. Further to the South than the Orange River, and between it and the mountain ramparts of the Cape, there are now many Colonists and flourishing Cape Colonies. The northern slopes here form a cold and yet healthy region, where winter is felt as in few other parts of South Africa. The railway from New London to which we have already referred, will greatly develop the agricultural resources of those districts. They are occupied by an energetic Colonial population, mainly Anglo-Saxon, and there are various Mission Stations, becoming so strong and consolidated that they will soon be in large measure self supporting.

CHAPTER V.

THE NATIVE RACES OF SOUTH AFRICA—
THE BUSHMEN.

WE have given thus some outline of South Africa and the extent of its Mission Fields. We have felt this to be the more necessary, as, while individual Missions may have excited interest, few are aware of the great breadth of Mission work that has been accomplished. Following up the general idea of this work which is to open up the relations of South Africa generally to the Gospel, we would study a little the native races to whom the Missions are addressed, scattered over these wide regions of Kloof and Karroos, of mountains, plains and howling wildernesses.

We begin with the Bushmen, probably the oldest race of immigrants who reached South Africa. While the history of the Bushmen has not the same political significance for the Colonies, as that of the Kaffirs, or even the Hottentots, it has also its special interests. Their language, for instance, is remarkable with its extraordinary clicks, quite unlike those of the Hottentots in many instances. It is a study which even German philology has not yet mastered. They are also curious as one of the smallest races in the world—the men averaging, some 4½ feet—the women 4 feet. Strange to say, Barth and Schweinforth found similar races widely separated in the North, and Du Chailly, also on the West Coast.* May we not conjecture also that the dwarf races with their poisoned arrows, described by Mr. Stanley in his descent of the Livingstone may be the same people.† Besides these remarkable peculiarities the Bushman's manner of life is also extraordinary. They cultivate no fields at all, digging only with their rude stone hammers roots out of the ground; they have no homes but clefts in the rock or holes burrowed in the ground. The Missionary has found them far up in the wild gorges of the Drachenberg, from 7,000 to 8,000 feet high, where the cold was intense —where they had no dwelling, only a few mats to shelter them from the piercing wind.‡ The bushmen have no cattle also. Some have fancied that they were poor Hottentot tribes who had been robbed of their cattle, but there is strong evidence that they never as a race led a pastoral life. Then they have no tribal organisation as with the Kaffir or the Arab. Their food, apart from roots, is chiefly the game of the wild. They are wonder-

* These races are the Doko on the East side of the Southern Nile—the Aka, east of the African inner Lakes and the Obongo on the West.

† Mr. Mackenzie in his "Ten Years North of the Orange River," writes indeed of a tribe of Bushmen between Sochong and the Zambesi remarkable for their tall and stalwart appearance. He says their features, their language, their mode of life all betoken them to be Bushmen, " yet a finer race than some of them I have not seen in South Africa." This is certainly an ethnological puzzle.

‡ Some of these Bushmen we have heard of as received in their old age by the Moravian brethren, into sheltered huts, but pining there for the want of the fresh air of the open heavens.

fully skilled in shooting and destroying game and wild animals with their poisoned arrows prepared from the sting of cobras and other venomous serpents, mixed with vegetable poisons. They are so cunning in entrapping, that clothing themselves in the feather of the ostrich and imitating its movements, they will approach these wily birds until they can pierce them with their arrows. Job's description of the Heronites who were Troglodytes, probably a kindred people, apply to them.* " Behold as wild asses in the desert go they forth to their work; rising betimes for a prey; the wilderness yieldeth food for them and their children." " They are wet with the showers of the mountains, and embrace the rocks for want of a shelter." "They were driven from among men, they cried after them as after a thief; to dwell in the cliffs of the valleys, in caves of the earth, and in the rocks." † Nothing can more strikingly describe the vagabond life of the Bushmen than these words, " they cried after them." As savages living often by theft and plunder, the other native tribes and the Boers declared deadly war against them. The latter indeed dealt with them as with the lions of the bush, and other wild beasts of the desert and sought to extirpate them. Vindicating his action in Old Testament phraseology the Boer was wont to speak of them as the Canaanites to be extirpated by them, the Israel of God, or they made them like the Gibeonites hewers of wood and drawers of water. One Boer,

* I am indebted for this idea to Merensky's Beiträge.
† Job xxiv. 5, xxiv. 8; xxx. 5, 6.

for instance, on the Northern Boundary of the Cape Colony, boasted that in six years he had caught or killed 3,200 Bushmen. Another that in the struggles in which he had taken part some 2,700 Bushmen had lost their lives.* The consequence has been that scattered and peeled, their numbers have greatly diminished in the Cape Colony. They are still indeed to be found in some of the clefts of the Drachenberg where once they were powerful, and there are scattered families of them in other eastern ranges, but it is only rarely. The wild Kalihari desert is now the last home of their liberty. They are skilful there to discover its rare springs of water, and then to conceal them. If pursued, the enemy in that wilderness is often baffled. He can discover no spring of water, and is obliged thus to retire.

These Bosjemens, children of the bush to whom the Boer gave this name as if they were like the wild orang-outangs, inferior creatures of the East with which the Dutch were familiar, have yet one remarkable gift. They possess undoubtedly some conceptive and imaginative faculty. Giotto, the famous early Italian painter was found by Cimabue when a shepherd lad scratching rude pictures on a slate, and yet this gift was developed by culture into lofty genius, and these Bushmen too possess the power of delineation, and we might add of music. Their rude, yet graphic pictures are marked by some artistic skill. They have graven them in the rock for ages indelible in a way scarcely known even to modern art. These sketches in

* Merensky's Beiträge, page 70.

their brown deep colouring, depict buffaloes, elephants, antelopes, and the various animals of the wild, with men, women, and children, human usages and warrior life. Similar pictures, indeed, telling of kindred races and gifts are found also in North Africa, amongst the rocks of the Sahara. They are surely a token that the gifts of genius may be found among the rudest tribes of earth, for are they not all the children of the Great Father?

The Bushmen and the Hottentots seem still to retain among them something of the Sabæan worship of the stars which we do not find among the Kaffirs. They have some faint idea too of a Supreme Deity who "made all things, to whom they are to pray." Mr. Merensky says of them that, "in their wild state they have rarely, if ever, yielded to Missionary influence, but when they have been obliged to adopt settled habits of life they have often shown excellent qualities. They have been found more honest and trustworthy than other native races, and they have taken in a higher life and become excellent Christians." They have been deeply and powerfully moved by Christian truths and have given much joy to the Missionary. The Bushmen have occupied but a limited place in Mission work. They are so difficult in their savage state to reach and their native tongue has been so little mastered. Probably the Rhenish Mission has done more than any other, to teach, educate, and christianise them.

CHAPTER VI.

THE NATIVE RACES OF SOUTH AFRICA—
THE HOTTENTOTS.

THE Hottentot race is quite distinct from the Bushmen. Their tongue is different, it has some clicks indeed as with the Bushmen, but the language is based on different principles, and is of a higher grammatical structure. The Hottentot differs physically from the Bushman. He is not a dwarf, on the contrary his average height is from five to six feet. He is well built generally with strong bones, small hands and feet, and arms and legs in proportion. He is of a healthy race—a number exceeding eighty years and ranging on beyond the 100 to 120. This he probably owes to the dry salubrious climate he inhabits. But there is no race of which it is so difficult to judge in South Africa as the Cape Hottentots, or Khoi Khoin, in consequence of their intermixture with the colonists and their changed habits of life. Their very complexion, if older descriptions of them be correct, has altered from a dark brown to a clear yellow.* One leading characteristic of the Hottentot is that he is not, like the

* For much interesting information regarding the Hottentots I must again refer to Merensky's Beiträge.

Bushman, a mere hunter of the wild. Nor is he, like the Kaffir, an agriculturist. He grows no Indian corn nor millet nor other vegetables, save exceptionally, but is a veritable Nomad, a herdsman, his cattle his chief treasure.

The Hottentot race seem to have emigrated from East North Africa. Their language, colour, and type point to this. Strabo's account of tribes in the Red Sea, their nomadic life and their usages seems to indicate a similar race. Herodotus speaks of these northern tribes as using a language like none other, and his description seems to indicate clicks. A later writer on ethnology, says, but without giving any definite authority, "Slaves with a language like the Hottentots are to be found in the Cairo Market." The Hottentots seem to have emigrated earlier into South Africa than the Kaffirs, later than the Bushmen. There are traces of them on the East Coast and their traditions seem to establish that they must have been once at Sofala and its gold regions. On the West tribes akin to them seem to have been discovered in the higher latitudes.* It may be added as some proof that they were earlier colonists than the Kaffirs, that the Kaffir tongue, which in its whole genius is so different, has appropriated some of the Hottentot clicks at least as regards its older tribes. This can be easily explained, for a people penetrating a new country, as the Normans, for instance, among the Saxons of England readily associates with and appropriates some of the peculiarities of the people it has annexed.

* Up to 12 deg. and 13 deg. Southern latitude.

The Hottentots were gradually driven by the Kaffirs from the East, they lost their rule in the South in consequence of the Dutch Colonists, their last centre of power has been in Namaqualand in the East.

The character of the Hottentot differs from the Bushman and the Kaffir. He has not the Bushman's rare gift of delineation, nor the Kaffir's breadth of intelligence, shrewdness, and perseverance; yet he has considerable capacity, as, for instance, in acquiring languages. Religiously, as we have said, they retained some elements of the old Sabæan worship ; but with their colonial intercourse, these religious usages seem gradually to have passed in large measure away.

The Hottentot is of a sanguine, emotional nature, he sighs, and weeps, and prays, but his religious impressions are apt to disappear as readily as they came. A venerable missionary among the Namaquas has said of them, " They are like the streams of their land, often full to overflowing, and then only the dry, sandy bed." But the grace of God can nobly fashion the savage nature, as in the case of Africanor, and so many more." The missionary has won from the Hottentots noble trophies of true, loving, and abiding Christianity. The Moravian Missions have been thus signally honoured and many more besides. There has been not only the rapid growth of sincere piety, but its deep roots, "Those that be planted in the house of the Lord shall flourish in the courts of our God."

The history of the Hottentots under Colonial rule has been a sad one. They were cruelly oppressed by the Boers, robbed often of their cattle, deprived of their land, and reduced to the conditions of serfs and villeins. Under the British rule they have fared better; still, even under it, they were long unjustly treated. The children of a Hottentot born on the land of a colonist were subject to apprenticeship till their twenty-fifth year, and then the older, from a rigid, vagrant law, were greatly hampered in their liberties. For this, no doubt, the Dutch rule was more responsible than the British, as it was with them the system originated, still we long tolerated it. It was the Mission stations which in these times of their oppression, afforded the Hottentots, especially, their shelter. The Moravian Missions set in this, a noble example, and the London Missionary Society and others followed them in this work of compassion and beneficence; but it was, after all, only a few, the Christian Missions could thus shelter; the many still remained oppressed. It is to the special honour of the London Missionary Society, and of its intrepid agent, Dr. Philip, that this grievance was, mainly by their instrumentality, brought to the knowledge of the British public, and that, after a long agitation, the wrongs of the Hottentots were redressed in 1828, so that they now enjoy all the security and freedom which British rule can afford.

As regards numbers the Hottentots are not a decreasing race, as natives under British and American rule are said to be; probably their numbers in the Cape Colony may reach 100,000. Dr. Wangemann, of the Berlin Mission, calculates them, as in all, amounting to some 350,000. The fact that they are so many, and that they have a future before them, may well inspire philanthropic and missionary zeal in their behalf. We may add, on good authority,* that a third of them are Christianised. We believe that later statistics warrant us in assuming the proportion as higher. The Christian cause is also making noble progress among the Namaquas, and Orlams of Namaqualand, who are of Kaffir origin. The superficial tourist who visits South Africa, or the egoistical, half-educated colonist with little Christian principle or feeling, may sneer at the Christianity of the Hottentot, but those who have carefully visited their Christian villages, their schools, their churches, and their homes, and seen the quiet order which prevails, will own that Christianity has not only saved the race from utter ruin and destruction, but has truly elevated it.

* Merensky's Beiträge.

CHAPTER VII.

THE KAFFIR OR BANTU TRIBES.

A MORE careful study of these races and their history is needed than of the Hottentots or the Bushmen. The future of South Africa must in large measure depend upon their civilisation and Christianisation.

These tribes are by far the predominating race in South Africa. If we take the River Limpopo, the northern frontier of the Transvaal, as the boundary, they are probably as six to one to the Hottentots and Bushmen unitedly, and they stand in nearly the same ratio to the colonists. If we include, again, the Kaffir tribes farther north up to the Zambesi, they may be reckoned, perhaps, in round numbers at three millions. But the same race stretches also widely east and west in Central Africa, and they have been reckoned as numbering some eighteen millions. According to other calculations, the whole of these Bantu tribes, allied in language, usages, and origin, may form fully one-fourth of the inhabitants of Africa.* If this estimate be correct it would raise their numbers to forty or fifty millions. But I shall not attempt so wide a survey;

* Africa, Keith Johnston, p. 530.

my limit will be South Africa; only the fact deserves to be noted from its bearing on the future civilisation and Christianisation of Central Africa.

I can glance only at some leading facts connected with these tribes, such as their distribution, origin, tribal characteristics, history, and probable future. The present sad crisis in South Africa may well suggest that some careful study of the Kaffir tribes is due, on the part of the British politician and the Christian philanthropist. It is, indeed, one of the greatest problems, we may say, that has ever arisen in our British colonial rule, how to put an end to these barbarous, sanguinary raids, so ruinous to life and property in South Africa, and how to educate and to elevate the Kaffir, so that he may be fitted to enjoy ultimately all the benefits of self-government. The Boers, indeed, cut the Gordian knot by enslaving or exterminating the aborigines; but this is a solution which England will not adopt, first, because it is opposed to that humane policy which has been nowhere more conspicuous than in our past relations with South Africa, and also because the Kaffir is not so readily to be extinguished. On the contrary, the black population is growing. In Natal there has been, indeed, an astonishing increase, far exceeding that of the European colonists, not only by natural growth, but by an immense black immigration into its territories. What are we to do with this growing population of semi-savage tribes? It is a question most hard to answer. Let me illustrate its difficulty. In the old Roman empire, which, in many features, had its analogies to our own, there was the Colonia and the Provincia, the former occupied by Roman citizens under Roman law, the latter governed by native law under Roman rule. We have the same thing in the British empire—the Colonia, as in Canada, Australia, or New Zealand; the Provincia, again, in India. But South Africa is not as in India, where the native population is governed, if wisely and justly, yet absolutely, by a superior race; South Africa is, on the other hand, colonial in its institutions, while yet the vast majority of its population is very far below the Indian standard of culture and civilisation. And yet the very idea of a colony must rest on the assimilation in culture of its races, without which there cannot be self-government. It may be said this problem is being solved in the United States as regards its southern negro population, but with what advantages? First, an overwhelming American civilised population, and then a black people, Christian, and trained in civilised usages. In South Africa, on the other hand, we have to do with races degraded, barbarous, polygamists, with the power of Christianity as yet imperfectly developed. Mr. Trollope, in his recent work on South Africa, has very well seized this point and illustrated how arduous must be its solution.

We would now glance at some leading facts relating to these tribes. There is their origin. All their traditions point to the north-east—Egypt or the sources of the Nile—as the cradle of their race. It is thus, for instance, as we have already noticed, that the Bechuanas still bury their dead with their faces turned in this direction. Mr. Merensky observes:—"The houses of the natives in Abyssinia are almost exactly the same as those of the Bechuanas or Basutos in South Africa. When we saw pictures of Magdala and other villages of the Abyssinians during the English campaign in that country, we had quite as correct pictures of the villages of our Basutos." I may add that the same applies to many of the photographs Mr. Stanley gives of East Africa in the "Dark Continent." Mr. Merensky further observes: "Many of the usages of the Kaffir tribes point to Egypt or its influence. In the same way it has struck us that the brown people, which are found painted on the walls as in battle with the Egyptians, or as prisoners, bear throughout the stamp of the Kaffir tribes. Weapons, the form of the shields of ox-skin, the clothing, the type of race are surprisingly like those of South Africa." The Kaffirs seem gradually to have emigrated to South Africa rather than to have approached it as conquerors. The Amatongas, or Knob-nosed Kaffirs, have probably occupied the low-lying country between the Zambezi and the Limpopo since three centuries ago; other races, as the Matabeles, followed them. The Amaxosas of Kaffraria, tribes which have come into greater prominence during our Cape colonial rule, probably reached the Kei, where there has been so much recent fighting, about 1670. The Bechuanas, among whom Moffat and Livingstone had their mission work, were probably among the last arrivals. It has been supposed by some that the Kaffirs are of Shemitic origin, and there are certain of their usages which seem remarkably to favour the idea: as, for instance, circumcision, the law of marriage

D

and the widow, the distinction of clean and unclean animals; and one of their tribes towards the north, the Makalakas, seems still to hold sacred a seventh day. The structure of the Kaffir language does not, however, support this idea, which is now abandoned. It is probable, at the same time, that in their southern wanderings there may have been added a considerable mixture of Shemitic blood, as Arab rule long prevailed on the east coasts of Africa; and this may in part account for these usages. It is a question of greater difficulty how far the Kaffirs are a Hamitic race. Much mystery still hangs around that great people whose history begins for us at the time of Babel, and culminates in the early splendour of Egyptian civilisation. It was they, too, whose races aided so powerfully the great Shemitic invasions of Europe by Hannibal, and in the middle ages by the Moors. There is every likelihood that the affinity is close of the Kaffir to the Copt and the Berber of North Africa, the ancient Numidian, and to those warlike tribes represented, for instance, still by the Turcos in the French army.

Passing from the origin to the distribution of the Kaffirs in South Africa, to enumerate all these tribes would be beyond our limits, and would scarcely interest our readers. Those who care for the study will find a very complete classification of them in the pages of Dr. Fritsch, an eminent German anatomist and anthropologist.‡ For the practical purposes of this paper, the following enumeration may

‡ The races of South Africa is the subject of his work; I forget the exact title. It is published in German.

be enough. There are the Amaxosa tribes of Kaffirland, the Galekas, Tambookees, Slambies, with the Gaikas. Kreli, with whom we have been at war, and with whom originated the present struggle, is the paramount chief of these tribes. There are also the Fingoes, Pondos, and Griquas in the same region. If we go farther north, and pass Natal, we have the warlike Zulus, of Zululand, with Cetywayo, their chief, whose present attitude to our colonial governments gives cause for just alarm. Farther inland, again, on the south, beyond that great range of the Drachenberg, separating Natal from the lofty plateau of the interior, there are the Basutos, of Basutoland. These are located near the sources of the great Orange river. Farther north than these, on the other side of the Vaal, we have in the Transvaal, kindred Basuto tribes, of which Sekukuni, lately at war with the Boers and now with England, may be regarded as the leading chief and representative. If we go still farther west, again, than these, we have on the confines of the Transvaal the Bechuana tribes, whose territories stretch on to the great Kalihari desert. And still west of these, on the other side of the continent, we have the Hereros. If we advance still farther north, beyond the South African colonies and the River Limpopo, but to the south of the Zambezi, we have the Matabeles, Makalakas, Banyai, and the tribes on the east occupying Umzila's kingdom.

And now to notice some of the Kaffir characteristics. Their language, for instance, may deserve a moment's notice. It is of a high character, melodious and soft; its grammar is marked by its regularity, with comparatively few exceptions. The forms of the verb are so varied that its paradigma would almost fill a book. It is a language nearer to the Shemitic than the Indo-Germanic, but it has still marked features of its own. "The development and beauty of the Kaffir languages," says Merensky, "which surprise every one who has really insight into them, have been to many a ground for supposing that these people must have originally stood on a higher platform of culture. We hold this for a false conclusion, for when the mental and intellectual culture of a people declines, its language declines all the more that it does not possess written records, and on this account the language, as it lives in its tongue, is always the exact expression of its mental and intellectual force. As, then, the development and beauty of the Kaffir tongue is not to be ignored, we believe that we are justified in the conclusion that the mental powers of the Kaffirs are greater than we are usually inclined to admit."

Another characteristic of the Kaffirs is that they are physically of a higher formation than the other South African races. We agree, indeed, with Dr. Fritsch, who has described with great care these tribes physically, that there has been exaggeration in some accounts of them, as if they were Herculeses in strength or Apollos in symmetry. This is quite an exaggeration. The European is generally their superior, both in muscular power and in proportion. Still the Kaffir is a well-built and muscular man, with good features, and were he civilised he might be more nearly on a level with the Europeans.

His mental capacities, as we have noticed his language implies, are considerable. He has undoubted sagacity in counsel and ready eloquence in the Pitso, or tribal assembly, where war and tribal questions are settled. He differs also from the other South African races industrially. He is not like the Bushman, a mere hunter of the wild, and a child of the rock or the desert, without a home, without cattle, without knowledge of agriculture, living on roots which he digs out of the ground with his rude stone hammer. Nor is he like the Hottentot, a mere herdsman of cattle. On the contrary, the Kaffir cultivates the soil and he understands so well the growing of Indian corn and millet, and other vegetables, that he has little to learn from the European. It is somewhat curious the division of labour among the Kaffirs. The man is the hunter, and also the herdsman, he tends the cattle and milks the cows, the women not being admitted usually into the cowstall. The woman, on the other hand, with her rude hoe, aided by her children, digs the soil and plants and reaps its fruit. She not only thus, indeed, grows the corn and the vegetables used, but she prepares the food for her husband, and makes the Kaffir beer. The life of woman among the Kaffirs is thus a great drudgery, and she is reduced almost to the rank of a slave. The Kaffir is a polygamist, more so, we may say, than even the Mohammedan, both because he can marry more wives, and especially because he can gain more profit by them. The more wives he can obtain the more land he can cultivate and the more wealthy he can thus become. The wives are purchased by cattle, a degrading usage, which has been a real obstacle in mission progress. Such a life as that of the Kaffir woman sadly crushes and terribly degrades her. The daughter of Africa is, we may almost say, the lost sheep of her sex, far from the fold and the shepherd, and from all that love and gentleness that should encompass her.

There is another difference betwixt the Kaffir and other South African races. They are far more of a people than the Bushmen or the Hottentots. Their organisation is tribal; their condition is not unlike that of our Scottish clans two centuries ago. All rally round their chieftain, who allots the lands of the tribe, decides with his counsellors judicial cases, and is, besides, supposed to possess supernatural powers. Dr. Wangemann, superintendent of the Berlin Mission, justly says on this subject. "The Hottentot has no feeling for nationality; even with the 350,000 of his people they are in no respect a race; while if but a few hundred Kaffirs live together they feel as Kaffirs. The Hottentot, too, is of a slavish mind, who sees in the white man his master; the Kaffir, on the other hand, looks on the European as an encroacher, whom he fears and hates, whose yoke he would willingly fling to the winds, to whom he can never resolve to submit himself slavishly as his master." We think the latter statement, although true to a certain extent, yet somewhat exaggerated. The Kaffir will certainly never be a slave; hence his hatred of the Boer. His tribal organisation will serve, too, as a rallying-point; so that, if oppressed, he will again and again revolt. But the language is inaccurate as regards the feelings of the Kaffirs towards British rule. It is just as regards, perhaps, many of their brutal chiefs, but not of the tribes generally, who have learned to appreciate the rectitude and mildness of our rule. Even as regards the heads of the tribes, we have Moshesh, the great Basuto chief, placing himself under British protection. Perhaps a still more decided proof of this native feeling may be gathered from the words of Moselekatze, the rude yet able chief of the Matabeles. "These," he said of the English, "are the masters of the world. When the great men in the white man's country send their traders for the ivory, do you think they give me beautiful things in exchange because they could not take my ivory by force? They could come and take them by force and all my cattle also; and yet look at them, they are humble and quiet and easily pleased. The Englishmen are the friends of Moselekatze, and they are the masters of the world!"* We believe that such impressions of our colonial policy are largely held among the Kaffir tribes, especially among those under our direct rule. It is by cultivating such feelings that our hold on Africa can alone be made secure and honourable, alike to the natives and ourselves.

We shall only add here, as regards the characteristics of the Kaffirs, that it is quite an error to suppose they have no religious ideas. What they possess, indeed, are probably only fragments of purer earlier traditions of Divine truths, but still they indicate a certain feeling after God and of the need of mediation. The Kaffir proper name for

* "Mackenzie's "Three Years North of the Orange River."

Deity signifies the highest existence, dispensing fate, giving life, sending good and bad fortune. But still their deity can scarcely be regarded as having any likeness to the God of Christianity. There seems to be no doctrine of faith in him nor of love towards him. He is destiny alone. In place of him the true objects of worship appear to be the manes of the dead, especially the dead chiefs of the tribes. To them offerings are brought, the priest praying after a certain ritual over the animal slain. There are traces also of human offerings being made, as, for example, the Zulu chief Chaka sacrificed ten of the virgins of the tribe, whom he buried alive at the grave of his mother. This was indeed but a small part of the holocaust offered by that savage chief to the manes of his mother. With the dead it is supposed also intercourse can be held. As in the Greek play of the Persians, Darius, emerging from the tomb, tells of the destinies of Xerxes his son, Chaka held thus that he had converse with the Induna, or minister of his father, and received inspirations from him. Then the dead were supposed by some of the Kaffir tribes, as the Zulus, to live in Serpents; and hence a form of serpent-worship like that of the Gallas in North Africa. But we do not dwell on these religious rites and ceremonies further than to show, what has been sometimes denied, that there is a religious element in the Kaffirs' nature. Christian Kaffirs, when asked what they thought of God as heathens, have answered, "We never thought, only dreamed of Him." Their religious ideas were vain and fantastical; still it is important to know, if we would understand the Kaffir, that these have been wrought into a compact and powerful religious system. They have their holy places, their holy mountains, holy springs, and their magical waters, by which they purify the tribe or strengthen it for the battle.* One strong form of their superstition is the dread of witches and of witchcraft—a belief of which, it is to be remembered, Christendom has only lately, if now, even, got rid. † The chiefs and their Indunas turn this credulity frequently to their own advantage as a means of plundering the rich native, or of getting rid of those they hate. Cetywayo, the Zulu chief, has thus, we have reason to believe, sought to free himself of the Christian Zulus. Kaffirs have, again, their sacred animals, as, for instance, the crocodile, a relic probably of their old Egyptian or Hamitic worship. We have already noticed how in circumcision and other usages they approach Shemitic forms of worship.

*It is said that Kreli's Galekas lately drank sea-water to strengthen them to fight with the British, the rulers of the waves.

† Lady Barker has given a lively sketch of the Zulu witches of Natal Her picture is really a caricature, as are many others of her South African descriptions. It is here fitted to do harm because it fails to bring out the dangerous, murderous character in many instances of this superstition.

CHAPTER VIII.

OUTLINES OF KAFFIR HISTORY.

AND now to glance at the history of the Kaffir tribes. We shall do so mainly as it may elucidate the present great crisis in South Africa, and its relations to the future. Two Kaffir races stand out prominently at present: the Kaffirs of Kaffraria, and the Zulus of Zululand. As regards the Kaffirs of Kaffraria, their later history is that of a long series of warlike conflicts with the Cape Colony. These began in 1811, not many years after our possession of the Cape, and the end is not yet, although it seems approaching. The uprising of the Kaffirs we have lately witnessed is the sixth in the long succession. The wars of South Africa almost recall to us those of the French in Algeria, although they have not been on the same scale. The resemblance is not wonderful, as in the Kaffir we have to do with a kindred, warlike, and obstinate race, with a similar strong tribal organisation. The Kaffirs have, during the course of these conflicts, been gradually driven back on the East Coast, first from the Fish River to the Keiskamma, and latterly the Kei has been the boundary. We presume it will be now the Bashee or Umtata, but a cession it seems has also been made of the western bank of St. John's

River. This has always been hitherto resisted by Umgekila and the Pondos generally; and it may issue in another struggle. But perhaps it is better at once to take a step of this kind which ultimately must be necessary for the security of our South African Colonies. This step brings the Cape Colony nearer Natal, and is thus some guarantee of the safety of South Africa. Within the Cape Colony, thus extended as we have said for more than a quarter of a century to the Kei, there has been naturally a larger Kaffir population under British rule. These were permitted to remain in their old locations, but subject to our control. Sandilli the Guika, chief of a tribe closely allied to the Galekas, has thus been allowed perhaps too much independence of action, and the result has been his recent fierce struggle with us, which has ended so disastrously for himself, his family, and his tribe.

We do not enter on the history of their long conflicts: we shall mark only the more important facts bearing on the present state of South Africa. One of these was the wise resolution, after a second severe struggle with the Kaffirs in 1818, to introduce into the East Cape Colony, British settlers. These arrived in 1820, and have infused quite a new life and enterprise into the Colony. We have already referred to the honourable place which the Wesleyans have occupied in this. These British Colonists, and we may add, some more recent bands of German settlers, have done much for the progress and development of South Africa. The Eastern Cape Province well deserves an honourable place in the future Federation that is contemplated. Another fact which stands prominently out as we review this Colonial history, is, that a firm, while yet a mild policy, is the best in dealing with the Kaffirs. It is necessary while cherishing the most benevolent sentiments, to act with firmness, for a savage interprets anything else as weakness. The administration of Sir Benjamin Durban was an honourable instance of this; and his ablest successors have followed the same policy. This intermediate course did not go far enough however, for many British philanthropists, nor for Lord Glenelg, at the time of Sir Benjamin's administration, the secretary for the Colonies. The whole native settlement proposed by Sir Benjamin was rebuked as unjust, and was unwisely reversed. New concessions proposed in favour of the Kaffirs were loyally tried and carried out; but the result was a miserable failure. The Kaffirs simply availed themselves of these to renew their depredations, until these became intolerable. A furious war broke out again in 1846; the Colony was boldly invaded, much booty was seized, many homesteads were ravaged and destroyed, many missions broken up, many valuable lives were lost. This policy, which had in the end to be quite reversed, not only inflicted terrible hardships on the Colonists, but untold miseries on the Kaffirs. We may notice another feature in the later colonial policy. It is the wise effort of the Colonial Government to educate the Kaffirs, and to train them to industrial habits. We may say here that it was under the able administration of Sir George Grey, this plan was mainly instituted, in which his successors have energetically followed him. Very many thousands of the natives are thus being annually educated with the help of the government, chiefly we may add in the mission schools. A large staff of native teachers are being trained up with care. Establishments are being formed with a special view to industrial training. Lovedale, a Free Church institution, receives thus aid from the government, we believe to the extent of some £2000 a year. With its large staff of missionaries, teachers, and European masters of industrial departments, and with its some 500 pupils and boarders, it is quite a model institution of its character in South Africa.

Another fact to be noticed, in its bearing on the present and the future, is the strength of the superstitious element in the Kaffir character. We shall have this great difficulty to grapple with until by civilisation and Christianity it be removed. We may take as instances, the fact, that the prophecies of a reputed Kaffir seer in 1850, chiefly led to that disastrous and deadly struggle. A still more striking instance of this fanaticism occurred in 1857. The Amaxosas then perpetrated a deed of madness scarcely to be rivalled in history. A prophet foretold to them the resurrection of all their dead warriors and chiefs, vast herds of cattle were to issue from the ground, corn without their culture was to spring up, the living were to be clothed in new beauty, and the white man was to fade away. Only this must hinge on a heroic faith—they must kill all their cattle, and destroy all they possessed, save the arms of the warrior. This almost incredible prediction was accepted, with the connivance of their chiefs, who probably acted for their own purposes, to rouse their tribes to the last effort against the colonists. But if this were their policy, it turned out a futile one. The Kaffirs destroyed their corn, and killed their cattle, and then nearly 50,000 of them perished of hunger, and famished thousands invaded the Colony, not as conquerors, but as beggars.

It would be beyond our limits to attempt any description of the events of the late insurrection, now, we trust, happily suppressed. The full materials for such a narrative are scarcely yet to be had. But from the numerous Blue books on "the affairs of South Africa," recently published, some correct general ideas may be formed regarding it. The occasion of the insurrection was evidently an obscure brawl betwixt the Galekas and the Fingoes, but its real cause, as is well known, was the intense jealousy of the Galekas at the prosperity of a rival race occupying what was formerly their territory, and who had, at no distant period, been their serfs or slaves. The truth is, the Cape Colonial Government is partly to be blamed for this. They allowed Kreli, some years ago, to attack with impunity the Tambookies, another Kaffir tribe, and he probably fancied he might act in the same way as regards the Fingoes. But the latter owed, we may say, their very existence to us, as a people, and we were pledged to their protection.

The history of this insurrection is another instance of the need of energy and promptitude in grappling with native difficulties. Sir Bartle

Frere from his large Indian experience at once saw his position, and we cannot indeed read these South African Blue Books without observing in how many ways the experience of Indian Administration is invaluable, in the treatment of native races. Had Sir Bartle Frere been supported by his Cape government as Sir Benjamin Pine* was by Natal, in suppressing the insurrection of Langalibalele, probably the struggle might have ended in a few days or weeks, but the Cape ministry did not at first realise the peril. Even when fully aroused to a sense of this, and when they had taken energetic measures for the suppression of the insurrection, they still showed an unworthy jealousy of Her Majesty's military forces, and attempted to put down the rebels by their Colonial troops alone. This they succeeded for a time in doing and the greatest honour is due to the volunteers, police, and native forces for their valour and discipline. Unfortunately a premature disbandment nearly made shipwreck of the enterprise. The ministry seemed to have lost their heads, to have got perplexed in the mazes of constitutional puzzles, and but for Sir Bartle Frere and the commander of the British Forces, Sir A. Cunningham, the Colony might have

* The serious and lengthened injury to the Cape Colony, and to its Christian Missions by the uncertain policy of the Cape ministry, we venture to say vindicates, if it were needed, the energetic action of Sir Benjamin Pine in Natal. At the time his policy was supported not only by the Colonists but by a large majority of the Missionaries and ministers of Natal, with the exception of Bishop Colenso. The misrepresentations of Bishop Colenso, and, we must add, the signal weakness of Lord Carnarvon, led to an unjust estimate and treatment of an able and humane public officer. We believe the justice, wisdom, and even humanity of the course pursued by Sir Benjamin Pine is now generally appreciated.

been exposed to the greatest danger. The result might have been as disastrous to the Colonial Forces and their military prestige, as that which happened two years ago to the Boers in the Transvaal, when they were so ignominiously repulsed by Sekukuni. An attempt was made by Mr. Molteno and his Cabinet to call in question the rights of Sir Bartle Frere, the Governor and High Commissioner, and as from his office, the Commander-in-chief of the Forces in South Africa. To have conceded this would have been to disturb, if we may so speak, the whole hierarchical order of the British Army. This is a position which Sir Bartle Frere occupies, not only as governor, but as High Commissioner, having entrusted to him not only Colonial interests, but the protection and defence of the native tribes of South Africa. The theory of the Colonial Cabinet was, that they were at liberty to supersede the Commander of the Forces, at least as regards the Colonial Forces, and to take them under their own exclusive management, and they practically acted upon this. This was a clear invasion of the Royal prerogative, and would reduce the executive Power of the Empire to a position inferior to that of the President of a Republic. It would strike, in fact, at the whole unity of the British Colonial Empire, the connecting link of which consists for the present, at least, in the constitutional rights and authority of the Crown. Practically, also, this division of the military Forces under two separate commands, was most injurious in the Campaign, and but for Sir Bartle Frere's obtaining additional forces from England, and for the successes they won in the field, the state of the Colony might still be precarious. Fortunately the British Cabinet gave their sanction to this ruling of Sir Bartle Frere, and the majority of the Cape Parliament have, after a long and somewhat embittered discussion, also acceded heartily to it.

CHAPTER IX.

THE ZULUS.

My limits compel me to give the merest outline of the later Zulu history. The Zulus, as living further north, did not come so directly into collision with our Colonial rule as the Kaffirs, but their annals still touch profoundly the past, the present, and the future of South Africa. About some fifty years ago, Zululand, Natal, and the interior were convulsed, as by some great volcanic upheaval, the traces of which may still be marked in the whole position of the South African tribes. Results indeed, of this great revolution may be found now, even in Central Africa. Chaka, the warrior chief of Zululand, might have been justly named the Napoleon of South Africa. Beginning his career as a common soldier in the ranks of Dingeswayo, who first organised the Zulus into regiments, breaking up their old tribal system, training his subjects by an almost Spartan rule, to the severest discipline, forbidding his warriors with but few exceptions, to marry, and subordinating every thing to the aims of military conquest; his hardy troops burst like some wild tornado on the peaceful tribes of Natal, and so ravaged it, that a country, which had perhaps at one time a million of inhabitants, was reduced to ten or twenty thousand, hidden in the mountain clefts, and gorges. Many of the tribes were driven in wild despair before him. Some, as for instance, the Fingoes were enslaved for a time by the Amaxosas, but afterwards liberated by the wise and energetic policy of Sir Benjamin Durban, and are now one of the most prosperous of the South African races, and but lately, were fighting our battles with success. Others of those expelled tribes perished of famine, or became cannibals, or arming themselves in their despair, as the Mantatees, carried fire and sword among the less warlike tribes of the Bechuanas.

It was about this period, that Dr. Moffat entered on his interesting Mission labours, from which, such precious fruits have since been gathered. In the providence of God it was owing very much to this distinguished missionary, that the desolating progress of the Mantatees was arrested. The incident is one of such interest, in the Mission annals of the Central Kaffir tribes of South Africa, that we shall glance at it. The position of affairs looked almost desperate, for the Bechuanas, although among the most industrial of the Bantu tribes, are, compared with the Kaffirs, an unwarlike race. Fortunately an earlier scene of Dr. Moffat's Mission labours had been among the Griquas, or Bastards, a mixed race partly of Dutch, and partly of Hottentot origin. Speaking the Dutch language, trained to the use of fire-arms, and having something of the stolidity and tenacity of the Boer, these were a formidable race then, in native warfare, able not only to defend themselves, but to take the aggressive against the Mantatees. They then occupied a country which is

still called West Griqualand, including the district
now named the Diamond Fields.* They had been
christianised mainly by the efforts of the London Missionary Society. Their chief, Waterboer,
had been at one time indeed, a teacher in their
schools, and had owed his elevation, mainly
we believe, to the influence of Dr. Moffat. It
was to the aid of the Griquas, Dr. Moffat had
mainly recourse, in the extremity of Kuruman, and
the Griquas readily hastened with an armed and
mounted force to repel an invasion, not only
dangerous to the Bechuanas, but to their own
security. Vast multitudes of Mantatee savages were
now gathered for the attack. Dr. Moffat who had
gone out with Waterboer, Adam Kok and others,
to see if they could not yet come to terms of peace,
compares the scene to one unknown in these countries, but with which the South African traveller is
familiar. It is usual there, in order to secure fresh
grass, to burn the crops of the past season, and the
fields for a time, thus wear a dismal and blackened
aspect. So numerously, the describer tells us, did
these Mantatees now swarm on the hills, that for a
time they were mistaken for the blackened fields.
The Mantatees would enter into no parley. Dr.
Moffat, as a man of peace, retired, but the superior
army and discipline of the Griquas, speedily issued
in the repulse of the savage host. Nor was this,†

* There are now two Griqualands, one on the west, the other on the east, on the confines of Natal. I regret to notice the Griquas on both sides, in this late war, have scarcely merited the regard felt for them, as loyal to the British Crown.

† We do not remember if this incident is narrated in Dr. Moffat's Mission Travels. It was one, when he exposed his life

we may add, all the happy result of the signal Mantatee repulse. The fame of the Missions, and of Dr. Moffat the Missionary, became thus extended. They reached the ears of the sagacious chief, Moshesh of the Basutos, to whom we have already referred, a tribe allied to the Bechuanas and the Zulus. He felt that to obtain such men would be a valuable prize. He sent indeed a large herd of cattle to Philippolis to secure their aid, but these were lost on the way. Soon after, however, three French missionaries arrived there, they were told of the earnest desire of the chief, and, in the providence of God, their feet were thus directed to Moshesh, where they founded that interesting and most successful French Mission, to which we have already referred.

Nor were these all the results of Chaka's great revolution. Some of the tribes, as the Matabeles, under Moselekatze, an old soldier, and captain of Moselekatzes, were driven northwards, first into the Transvaal, and then beyond the Limpopo, to these north-west regions which they still occupy. It was among them that Dr. Moffat, whose influence with Moselekatze became so great, planted the mission at Inyati, the most northerly outpost now of the African missions, south of the Zambesi. The Mashonas, Banyais, and Makalakas, are now the the tributaries of Lobengula, the present chief of this race. The same victorious Zulu tribes spread also to the north-east, where now Umzila the Zulu

as on many other occasions, to great peril. We betray no confidence, we trust, in saying that we heard the whole graphic story from Dr. Moffat himself.

King reigns. Still another detachment of Chaka's great army deserves to be noted here. Defeated by the enemy, and fearing the vengeance of their chief, they crossed the Zambesi, and still survive in the warlike and dangerous tribes of the Mazitu and Watuta,* located near the lakes Nyassa and Tanganyika. As their language is quite akin to that of the Zulus, the fact is one of importance in connection with the future evangelization of Central Africa. We may add here, that Chaka's bloody reign met with its due reward. He was himself assassinated in a conspiracy headed by his brother Dingaan, also a ferocious chief, who, for a time continued to rule Natal, but was at last utterly defeated and driven out by the Boers, before Natal had become a British colony. He richly deserved this in consequence of his treacherous conduct in murdering a party of the Boers, who had gone unsuspectingly to his Kraal, to conclude a treaty of alliance, and in slaughtering all the other Boer families, on whom he could lay hands. Driven into Zululand he was soon afterwards assassinated, probably with the connivance of his brother Panda. We refer to this more especially as Panda was the father of Cetywayo, with whom our relations are at present, to say the least, so uncertain. Latterly, the arbitrariness of his rule, has assumed the form nearly of open hostility. He still retains the same severe regimental discipline, and his forty or fifty thousand warriors are now

* Perhaps these tribes are the same, but with different local names. Mr. Stanley in his last work makes frequent reference to the Watuta. Lieutenant Young who so ably conducted the Livingstonia Mission, had a conference with the Mazitu, near the Lake Nyassa.

armed with guns. He and his tribe are sunk deep as ever in Zulu Superstitions. He is himself a sanguinary tyrant, whose hands are stained with the blood of Christians, and of a great multitude of his heathen subjects.* It is extremely doubtful if there can be peace to South Africa until Cetywayo is either driven from power, or brought under effective British control. The instance of the unfortunate license allowed to Kreli, to go to war with another neighbouring tribe, shows the great peril of permitting a savage to act as he pleases on our frontiers. The case, of course, which is being submitted to arbitration, of his rights to certain frontier limits, ought to be justly dealt with, and if he can establish these, they should either be returned to him, or compensation should be given.

* See *Blue Book* respecting affairs of South Africa. c. 1883, Pages 2 and 3. There is abundant other evidence also.

CHAPTER X.

BRITISH COLONIAL GOVERNMENT OF THE ZULUS IN NATAL.

WE wish to refer, in this chapter, shortly, to our rule of the Zulus in Natal. This has been lately brought under the consideration of the House of Commons, and very hard things have been said on the subject. The wide question of Zulu rule we shall not discuss, but limit ourselves to the special questions raised. The chief of these was polygamy in Natal. On this subject, more correct information can now be obtained, than was perhaps then in the possession of the Members who spoke so severely. The native laws of Natal have been lately codified, and only very recently published. I trust I have sufficiently expressed my detestation of polygamy, and my opinion that it is a greater curse even in South Africa, than in Mohammedan countries. But, I presume, we are not prepared at once to supress it among the Kaffir tribes of South Africa, any more than among the Mohammedans, for instance, of India. It would certainly be better almost to abandon South Africa altogether, than at once to pass an enactment, which if executed would lead probably to a war of native or colonial extermination. The subject of polygamy in Natal cannot be well understood without some knowledge of the history of the Colony. We took over the rule of Natal, with its native usages and customs, and among them was polygamy. One speaker in the House of Commons seemed indeed to be under the impression that polygamy had been formerly limited to the chiefs and great men. This would if true, amount in fact, to the serious charge that our Natal Government had favoured the extension of polygamy. The statement was made, *it was said*, on the authority of a Member of the Legislative Council of Natal; how far he was responsible for such an averment, we do not know, but it is unquestionably an error and an injustice to our Colonial Government. It is true that under Chaka's regimental rule, marriage was altogether prohibited to the soldiers, unless to a favoured few, but the statement is quite incorrect as regards the Kaffir and Zulu tribes generally. While accepting the native usages of the Kaffirs—it was on the part of the Colonial Government with this decided reserve, that anything contrary to the laws of justice and civilisation, would not be tolerated. Now this, under British rule necessarily excludes slaveholding, and we presume it will apply in the same way now to Cyprus. If native women in Natal are now compelled without their consent to marry, we should say that the charge of slaveholding, which has been made, was proved, and that under our Imperial laws it could not be tolerated. But without entering on the rules of the Native Code in general, there are two which clearly establish, first, that the consent of the woman is necessary, and secondly, that provision is made to see that this rule is properly carried out. To obtain these two things, there is one law of the Code, that no marriage can take place without due attendance or recognition of a proper official witness. (Law 7.) Again, the official witness is to make public inquiry of the intended wife, whether it is of her own free will and consent, that she is about to be married. (Law 4.) And then, still more strictly, the official witness is required to prohibit any marriage being proceeded with, where the intended wife has not publicly stated her consent thereto, and he is, as soon as may be, to report the circumstances to his magistrate and to the chief."* It may be inquired, Are these enactments carefully administered. I have every reason to believe, on high authority, that the Magistrates of Natal are most conscientious in the discharge of this duty. As regards the Code generally, no one can read it with anything but deep regret, that any British subjects should be ruled by such laws. We cannot reconcile much in it, with the usages at least of any higher civilisation. At the same time on the principle "Thou shalt not speak evil of the ruler of the people," we think these provisions of the Code which we have quoted save the honour of the Colonial Government from the charge so strongly made against it, that as regards women, there is actual slaveholding in Natal.

There is another charge which has been so publicly made that it deserves notice and some explanation. It has been said in the House of Commons that wives are sold in Natal to the highest bidder.

* These laws apply equally to widows.

It so happens, as the code conclusively shows (Law 11), that, with the exception of the hereditary chief, this is an impossibility legally. In Natal, as in the East generally, no woman indeed is married without receiving a dowry. This is paid to her father or the nearest male relative, and she and her family have, I believe certain claims on it.* As the Kaffirs have but rarely pecuniary transactions, this payment is generally in cows. Were it not a matter of so great seriousness one could scarcely but be amused at the fixed tariff of Kaffir dowries, laid down in the native code. The hereditary chief alone may bid what he pleases for a wife, and hence probably Langalibalele was so rich in wives. But this is forbidden to any other, and the chief is to seize the superfluous cattle and report the circumstances to the magistrate. The son of a chief must not pay more than 15 cows, the head of a petty tribe 15 cows, and ordinary Zulus must each pay 10. (Law 11). This last may represent the sum of £50 to £100. I do not vindicate for a moment such an enactment. It seems too much like giving some British sanction to polygamy, as if regulating a system against which we earnestly protest. Still it shows that the sensational charge, of Natal native wives being sold to the highest bidder, is about as just, as the common belief spread over the Continent, that Englishmen sell their wives at Smithfield. I have been assured on very high authority, that fixing thus the dowry of a wife has been practically favourable to young

* There is an iniquity in the code we cannot however overlook. Women are incapable of succeeding to property. (Law 32). This is an injustice which should be rectified. The dowry should be settled on the wife.

men getting wives, and thus to the cause of morality, and that statistics establish also that the law has tended to lessen polygamy. For my own part, however plausibly it may be thus defended, I think it should be abolished.

There are several other topics to which in the cause of truth and fairness, I might refer in connexion with the late Parliamentary discussion. One of the speakers, for instance, insinuated that Christian native marriages had no validity in Natal. On the contrary, I know that the aim has been to raise them to a higher position than native ones. For instance, the Christian parent must present himself before the Resident Magistrate, and declare the consent of his daughter to the marriage, and he must also abandon the right to the payment of a dowry. (Law 3). More, I think, might or ought to be done in this direction. A Christian marriage might justly be regarded, at once as raising those who celebrated it to the same rank as the colonists. The very fact should emancipate them from native law. This might require, of course, some careful guarantees, but these would present no great difficulty. Another advantageous change in the native code might be to recognise, first native marriages as alone legally binding, and the rights of succession as belonging thus to the children of the first wife. Let me add here, that the greatest blow we can perhaps strike at polygamy in South Africa, apart from the higher influences of Christianity is the development of industrial education, and of personal tenure of land. The introduction of the plough will do much to emancipate the Kaffir wife, for so long as the land can be cultivated with the rude hoe, her labours and those of her children can be profitably used, but she cannot hold the plough. Kaffir male labour must then intervene. Hence, indeed, the elevation in some measure of women among the Basutos and the Fingoes, as the plough has been largely introduced. They are the most advancing native races.

In connexion with the morality of the natives, let me add here that there are infamous rites, as regards the Kaffir youth of both sexes, quite as degrading as the worship of the Paphian goddess. Any one who has read Dr. Fritsch's work on the South African races must know this. The missionaries have long lifted up their earnest protest against them. They poison the moral life of the Kaffir youth at its very springs. They ought not to be tolerated under our British rule.

There is just one other topic to which I shall here refer, as regards the Zulus of Natal. It is the alleged difficulty of their being relieved from the operation of native law, and obtaining the rights of colonial citizenship. The Aborigines Society has pressed this question on the attention of government. I have the law of 1865 before me and I have arrived at an opposite conclusion. I venture to affirm, from having seen something of it, that a German wishing, say to emigrate, would have greater difficulty in obtaining permission than a Kaffir to enjoy full Colonial rights Civil rights involve duties and responsibilities of a grave character, which a mere savage can scarcely be expected to fulfil; take for instance the duties of a juryman. These ought not and never can be conceded without those who receive them being taught that it is a great privilege they have obtained. So must it be with the blacks of South Africa. Having looked at the questions which are asked, they are such as, place of birth, age, residence, time of abode in the Colony, trade or occupation; if the native be married? and the importance of this inquiry I shall immediately notice, if he can read and write? &c. We do not find, as the Aborigines society, any great technicality in these questions. But then it is said, this "law of naturalization has been a dead letter since it was passed." The Aborigines Society might surely know the reason of this. It is simply this, that the act of exemption from native law, is a deadly blow at polygamy. Civil rights are refused to any native, who is not the husband of one wife. His children, if by former wives, may be naturalized, but he is debarred from any application, if still living in polygamy. If a native should obtain these rights, and continue a polygamist he exposes himself to fine and imprisonment. Every one knows that this is the real stumbling block with the natives in applying for Colonial Rights.*

But my readers may think I have pursued this subject far enough. I should hardly have gone so far, had I not known how little South African affairs

* I may notice that to obtain the franchise along with Colonial rights requires a somewhat lengthened period of residence. This might be reduced, were an educational test introduced. An experienced South African statesman has suggested to me, that the personal possession of land by a native might be a sufficient guarantee. It is quite plain that care must be taken lest the black vote should, in the end, swamp the higher Colonial influence. Lord Carnarvon has pointed to this somewhere in his despatches.

are understood at home, or rather how unfairly they are often represented. As regards the Aborigines Protection Society, while respecting highly their motives, I have yet often asked myself as regards South Africa, whom do they desire to protect? Is it to maintain that wretched tribal system, with its degrading usages, and with its ignorant, ferocious chiefs, such as Sandilli, and Kreli, and Cetywayo? Is it to allow such men to maintain a reign of terror over their people, and to allow them in their reckless license, under the wretched plea of witchcraft, to despoil the more industrious of these tribes of their wealth, and to murder them in cold blood without a trial, as Cetywayo does. Or does not rather Aborigines Protection mean to obtain for every native a court of justice where his rights shall be guarded, his life defended from violence, and security afforded for Aborigines progress, education, and civilisation? I cannot doubt that the latter is the design of the Society, and that their advocacy of native rights, aims at such beneficent designs; but if so, I think this might lead them to be more careful and discriminating, and fair in their judgments, on South African Colonial rule—to regard its native administration with a far less jealous eye, and to acquiesce in, rather than to oppose the extension of so beneficent a Protectorate of the natives, as British rule has been; the happy results of which we see in the quiet rest, Natal has enjoyed, and in the advancing wealth, prosperity, and civilisation of such tribes as the Basutos.

CHAPTER XI.

OUTLINES OF THE SOUTH AFRICAN MISSIONS.

Our idea in this volume, it will have been seen, has not been to look at Missions exclusively, but to give some sketch of South Africa, its physical conditions, its native races, its Colonial progress—at the same time the main idea we have had before us, is to open the way for our taking some intelligent and comprehensive view of the wide Mission fields of South Africa, and of the work that has been, and is being accomplished. Many of our readers are no doubt familiar with the facts of individual Missions in which they are interested, but our design is to awaken interest in the whole Christian work being carried on by the different churches and by various Christian agencies. The field is wide—there are German, French, Norwegian, English, Scottish, American, even we may add, as an interesting fact, missionaries from Russian Finland at work. This general study is of value, we think, for over all these wide Mission fields, the seeds of Eternal life are being sown, and in some of these they begin to ripen, or they have ripened. It is interesting to reflect on what the results of all this may be for the civilisation and Christianisation of South Africa, and the view is even wider, as we think, of the bearing of

South African Mission progress on the emancipation of Central Africa from its crushing evils, and its abodes of horrid cruelty, and on its entrance on the nobler career of civil and Christian progress. We think this all the more important as our current literature which has latterly turned with some interest to South African travel and its hunting grounds, or to the Gold and Diamond Fields, or to Colonial politics even, or to sensational and exaggerated sketches of South African manners and climate, has scarcely noticed Missions at all, or only it may be to undervalue them. We take, for instance, a very popular writer of the day, Mr. Trollope, who has recently favoured South Africa with a visit. These are some of his observations on Missions, "A little garden, a wretched hut, and a great many hymns, do not seem to me to bring the man nearer to civilisation, work alone will civilise him." He remarks again, regarding some observations of M. Casalis, a distinguished French Basuto Missionary, "The noble simplicity of individual missionaries as to the success of their own efforts, is often charming and painful at the same time, charming as showing their complete enthusiasm, and painful when contrasted with the results." We may say here, to do Mr. Trollope justice, that when he sees Mission work with his own eyes he is far from being a prejudiced judge. Thus for instance, he gives a glowing description of Worcester, one of the Educational Institutions of the Rhenish Mission, "I do not know," he says, "that I ever saw schoolrooms better built, better kept, or more cleanly. As I looked at them, I remembered what had been the big room at Harrow in my time, and the single schoolroom at Winchester, for there was only one." Had Mr. Trollope been able to follow the lessons given in that Rhenish establishment, he would have also found as we know, on good authority, that they were almost abreast of similar German Institutions, and higher than many English. But after all, would this have been very satisfactory to Mr. Trollope? we have difficulty in saying, as it is hard to gather from his book whether education is of value or not, at least we quote here these puzzling sentences, "The Kaffir at school, no doubt, learns something of that doctrine, which in his savage state, was quite unknown to him, but with which the white man is generally more or less conversant, that speech has been given to men to enable them to conceal their thoughts. In learning to talk, most of us learn to lie, before we learn to speak the truth. While dropping something of ignorance, the savage drops something of his simplicity." We must observe on this, that if Mr. Trollope believes in the savage simplicity of a Kaffir, of his knowing nothing of lies till the school has taught him, he has an idea of the race singularly contrary to what Colonial experience teaches. We might add, is not Mr. Trollope's view of education, a somewhat cynical one?—for it evidently means that for the civilised, as the savage, education is, as regards moral value, a very uncertain quantity indeed.

Elsewhere, we may observe, that Mr. Trollope does great justice to another large educational and industrial Mission Institution, we refer to Lovedale. "Lovedale is a place," he says, "which has had, and is having very great success," but then he adds, "It has been established under Presbyterian auspices, but it is, in truth, altogether undenominational in the tuition which it gives. I do not say that religious teaching is neglected, but religious teaching does not strike the visitor as the one great object of the Institution."

In regard to all these statements of Mr. Trollope on Missions, there is not one of them that is not quite inaccurate. Take Lovedale, for instance, he would scarcely place it in the category of religious Institutions at all, yet it is well known in South Africa, to any who know anything of the subject, that while Lovedale is a model Educational and Industrial Institution, it is pre-eminently, not simply evangelical, but evangelistic in its whole system. It is no doubt undenominational, as Mr. Trollope says, but it is not less intensely Christian in the whole teaching that pervades it. As regards M. Casalis again, of the Basuto Mission, Mr. Trollope could not possibly have stumbled on an instance more unfavourable to his authority as a witness regarding South African Missions. It is the poor results of Missions that pain him, yet if the Basuto French Mission in South Africa is esteemed for anything, it is for the valuable results that have accrued from the work of the missionaries. It has remarkably educated and civilised the Basutos, and it has done a great deal to develop, what Mr. Trollope seems to regard as the sovereign civiliser, work. I shall on this subject quote a few sentences from a Colonial Blue Book giving the testimony of Mr. Griffith, the late Colonial agent and magistrate in Basutoland.

He says, "The work of forty years has not left the missionaries of Moshesh without valuable testimonials to the faithfulness and efficiency of their labours in this country, testimonials which consist not in elaborate reports to Societies at home, but in the religious life and Christian conduct of thousands of natives who would otherwise be enveloped to-day in all the darkness of their primitive heathenism." "The quality of the work done in the field is of more moment than the quantity, and in this respect, no missionaries could have been more conscientious and successful than those who have charged themselves with the duty of evangelising the Basutos. To this fact may be attributed in great measure that superior intelligence, spirit of inquiry, desire for improvement, and appreciation of good government, which prevails among this people, more than amongst any other South African tribe except the Fingoes." Here are certainly two very strongly contrasted opinions as to results. We may look upon this and upon that, the one the opinion of a casual visitor to South Africa, who never in fact went near the Basutos; the other of an able experienced Colonial magistrate who knows Basutoland better perhaps than any other. We venture to suggest, that Mr. Trollope may spare himself the pain inflicted on his feelings by M. Casalis' enthusiasm.

As to hymn singing, it is really a very innocent thing. The Moravians, the Germans, the French, all the missionaries, we may say, are addicted, so to speak, to this. They think that it is enlivening to the rude native, and that it has an elevating religious tendency. But if Mr. Trollope supposes that the time of the Mission Schools is thus engrossed, we assure him he is quite mistaken. We may refer here to the Cape Blue Books, or to Mr. Dale, the able superintendent of education in the Cape. Many of these Mission Schools are of a highly efficient, educational character, almost abreast of the same class of schools in France, Germany, England, America, or Scotland. I can testify myself to the high class of teaching I have seen in Natal. In reference again to labour Mr. Trollope's specific, the missionaries have certainly not fallen short. Many of them might justly say with St. Paul, that they had wrought with their own hands. Their houses, their very churches, many of them considerable edifices, have been raised chiefly, not only under their direction, but with their own manual labour. It was a pity, I may say, that Mr. Trollope, in his tour when at Maritzburg, a town which so pleased him, had not also ridden out to Edendale at a few miles distance. He would there have found, in contrast with the poor kraals of the heathen, one of the most thriving Christian villages in South Africa, and he would have learned that it owed all its busy life as a hive of industry, to Alison the missionary. If also, on his dreary journey in the upper districts of Natal, his eye had caught a native busy erecting a Colonial or native cottage, had he inquired who he was, or how he had learned his trade, he would probably have been informed—he was one of Alison's school Kaffirs.

We have no desire to undervalue many of Mr. Trollope's clever if rapid sketches of South Africa, nor his shrewd observations on Colonial life, but he may rely on it, that the missionaries of South Africa have not absorbed their energies in teaching the natives to sing hymns. I do not know if we review the Mission annals of South Africa with care, where we shall find nobler qualities and virtues displayed, than by many of its missionaries. Count Montalembert has given us noble sketches of the self-denial and heroism of the early monks of the West. We think the achievements of many South African missionaries might well be compared with theirs, as regards courage and endurance, while, along with this, there has been a far more intelligent zeal, or let us call it with Mr. Trollope, enthusiasm. With what heroism many of them have lived among savage tribes, with their wives and families, with no other protection than their heroic faith! With what noble courage some of them, as a Moffat, or a Calderwood, have confronted angry and cruel tyrants, and awed them into submission by their very boldness and fidelity! With what splendid success, bent on great Mission designs, a Livingstone penetrated Central Africa—patient, intrepid, a peace-maker, the most illustrious of modern travellers. With what sagacity, energy, and educational skill, have such Institutions as Lovedale been established. And how great has been the triumph of the Rhenish missionaries, on the desert, wild and arid coasts of Western Africa, in training the wandering tribes to a settled life, in introducing among the most degraded races civilisation and Christianity, and in rendering it thus possible for the British Government to extend its beneficent rule to them, and to end for ever their deadly strifes.

CHAPTER XII.

THE RHENISH MISSION.

THE Rhenish Mission has just celebrated its Jubilee. It would, as an appeal it addresses to its friends says, "offer unto God thanksgiving, and pay its vows unto the Most High" for all His merciful protection, and for all His living Presence with it in its many labours. It is half a century ago, when in the Wupperthal, that great centre now of German industry, there were gathered together the representatives of three leading cities in the Rhenish provinces, Cologne, Elberfeld, and Barmen, to form one united Mission to the heathen. This was the beginning of the Rhenish Mission—other Mission Societies, such as that of Wesel, speedily joined themselves to it, until it has now become the representative very much of all the ancient and noble Evangelical Churches of Rhenish Germany. The interest in the Mission cause had been advancing there, even from the end of last century, when faith and love seemed in so many parts of Christendom to be dying out. But if among the higher class, the illuminati, as they fancied themselves, it was so on the Rhine as elsewhere; the smoking flax of old Rhenish Evangelism was not quenched in the lower middle class, nor among the Bauers (peasants). There was

still among them earnest piety. There were no great
religious gatherings indeed, such as we have now—
they would rather have shrunk from these, still
"they that feared the Lord spake often one to
another." In little companies of twelve, or even a
smaller number, they would gather together once a
month, to hear what the Lord was doing, to cor-
respond with their Christian brethren in Frankfort,
and Basle, and Holland, and England, or to listen to
the refreshing story of the voyage of the good ship
Duff, with her precious Missionary cargo; and if
they met often depressed at the day of small things
then; yet after their prayers, and readings of the
Word, and counsels one with another, they would
depart refreshed and rejoicing. We cannot pursue
the details of this progress, as it is so well told in
the Missionary narrative.* At last, with the good
hand of God upon them, their counsels and delibera-
tions, and prayers issued, as we have stated, in the
Rhenish Mission. The same Jubilee appeal, to
which we have referred, says truly, "Still and noise-
less are the works, which thrive and bring forth fruit
in the day of eternity." We may say that this
applies to much good work that has been accomplished by the Evangelical Christianity of the Rhine.
Its unobtrusive, yet earnest Evangelism and Philan-
thropy have issued in great results. Kaiserswerth,
with its many Christian agencies and establishments
crowned with its noble Deaconesses' Institution, is an
instance of this, but there are many more less known.
The Christian tourist, if he inquire, will find

* The history of the Rhenish Mission to which already reference
has been made.

that he will not readily exhaust the interest the district may afford him in its Christian institutions. He may complete his investigations by a visit to Elberfeld, with its admirable organisation for the Christian relief of the poor, and then he may pass on to Barmen situated so near, with its commodious, well equipped, well organised training Mission Institution.

Such a visitor now however, will have lost the opportunity of witnessing the Jubilee of the Mission, celebrated on the 14th and 15th of August last. It was an occasion of deep interest to the Evangelical Churches of the Rhine, especially to those Christian brethren who had long known and loved the Mission. Its Jubilee had at last come, fifty years of Christian work in the vineyard had been left behind. Those who have been at such religious festivals in Germany know with how much heart they are conducted, what enthusiasm is evoked, what pleasant gatherings there are of Christian brethren, all the more firmly attached to their principles and faith, because around them the proud waves of infidelity and socialism are beating. They will recall the simple yet solemn pomp of these occasions, the German clergymen in their talars, some of them with portly figures and broad massive faces, that recall to you the portraits of Luther, others again reminding rather of the spare student features of Melancthon. Then there is the glorious singing, as it were with one loud voice, of the great congregation; all this religious enthusiasm characterised in a high degree this Rhenish festival. There was a large gathering, many friends not only from the Rhenish Provinces, but from Holland, Switzerland, and Norway, with greetings also from England and Sweden. Many of those guests came not with empty hands, but bringing rich gifts, so that the treasury of the society is this year enriched by £3500. Professor Christlieb, of Bonn, gave, as it were, the keynote to the whole jubilee services in the opening address. In his sermon there was a retrospect of the past, and a recognition of the truth and faithfulness of God, to whom the honour was due, and the hope was expressed, that as links in the chain of the generations, they might have trust in the continued faithfulness of the Eternal King. The sermon was deeply and finely thought out, warm and glowing in its tone. Then there followed the ordination of four young missionaries, who were addressed by Dr. Nieden, the general superintendent of the Rhine, in words full of heart and power. Other addresses followed. Dr. Fabri, the able superintendent of the Mission College, gave a life-like picture of their Mission fields in South Africa, China, Borneo, and Sumatra. German pastors and Christian strangers who were there as guests added their cheering words. "It was altogether," as the Mission report for September says of it, "an elevating, rich, and may we also add, richly blessed festival, which none who took part in it will soon forget."

The Missions of the Rhenish Society embrace Southern China, Borneo, Sumatra and Nias, an adjacent island, and in all of these it is doing good work, full of promise for the future, but it is its South African Mission in which we are here interested.

This is its earliest Mission, where it sent its first labourers nearly half a century ago, and here we venture to add, it has won its noblest success, noblest, not only on account of the far larger number of converts it has here made, its numbers in South Africa amounting to some 15,500, but noblest in this higher sense, that it has here deliberately chosen for its sphere of work, races that seemed the most degraded, and which had been the most overlooked, and regions the most sterile and arid, appearing as unpromising for Mission stations and Mission agents as any in the world.

Most young Missions when the Rhenish Mission was started, looked to the London Missionary Society for advice. It occupied then, deservedly, the most prominent place. We may add, that that Society gave its counsels to those entering on the Mission work, always readily and wisely, and magnanimously. If it saw that the great cause was to be advanced, in a fine catholic spirit, it was willing to sacrifice what might have seemed its own interests. It was thus, for instance, that both the French Basuto Mission, and the Rhenish Mission, then entering on the work, were greatly indebted to the wise counsels of the Rev. Dr. Philip of the London Missionary Society. The latter resolved to begin its labours in the Cape Colony, and four missionaries were solemnly ordained to the work at Barmen. There was on the occasion a large Christian gathering, for it was an event of note in the Evangelical annals of the Rhine. Dr. Philip was himself present, twenty-three German ministers united in laying their hands on the ordained, and Dr. Krummacher, the eloquent preacher, offered up the closing prayer.

It is quite impossible for me to do more than glance at the Mission work accomplished by this Society during the last half century. How little can we in so rapid a survey of the outer things of a Mission, judge of the far deeper history that belongs to all such—"the rich capital," as the Society's appeal well expresses it, "of love's holy zeal, and of faith's work hidden behind. How much labour, how many prayers, how many tears, what joys and thanksgivings have been offered up, ere we now, in the review of half a century, in the great gathering, can thus loudly praise the blessed, wondrous, faithful keeping God."

We shall first notice the labours of the Rhenish Mission in the Cape Colony. It began its work there, and as these stations are the oldest, so are they the most firmly rooted and grounded. The number of converts is also the largest, amounting to some 10,000 baptized. The incidents of its Mission life are, perhaps, less striking than among the ruder tribes in the more sterile regions further north—still there are some things worthy of note.

The Missions in the Cape included two classes, the Hottentots and the slaves, for slavery existed in the Cape half a century ago, as in the West Indies. As regards the Hottentots of the Cape, we may notice that they are not the old Hottentots, or Khoi Khoin, whom the Dutch found on their first arrival. These, with their free nomad life, and their numerous herds, have long since been driven from the Colony. We shall find some traces of them as we proceed further north. The existing Hottentots of the Cape are a mixed, or we might rather call them a mongrel race, with Dutch and Hottentot blood, born of Hottentots and slaves, and Hottentots and Europeans. They have lost their original language, and speak Dutch, they occupy chiefly a servile condition, possessing but little land. They are, at the same time, more civilised than the tribes of purer Hottentot origin further north, and they have been in the main Christianised. From their sanguine, emotional nature, intoxicants are a great danger to them, brandy or Cape smoke, as it is called, is the frequent cause of their ruin. Yet, as we have already noticed, they are not a decreasing race in the Cape. The Rhenish Mission has accomplished a good work among them. There are large flourishing Christian communities, such as Worcester, with its 2000 members, and there are included among these Hottentot converts, many sincere, pious, and steadfast Christians.

There is the other class, the slaves. Almost the first, if not the first work of the Rhenish Missionaries on their arrival, was ministering to them as at Stellenbosch and Tullbagh. The Dutch Christians gave to this at first their hearty countenance and support, and the work was crowned with much success. But then there came the Emancipation of 1835. We notice it for a moment, generally because upon it hinges so much of the later history of South Africa. The Boers never liked the firmness of British rule, but this measure quite enraged them. It was the Canaanite obtaining equal rights with the Israel of God, in place of being exterminated, or at least of being held in the place of hewers of wood and drawers of water. And the Boer was not satisfied with grumbling as our West Indian planters did; in his indignation he resolved to trek northwards so as to escape the hated British rule. Hence the foundation of Natal, the Orange State, and the Transvaal, Colonies with which now the future of South Africa is so intimately bound up. But this is a digression. To return to the Rhenish Mission, it now no longer enjoyed the favour of the Boers. Thousands of the emancipated blacks poured, for instance, into one of the Rhenish Mission stations,* and the Mission chapel was found far too small, but the Boers would now give no help. The emancipated blacks, however, flung themselves into the breach, and as an expression of their attachment to the Mission and the Missionaries, raised £1000 to build the new church, and prepared themselves some 30,000 bricks.

We do not notice the details of these Cape stations. There are ten larger, with a number of subordinate stations; they are doing much for education and industrial progress. Many of the Rhenish schools are of a high order. We have noticed Mr. Trollope's high estimate of the Worcester Institution, which is one of the best in the Cape Colony. The Rev. Mr. Esselen, its head, belongs to the very front rank of South African Missionaries. But what to us is most interesting and encouraging in these Cape Rhenish Missions, is that they have almost attained to their manhood. They are nearly, if not altogether, self-supporting. This has been partly effected by the stronger stations, from their resources helping to aid the weaker, and the

* Stellenbosch.

weaker pledging themselves to raise a definite and increasing amount. This is in fact a South African Sustentation Fund. This purpose has not been this year, we believe, so fully accomplished as had been hoped for, but there is every reason to believe that the Missions will speedily attain to it. All the other evangelical Missions in South Africa, we may say, are striving in the same direction, so that leaving the Churches they have founded with so many labours and prayers, they may be enabled to pass on into that immense field of the world which yet lies before them, and toward which it is their special vocation to pioneer the way. Such an organisation and such mutual aid also is fitted and will doubtless inspire the native Churches more and more with an evangelistic character. It is theirs in the future, we trust, to subjugate Central Africa to the Cross.

Lesser Namaqualand is included by the Rhenish Society in its Cape Stations. Here the country no longer wears the same aspect as the South. The region was not formerly so desolate, for the slopes of the mountains were covered with woods when the Dutch first settled, but the Boers gradually cleared away the great forests, and the rains became thus ever scarcer. As a compensating circumstance for the fortunes of this district, copper mines have been lately discovered, the richest, it is believed, in the world, and which, it is said, have already made the fortunes of their possessors. These are naturally attracting the colonists, and inducing a number of the natives to abandon their nomad life for more regular work. Two other Mission

societies besides the Rhenish have penetrated so far
north ; the S.P.G. and the Wesleyan. As both of
these societies are Colonial as well as Missionary, it
is perhaps the Colonial element which has chiefly
drawn them, at least the former. Much further inland again, not very far from the great Orange River,
the Roman Catholic Church has lately sent pioneers,
doubtless to survey these fields, which she has never
hitherto occupied. She has taken possession of Pella,
a station occupied by the London Missionary Society,
and the Rhenish, but abandoned by each in succession. She doubtless hopes that she will be able to
resuscitate it to a new life.

We proceed further north beyond the great
Orange River, barred with its " hopeless sandbanks,
which all the rains and snows which fall on the
peaks of the Maluti, and the other great eastern
ranges, as well as on the wide plains of the
Sovereignty" fail to wash away. "Not one constantly flowing stream enters the Atlantic between
Walvisch Bay and the Orange River, a distance
of 400 miles."* Further inland few traces of
timber, or rather even of native bush, are to
be found on the bare flats or heights, and the
pastures for the cattle must be sought with weary
toil, in a wide circuit. In most years the land
retains its parched and thirsty look, and when here
or there a thunder-shower falls, the inhabitants
of the waste hasten thither until, if exhausted, a
richer or scantier table is spread for them elsewhere.
Only Nomads can live in such a country, an agricultural race could not do so permanently. The

* Silver's South Africa.

names of the localities are often taken from their water springs, as the "fontein or fountain," is the great geographical feature. There is almost recalled to us the story so graphically told in Genesis of the patriarchal wanderings—of Isaac digging and searching for wells, and then recording the name of the precious possessions he had obtained. But there are other times, again, in Namaqualand, when it is refreshed with plenteous showers, and "when the whole land is covered as by magic with the loveliest carpet of flowers and plants, and the brows of the hills are encircled with fragrant blooming crowns."*

Limited as the population of great Namaqualand is, estimated by the missionaries to be, probably some 40,000 in all, there are no less than four races, among three of which the Rhenish Society has established flourishing stations. One of the races are the wild Bushmen living in the more desolate and remote districts. We have already described the characteristics of this tribe, and that while there have been interesting instances of individual conversions, in their wild state no missionaries have been able to establish stations permanently among them. Among the Namaquas again, a second race, the Rhenish Mission has, after long and patient efforts, obtained important success. They have mastered the

* Geschichte der Rheinischen Missions Gesellschaft. This extends even further into the desert. Sir Bartle Frere in an interesting dispatch writes—" The great Kalihari desert, so dreaded as a rainless and waterless waste by former travellers, has turned out to be neither rainless nor waterless. The rainfall is very uncertain but when rain falls there is much fine pasture. There is sufficient water always to be found in some of the ravines and fiumaras, which seam the surface of the desert if the traveller only knows where to look for it."

G

Namaqua tongue, the purest, perhaps, of the Hottentot dialects, and they have not only translated into it the Scriptures, but other Christian books and many hymns. Many of the stations among these tribes are large, in one there are 900 members. Commodious, well-built churches have also been erected, the services are conducted with great religious order and decorum, and fruits of sincere piety have been gathered. There is, again, a third race, the Orlams, among whom the Rhenish Society has important stations. The Orlams seem to be the remnants of the ancient independent Hottentots, or Khoi Khoin of the Cape, who preferred rather to emigrate, than to remain the serfs of the Boers. They are a people somewhat more advanced in culture than the Namaquas, and they are accustomed to the use of firearms. This long gave them a great advantage over tribes not practised in using them. It may be interesting, in passing, to notice that Christian Africaner, whose conversion, as described so graphically by Dr. Moffat, is one of the most striking incidents of modern Missions, belonged to those tribes. But piety is not hereditary, and his son, Jan Yonker Africaner, lately deceased, certainly did not walk in the later steps of his father. On the contrary, he was a bold, restless, ambitious, ferocious chief, always ready for any raid and aggression on his neighbours—the Rob Roy, shall we call him, of Namaqualand, only the name would do him too much honour—a constant disturber of the peace of its tribes, and a source of great disquiet to the Missions, and the Missionary Stations. We shall meet his name again, when we advance into Damaraland.

Amid these tribes, now more peacefully settled, the Rhenish Mission has won many trophies to Christianity. It has some large stations, one with 700 members, it has built excellent churches, and it has gained a predominant position. The last race which has also its settlements in Namaqualand, are the Bastards, tribes akin to the Griquas, and of mixed Dutch and Hottentot origin. They are, as a people, the most advanced, not simply good herdsmen, but understanding also the cultivation of land. They, too, have been trained to the use of arms. Among them the Rhenish Mission has flourishing stations, one numbering some 400 members.

It is a remarkable and noble achievement, that in so desolate a country as Great Namaqualand, the Rhenish Society has now no less than 11 stations with about 5000 members, and that Christianity has there won such a position among these wandering nomad tribes. "The Mission," we translate from the records of the Society, "which was begun by the London Missionary Society in 1810, continued by the Methodists in 1817, since 1840 gradually, but now entirely, fallen into the hands of our Missions, has a very great significance for the entire existence of the Namaquas and Orlams. The Mission Stations are the middle point, around which the people has gathered, and continues to gather. The Mission schools and the special instruction of the Missionaries, are till now the only means to teach, and to advance the natives, and what is weightiest of all, in the Mission lies the alone deliverance from the destructive influence of European communication, especially as regards brandy, which the natives are quite unable to resist of themselves. The resistance of the heathen seems everywhere to be broken, and there is shown, by all the races, a more or less universal approach to Christianity."*

We have now reached the most northerly stations of the Rhenish Mission in Damara or Hereroland. Hereroland, we use the latter name, lies, as our readers will observe, on consulting any good map,† to the west of Walvisch Bay, the most northerly port, we may say, in West South Africa. We may notice here, that Walvisch Bay is by far the easiest way of access to reach Central Africa, at least, on its western side. To take it, saves unnecessary fatigue, and a long protracted land journey.

The history of the Rhenish Mission here has been one of great vicissitudes, of seeming defeat for a time, and yet in the end of triumphant success. But to understand its present position, we must take a rapid view of the tribes of Hereroland, and of their recent history. The subject, we may say, has not only its Mission interest, but its value in connection with South African Colonial progress. It is a chapter of our later history, not so important perhaps, as the annexation of the Transvaal, but which has also its bearings on the future of Central Africa. We may say also, that it is comparatively unknown, at least, in its details to the British public. We glance first at the Herero tribes. In these we meet for the first time on the West Coasts of Africa with Bantu or Kaffir tribes. They descended probably from the

* Rheinischer Mission Atlas, &c. Barmen. 1878.
† We have not thought it necessary to supply a map for this book. Any good South African map will sufficiently indicate the places that we note.

Zambesi, attracted probably by the country, which is well suited for herdsmen. We may say that in Hereroland, the climate of West South Africa begins to improve—if still the country is somewhat of the same structure as Namaqualand, it has more rain, and offers thus larger and richer pastures. "The Hereros are a large, strong, rude but dirty race of herdsmen, who care for their flocks with much skill, but to whom their oxen are above everything. The clothing of the Hereros is, at least, somewhat richer and more presentable than that of the Kaffir. The men and women wear aprons and mantles of skin, both men and women have sandals also, and the latter, heavy leather caps. European dress has also found its way in largely."* This is certainly a much more elaborate toilette, to say the least, than that of the Kaffirs of the east. The Hereros as a people, we may add, amount probably to 100,000.

The Hereros were long the dominant race in the country, until, in 1840, the Orlams from Namaqualand, under their bold, unscrupulous chief, Jan Yonker Africaner, invaded the country, invited by Katyamaha, a Herero chief. Although an inferior race physically the Orlams, and with them the Bastards also came, had the immense advantage of being trained to the use of fire-arms. Speedily they made large booty from among the immense herds of Herero cattle, and for a time they reduced the Hereros almost to slavery, and in all likelihood the race must have succumbed, but for two circumstances. First, there was the presence of the Rhenish Missionaries; these had so far civilised

* Rheinischer Missions Atlas, &c.

them, and there were also some genuine converts among them, and this gave the Hereros moral support. Meanwhile, however, the Missions were themselves in great part broken up.

But help came also to them from another source. As the subject is of interest, and throws light, if we may so express it, on the Colonial economy of South Africa, we shall briefly notice it. At the time of this Orlam and Bastard invasion there was the beginning at last of a Colonial element in Hereroland, able to afford some help to the Hereros, and which did, in point of fact, come to their rescue. Some were pioneers in search of copper-fields, some, travellers going or returning from the Zambesi; but the most were the Colonial traders. As the character of this class is somewhat curious, and they are likely to occupy a considerable place in that Colonial progress which may ultimately bring us to the Zambesi, I shall notice them. They are extremely well described by Sir Bartle Frere in the dispatch to which we have already referred. "Such a region" as Damaraland and the interior "has a certain charm for a large section of the population in South Africa, where energy and enterprise are apt to seek a field of action in a life of wandering through the less civilised regions of the Colonial border. Avoiding the more frequented and well explored roads, and combining shooting and hunting with barter for skins, ostrich feathers, ivory, or whatever the native tribes may have to sell, the traveller enjoys a roving life at little expense: often returning from a long journey with sufficient to leave a considerable surplus on the outlay he has incurred. This process of smousing, as it is termed in local slang, has a larger share than even the trekking propensities of the frontier Boer population in carrying European trade into native States beyond the Colonial boundaries, and in some respects paving the way for European civilisation."

By the help of these various Colonists the Hereros were rescued from their perilous position. Possessing by their means fire-arms, they succeeded not only in resisting the Orlams, but in repulsing them, although they still continue to occupy a part of the country. Kamaherero, a Herero chief, seems now to be recognised as the paramount chief of the country.

Amongst the Hereros the Rhenish Mission has some flourishing Stations. There are in all some 1200 to 1300 members. At Okahandiya, the residence of the paramount chief, a stately church (for South Africa) has been erected, capable of holding some 700 hearers. One of the churches has 300 members. The Hereros have shown themselves also liberal. In addition to supporting their teachers; they, with the Namaquas and other tribes living in these districts, have contributed £1040 to the Missions.

It is satisfactory, such a report as this of the Rhenish Mission regarding the Hereros. It is only indeed a small part of the Hereros who yet live at the Mission Stations, and are brought under the influence of the Gospel; the greater part still keeps itself apart, and clings to its heathenism and its rudeness. Yet the revolution now effected, compared to the former state of the country is so remarkable, and these Herero Christians show so much firmness and zeal for their new faith, that we may hope that gradually the whole people will be Christianised.

There are also in Hereroland the Damaras, a race, we may say, which is still an ethnological puzzle, in some things akin to the Bushmen, in others widely different. Like the Bushmen they love the solitudes of the desert, and like them they care not for dwellings, but in contradistinction to them again, they are eager to possess flocks, and they are skilful in garden and in land cultivation. They are a small, weakly people, and seem to have been enslaved successively by the Namaquas and the Hereros. Their number is from 40,000 to 80,000. They seem to approach Christianity, and there are a number of converts from their ranks. The Rhenish Society feels that they merit attention. " Tribes to whom, as to them, Christianity has been a deliverer from slavery, are those who not rarely turn as a united people to the Gospel."

There are in Hereroland, still further, the Orlams and Bastards. Among these there are some 1200 members occupying five stations. In one of these there are nearly 700 members. While the number of members is nearly the same as among the Hereros, the number of church-goers is very much greater, and the schools are often very well attended.

The Rhenish Society has thus its flourishing Missions among all these tribes; its influence, especially since these feuds, to the termination of which it contributed so much, has grown as a mediating, civilising, and Christianising power. Still the recollections of the past, and of the stations scattered then or destroyed, and the knowledge that the seeds of discord were widely sown among these tribes, could not but give rise to misgivings for the future. In addition to these tribal differences already beginning to emerge, there was the fear of the Boer. It has been ascertained that further north than the settlements of the Hereros, there is a fine country, the Kaoko, scarcely inhabited yet, only traversed by the Bushmen and the Damaras. It is also known that the Boers have reached the west side of the Lake of Ngami. To what complications might not their approach give rise? In these perplexities, we believe, it has been greatly to the relief of the Rhenish Missionaries to have heard of a probable British Colonial Protectorate. Mr. Palgrave, a friend of the Rhenish Missions, was appointed by the Cape Government to confer with the Namaqua and Herero chiefs on the subject, and the missionaries undoubtedly paved the way for him in this. The result has been that their chiefs having had guaranteed to them large possessions, were willing to accept British Suzerainty in return for British Protection. The Colonial Government on its side, while wisely acting tentatively, seems ready to extend this Protectorate for reasons of Colonial security. Sir Bartle Frere writes: " It may be said that whatever risk exists, is to be found in the eastern rather than in the northern frontier of the Colony, but there are unmistakable signs that the Colony is at least as much exposed to it in Damaraland, as in Kaffraria or Zululand. An alliance with a few South African filibusters might have enabled a freebooter and murderer like Jan Yonker Africaner to found a dynasty, which the advent of the Boers who are trekking thither via Lake Ngami, might convert into a republic. On the eastern frontier the element is likely to be of English extraction. In Damaraland there is every chance of its being of foreign, European, or American origin, and much more dangerous to the peace of the country."

We may briefly state the result. Mr. Palgrave returned last year as the Colonial Commissioner and the British flag has been hoisted at Walvisch Bay. He has since held a conference of the chiefs at Okahandiya, the Herero capital. He informed the chiefs of his appointment as Commissioner. The place where they met is to be the residence of the highest Colonial official, and plans are to be prepared for the erection of a Council House. Mr. Palgrave "bore himself in a friendly manner to the Missionaries, and stated that it was in contemplation to aid the Rhenish Mission Schools."* Mr. Brownlee, the late Secretary for native affairs, we are interested to see, has enjoined on Mr. Palgrave to direct his "most serious attention with a view to making such arrangements with the Damara and Namaqua chiefs, as will effectually prevent the introduction of drink into their respective countries." This is really a question on which the future of the South African races depends. If for nothing else, a South African confederation would be a benefit, were it able to pass a decided, well judged, comprehensive

* Jahresbericht *der Rheinischen* Missions, Gesellschaft, 1877, page 21.

measure on the subject. If even in Scotland and Ireland, a regulation of the liquor law is needed, it is absolutely essential in South Africa to prevent the corruption and destruction of the native population.

I close this rapid notice of an interesting event, our Protectorate of Herero and Namaqualand, by observing how Colonial Government and Mission action can thus co-operate beneficially the one with the other. But for Missionary work, these dreary countries, and their degraded Nomad races, could scarcely have been brought at all under a civilised rule. On the other hand, the British Protectorate may greatly tend to the security of these Mission fields, where, with many tears and trials, so much good seed has been sown. It may so strengthen, we trust, the hands of the Missionaries, as that these native communities may become ever more deeply penetrated by the principles of a living Christianity.

While the Rhenish Mission extends so far on the west, there is still a large intervening country betwixt it and the Cuanene, the Portuguese boundary. There are here the lofty and rich plains of Ovampoland, a country fertile in corn and garden produce, with a people of the same Bantu origin as the Hereros, but more advanced and industrious, and with a more formed government. One of the Rhenish Missionaries, the Rev. Mr. Hahn, long settled in Hereroland, and who belongs to the highest order of South African Missionaries, made an attempt in 1857 to enter this country; but the way was barred to him by hostile chiefs. It was said that the king died with fright at the approach of the Missionaries, who seem to have had the character of being great magicians. In 1866 things had, however, changed. Yonker Africaner had with the Orlams been beaten by the Hereros, and the idea seemed to have spread to Ovampoland that it was the Missionary Hahn who had accomplished it, and that his magical powers should be propitiated. An invitation was thus addressed to him to return. He was most cordially welcomed by King Tyikongo, who entreated him to remain; but when he declined, he entrusted two of his sons to be educated by him. While the Rhenish Mission could not see its way to extend its work here, the Rev. Mr. Hahn bethought himself of other co-operation. He had been very warmly received when in Europe, not only in Germany, but in Holland, England, and Russia, and it was resolved to apply to an Evangelical Mission Society, whose seat is at Helsingfors in Finland, known for its mission zeal and for its sufficient resources. The proposal was very cordially received, and a well-equipped Mission body, consisting of seven missionaries and three Christian handicraftsmen, were sent to occupy this new Mission field. They began by spending a year with Mr. Hahn in Hereroland, in order to study native usages and the native languages. They then proceeded to their field of work, where, like most young Missions, theirs has been a chequered career. Some of the chiefs had hopes that they were to supply them with gunpowder, and help them as the traders, and were disappointed, and did not care for their teaching. One forbade them his territory, and stations had to be abandoned, still the King Tyikongo continued friendly. They have as yet, so far as we have seen their reports, had no open conversions, but their presence as Christian men has already had its savouring influence on the natives. The fact of this Mission is an interesting one. May the great Russian Empire yet take its share in the work of evangelising the world; as its Finnish Evangelical Mission is now doing, so bravely confronting its initial difficulties!

CHAPTER XIII.

MISSIONS OF THE CHURCH OF THE UNITED BRETHREN.

THE Missions of the United or Moravian Brethren are chiefly situated in the Cape Colony; indeed, if Kaffraria be now formally annexed, they will all be within it. It was the Brethren who had the honour first to occupy this Mission Field for Christ, and they may be justly said not only to have been the first to direct attention to South Africa, and to achieve a noble work there, but to have given, by their success, a mighty impulse to the whole Mission cause in the world.* The first movement towards the establishment of such a Mission was given by an account which the Missionary Zugenbalg gave of a visit to the Cape in 1715, and of the state of the natives. This called forth much Christian sympathy and compassion. In 1737, Georg Schmidt, a Moravian by birth, but who had been later an evangelist in Bohemia, where he had lain in prison for six years for the gospel's sake, was the first Mission agent of the Brethren to arrive in the Cape Colony. His

* In Dr. Chalmers's works, for instance, there will be found a Missionary sermon in which there is a noble and eloquent portraiture of the Missions of the Brethren, and of the Evangelical source of their success.

arrival in Capetown caused no small stir, exciting the animosity or mockery of many, but securing also the support of some pious men. After some time had passed, and some persecution had been endured, he was permitted to occupy the station which is now called Genadenthal, or the Valley of Grace,* a place still occupying great prominence in the South African Mission Field as the largest of its settlements, with its 4000 or 5000 converts; and which is also still more sacred from its memories of the past, as the scene of the labours of Schmidt, whom the annals of Missions have enrolled for ever among their illustrious names. Georg Schmidt laboured for nine years at Genadenthal, and gradually gathered together a little, but attached, Mission company of some 47 adherents, with 50 children in the schools. But the opposition to him continued, and when, after his ordination, he baptized some of the blacks, it burst into a flame. The Boers could not tolerate it, that the Hottentots, "Schepfels or creatures," as they called them, should be regarded as men, to whom the sacraments were to be administered. Calumnies were heaped upon Schmidt. He was forbidden to baptize any more, and at last his enemies so prevailed, that he was summoned to Holland, to answer for his conduct. Many a year passed over him in Germany, a poor day-labourer in his old age, with his eye turned to that southern land, and its southern Cross, which he was never to see again, but where he had sown the

* Its original name was Affenthal, or the Valley of Apes, but a Dutch governor, at a greatly later period, struck with the good work which the Brethren had wrought, suggested that its name should be changed to Genadenthal.

seeds of life eternal. At last, in 1785, at Niesky, he fell asleep in the Lord.

It was nearly half a century later, that the Brethren obtained permission to resume their work in South Africa. Three of them arrived in 1792, all of them, and those indeed who followed after a little time, of humble origin—Christian artisans. The governor directed them to settle at Bavianskloof, Genadenthal, where Schmidt had been. They found there the remains of a wall and some fruit trees, among others, a great pear tree, and under its shade they held their first meeting with the Hottentots. With others who visited them, there came the poor blind Lena, an aged pupil and convert of Schmidt's, bringing with her, wrapped up in its sheep skin, her old treasured Testament, a gift of Schmidt to her—with the truth, we may trust, these Scriptures had taught her still fruitful in her heart. The Mission work thus begun, speedily prospered, and at the Christmas of another year, there gathered beneath the same old pear tree, said to have been planted by Schmidt, seventeen persons who had abjured the old heathenish life, and of whom five had already received baptism. The change wrought by the Mission was speedily very marked, even the Boers observed how different the Hottentots were, as compared with their old rude state, and could not but admire the industry of the brethren under whose care the now well-watered gardens of the station throve luxuriously. It was not very long after the arrival of these brethren, that the Cape Colony was for the first time occupied by Great Britain. The speedy result was the growth of the Mission. Multitudes of Hottentots flocked to it. The number of the brethren was also increased, and as they all could teach useful arts, the industry of the natives was greatly advanced. There was also more order and cleanliness, and garden culture made such progress, that even an opponent who did not care for the Mission, could not but express his admiration at the sight of the friendly industrious village with its 200 cottages embosomed in their gardens. The chief edifice in Genadenthal was the church, which even in 1802 had been so enlarged as to hold from 800 to 1000 hearers. Those who visited the station felt how happy was the change which had been wrought in the Hottentots by the power of the gospel faithfully declared and administered. So widely had the news spread of this wonderful place, that even so early as 1799, head men of the Bushmen had been sent from the Zak river, a distance of 600 miles, begging that such men might also be sent to them.

We may here give a short description of Genadenthal, which is still the great western centre of the Moravian Missions in the Cape Colony. It is the notice of a visitor of a much later date, bringing before us, in certain aspects at least, rather what Genadenthal is now, than what it was. Genadenthal lies about 80 miles to the eastward of Capetown. "Lofty mountains," the writer says, "form the background, and the view is bounded on either side by considerable eminences. The peaceful valley which spread itself before us was thickly grown over by numerous clumps of oaks and poplars, together with some gigantic Australian

H

trees—one of which, the blue gum tree, here reached the height of 100 feet. A road winding among the houses, gardens and trees, conducts the visitor to the centre of the settlement, consisting of the Church and other Mission buildings, arranged around an open space. On one side is the church, a very simple, but neat and commodious building, which, on the ground floor and in the galleries, accommodates about a thousand persons. The dwellings and workshops of the Missionaries, occupy the opposite side of the square. Near the church stand the school buildings, of which the newest is the most important—it is mainly a training institution for native teachers."*

We may add in regard to this last Institution which is only on a limited scale, that the usual branches of a higher ordinary education are given, but scarcely the secondary. "Mathematics and languages," one of the brethren writes, "have never been liked by our pupils, and consequently, but little progress has been made in these branches. Bible knowledge, history, geography and music, are the favourite branches of study of all without exception."

From Genadenthal the Gospel has gradually sounded out in South Africa—stretching from west to east. If the work of the Brethren for a time seemed rather one of inner development than of outward progress, yet the smouldering fire again burst into a flame, and never has its Evangelistic work been carried on with greater zeal and success, than by the Brethren in these later Eastern Stations, to which we shall immediately

* Periodical Accounts, U. B. Missions, Vol. xxv., p. 34.

refer. Meanwhile, we observe that in West South Africa there are now seven principal stations, with four out-stations. Mamre, not far distant from Genadenthal, was among the first of these, and has now some 1300 native Christians, and its pecuniary resources, to judge from later reports, seem considerable. Other stations—some west, others more to the south-east—have grown in numbers. We do not quite know what are the intentions of the Brethren, but it would seem to us that these Churches are as prepared as those of the Rhenish or the London Missionary Society, in the western districts, to be self-supporting, especially if the stronger will bear up the weak. We may add the latest statistics here of these western stations. * There are 39 European Missionary labourers, male and female, 4 native Missionaries and assistants, 200 native helpers, 1869 communicants, 1203 adult non-communicants, 3271 baptized children, 2047 enquirers and candidates for baptism, 15 schools, 1974 scholars, 28 teachers, 52 monitors. We have already referred to the higher educational institute at Genadenthal. In all there are some 8390 under the pastoral care of the Brethren in West South Africa.

The eastern Stations of the United Brethren were at a much later period established among the Kaffir race. The more special aim of these Missions was the Tambookie tribes, among whom they have indeed gained considerable success, but there are found other Kaffir races also at these settlements, and a number of Hottentots. Some of the stations are of

---

* These have been kindly furnished to me by the Rev. H. E. Shawe, Secy. of the Missions of the United Brethren, London.

very recent origin, four begun during the last four or five years, indicating thus an earnest evangelistic purpose of pressing on into new fields of work. One of these stations, again, Shiloh, the oldest of all, is this year, like the Rhenish Mission, celebrating its jubilee, being just half a century old. Shiloh may be said to occupy among the eastern Stations of the Brethren, a place somewhat analogous to Genadenthal in the west. It is, as it were, the mother Church, and its membership is still the most numerous. It is situated in an elevated country, some 3500 feet high, to the north-west of the Amatolas, not far thus from the strongholds of the Gaikas. Placed in such a situation and surrounded by warlike Kaffir tribes, we may readily conceive that its history has been an agitated one. Like some of the villages on the slopes of Vesuvius, which seldom altogether escape when there is a great eruption, Shiloh has shared in all the protracted succession of Kaffir convulsions. The interesting story of Shiloh, its disasters, its survival after events which threatened its ruin, its gradual growth, and now its firm settlement, are very well and simply told in a recent sketch of its history, in the periodical accounts of the Brethren.*

As it is impossible in South Africa, generally, to obtain good harvests without irrigation, it is the first business of a Mission station to construct water conduits to their fields. This the Missionaries were obliged to do with their own hands and toil at Shiloh,

* This has been reprinted separately in a small publication, entitled "History of Shiloh, and the Missions of the Church of the United Brethren in Kaffraria." London, 1878.

as the Tambookies looked upon all manual labour as a disgrace to men, fit only for women. Gradually, however, the example of the Missionaries, and the success of their work, made an impression. They began to feel that labour was more honourable than they had fancied it. They abandoned their old rude Kaffir mode of farming, and thoroughly ploughed and cultivated their fields. Stone houses were built in place of their miserable kraals, and the decencies of European clothing were preferred to their insufficient native attire. Skilled labour was taught them by the Brethren, themselves artisans, and they learned to become good farmers. Now, some of the natives possess waggons, with numerous teams of oxen, a source of great wealth at present to the Boers, and natives in South Africa. I have specially instanced these facts as they are told by the Brethren in the story of this Mission as an illustration of the bearing of Missions generally on native industry in South Africa, and as the best answer to the sneers of Mr. Trollope and others, who have not taken the trouble to acquaint themselves with the real facts of Mission economy.

Meanwhile, also, in the far higher spiritual field, the fallow ground was being broken up, and the precious seeds of a life higher in its moral tone, and in its religious and spiritual character, were being sown. Dark superstitions were being dissipated by Christian light, and advance was made to a purer and better life. But it is quite beyond our limits to note all the periods of crisis at Shiloh during the last 50 years, and we glance at them only as a picture of the trials of many another Kaffir station.

Sometimes their experiences were clouded and adverse—their station was assailed by hostile natives—they were despoiled of their property, and their cattle were plundered. Again they were attacked by jealous and suspicious Colonists—their church battered by a cannon, and their houses destroyed. Sometimes they were obliged to flee as exiles to a distance, scarcely hoping to see Shiloh again. But harder trials than even these vexed the Brethren— there was the declension of their converts, their falling into drunken habits, the bitter strifes of the Hottentots, the Tambookies and the Fingoes, at the station. Sometimes, too, especially during the rising of the native tribes against the Colony—there were unmistakable marks of disloyalty. It must be remembered how strong with the Kaffir the tribal attachment has been, just as with the Gael in Scotland, some century or century and a half ago. No doubt there were the new and higher influences of a Mission life, but there was often a hard struggle, and sometimes a failure. I refer to this because it bears on the present as well as the past. I quote from the history of Shiloh one incident as illustrative of this. It occurred during a Kaffir rising. The narrative says—"Some deliberately entered upon treason—others followed their leaders without thought, until they were too deeply involved to withdraw. But very many were evidently carried away by the influence of the prevailing spirit, and were unable to obey the dictates of their better feelings and judgment. To the Missionaries' faithful exhortations and entreaties to continue loyal, they yielded a ready assent, and then Tambookies and Hottentots, bursting into tears, would go over to the rebels." We believe that during the late rising, if indeed we can yet regard it as quite past, there have not been many instances of disaffection or rebellion on the part of native Christians, but such have occurred, and this narrative of the Brethren may throw light upon them. The Missionaries have inculcated loyalty strenuously where the tribes were subject to British rule, as in the Cape and Natal. But it is scarcely to be supposed that they should or ought to do so among tribes not yet subject directly to our sway, and regarding whose exact relations to ourselves there has been room for doubt. We may state, however, that all the Missionaries, including those representing Foreign Societies, have been most friendly to British annexation where it has actually taken place, as in Basutoland the Transvaal, Namaqualand, or Kaffraria. We must add here that while the Missionaries have ever sought by their mediation to promote the cause of peace, the action of some of the government officials, not as regards them, but the natives, especially in reference to their rights to land, has been such as to have furnished an apology, if not for open war on the part of the independent natives, or of disloyalty to the Suzerain on the part of the subject tribes, yet for a bitter sense of wrong and injustice.*

But while there are darker, there are also brighter moments in Mission annals, and such there were at Shiloh—times of steady progress in education, in

* We have not beside us the document, and shall not therefore refer to it more specially, but we believe a late eminent Colonial official has stated that considerable wrongs have been inflicted on the Griquas of the west.

intelligence, in moral and religious habits—times of serious impression—times, too, when everything external again shone upon them—when the Government liberally provided them with wider lands for their increasing numbers—when a Governor could assure them that he would rather have the frontier guarded by 9 Mission stations, than by 9 military posts, and when, having attended their religious services he remarked, "I have been in many fine churches, but my heart has never been so touched as it was in this humble temple of God in the wilderness, in which black people and white sit side by side, as brethren in Christ."* In point of fact, latterly no British Colonial Governments are less liable to reproach, as regards Christian Missions, than those of South Africa, although, in reference to Mission lands there are still, we believe, some causes of grievance.

Around Shiloh there have gradually grouped themselves some stations which are now steadily growing. Further to the north-east, in Kaffraria, there is a central group of stations chiefly among the Tambookies, while further north again, there are growing stations among the Hlubis. The latest statistics of the Brethren's eastern stations are the following—There are 8 stations and 2 out-stations, 20 European and 2 native Missionaries, 53 native helpers, 481 communicants, 149 adults, non-comunicants, 656 baptized children. There are 9 schools, 512 scholars, 12 teachers, 1 monitor. In all, there are 1990 under the pastoral care of this Mission. We may notice here, that only one station,

* Sir Harry Smith. History of Shiloh, p. 26.

Entwanzana, near the territory of Stockwe, one of the rebel Tambookie chiefs, had to be abandoned during the war, and was in great measure destroyed, but is now re-occupied by the missionaries.

I may be permitted, in closing this rapid and imperfect sketch of the Missions of the United Brethren, one or two remarks. One is, that we cannot read these periodical accounts they publish, without observing how truthfully and candidly and unreservedly the Mission story is told. If Mr. Trollope fancies Missionaries to be credulous and sanguine in their views, drawing on their imagination as they paint Mission scenes, let him read these simple narratives; they certainly tell no romantic tale. On the contrary, while there are hopes expressed of some of the converts, and joy in the progress of others, the story is full of the sorrows of the Brethren over many of them, their little progress, their weaknesses, their strifes, their immoralities, the drunkenness of some. One almost feels at times, as if in their desire to be truthful, the Brethren sometimes allowed themselves to take too morbid a view of things. There is another remark we would make —the Moravian Missions may not have some of the qualities of later Missions; the work is indeed the same, but the machinery may differ. And perhaps, from their older history, their methods may seem a little antiquated, and the movement a little slow. The conduct of missions has undoubtedly changed considerably. Half a century ago, it had less perhaps of that alert, energetic, business character, if we might so describe it, which it now possesses. There may be less of sentiment now, but more perhaps of intelligent and vigorous action. The whole scheme of Mission work has been more fully thought out, and has in practice been more completely developed. To be a well-equipped missionary affords now as large a field, not only for Christian graces, but for all Christian gifts and accomplishments, as any department of the ministry; perhaps more so, indeed. Then again, our modern missions have a far wider field than the United Brethren, from which to gather in men thoroughly furnished for mission work, by their biblical studies, their facility in languages, their acquaintance with medicine, besides those rarer qualities of energy, indomitable patience, courage, sagacity, all so needful to influence the savage mind, and mould it to the gospel. We do not exaggerate, when we say, that such missionaries are now to be found in the Mission fields, of as high a type of intellect, and moral force, and with as varied gifts as any order of men in the ranks of the Christian Church. If the Brethren have not so many of these men, yet it is evident that they are, so far as their resources allow, determined not to lag behind, but to stir up every gift; and while they have had in the past so limited a choice, comparatively, of men, yet who will deny the great success they have gained, and continue to gain by what are, after all, the main essentials of mission success—the graces of meekness, brotherly kindness, Christian fidelity, guilelessness, Catholic charity? These their whole annals brightly display. These are far higher in Mission work than all the zeal of the Ecclesiastic, or the pretensions of sacerdotalism. We cannot read the records of the South African

Missions of the Brethren without finding many pleasing tokens, that the old type of Moravian piety is vigorous as ever. There is the same beauty of character, the same fidelity to their old fervid evangelical testimony, the same unshrinking boldness to declare it, the same readiness to embrace in the Christian brotherhood other Churches than their own. There is also the same successive gathering of souls into the heavenly garner, the same evangelistic earnestness, ready to leave old cultivated fields for new and difficult work. Unhappily, too, there is the same story of severe privations and trials to which the Brethren expose themselves in their arduous self-denying work. Brother Meyer, lately labouring in the Missions to the Hlubis, deserves to be held in Christian memory in the Churches for his long, unwearied, and successful labours among the Kaffirs. From his thorough knowledge of the Kaffir tongue, he was able to render great services in the preaching of the Gospel, and he wore himself out spending and being spent in his Master's work.

We shall add to the name of Meyer another which deserves not to be forgotten in Mission annals, Wilhelmina Stompjes. She was born in Kaffraria, but had in the providence of God been led to Genadenthal. When the new station at Shiloh was to be founded fifty years ago, she, with her husband, accompanied the Missionaries there. "The strong and admirable features of her Christian character," says the Mission narrative, " her intense love for her Kaffir countrymen, and her mastery of the language of the people, gave her a great advantage over the Missionaries, who could only hold intercourse with them with the aid of an interpreter, and she faithfully used it in all humility for the furtherance of the Lord's work. With a warm heart and overflowing lips, she would tell of the love of God in Jesus Christ. Her word had such weight even with the proud chiefs, that they were often swayed by it, and did not deem it beneath their dignity to send special messengers to the lowly maiden in the Missionaries' household." When acting as interpreter for the Missionaries it is said, "she could not help adding copiously to their words in order to make the message more impressive and more intelligible." On one occasion, but for her the Missionaries would probably have perished, Mapasa, a murderous Tambookie chief, came to the settlement in his war dress with fifty armed men, bent on its destruction. But Wilhelmina heard of it, and suddenly appeared. "Pressing through the group of savages, each of whom held his spear ready to strike at a word from the chief," she, with undaunted courage, reproached Mapasa for appearing in such warlike fashion, and ordered him to depart. "The fierce and cruel chieftain's son, completely overcome by her manner, instead of killing the missionaries, and the woman who dared to intrude on an assembly of men, withdrew peacefully, and apologised later for his conduct." On another occasion, when Sir George Grey visited the station with many tears she said to him, "Oh my Lord governor, I am deeply concerned about my poor people the Kaffirs. How many of them know nothing about the Word of God! Do show your power by causing more missionaries to be sent, and new stations to be founded." The Governor's heart was touched by this fervent appeal, and adopting her views, he advised her to urge the missionaries to go forward from Shiloh to occupy new ground. Wilhelmina died in 1863, probably seventy-five years of age. " A consistent follower of our Saviour, it was her delight in public and private to tell of His exceeding love for sinners, and she was able to do this with such tact and power, with the accompanying influence of God's Holy Spirit, that many were brought by her to rejoice in Jesus as their Saviour. All her rare talents were freely devoted to the Lord's service. Nowhere was garden and field in better order than under her busy hands, and the produce was, with most unselfish liberality, carefully appropriated for the furtherance of the cause of Christ. Her memory will long live in Shiloh."

CHAPTER XIV.

THE LONDON MISSIONARY SOCIETY.

THE chief work of the London Missionary Society lies now in the distant interior in Bechuanaland, yet its association with the Cape, which was the basis of all its operations, is so old, and the tie is still so strong, that we shall notice its labours here. In 1799, a few years later than the Moravian Brethren who followed Schmidt, the four first Missionaries of the London Missionary Society arrived at the Cape. They were welcomed by some of the pious Dutch— especially by Bos, an earnest Dutch minister, who was the means, indeed, of establishing there a South African Mission Society, which has since struck deep roots in the country. Two of the Missionaries accepted an invitation to visit the Bushmen, in their distant settlements—another left speedily for India—the fourth, and by far the most remarkable man of them all, went to the Kaffirs. The name of Dr. Johann Theodosius Van der Kemp, is one that will ever be illustrious in Mission history. This devoted, gifted, self-sacrificing Missionary, was born at Rotterdam, in 1747, where his father was a preacher. He was, as a student, not only a distinguished classical scholar, but said to be conversant with most modern languages, for acquiring which, indeed, the Dutch have a gift. His first career was as a cavalry officer, in which he distinguished himself, but which he left in consequence of some quarrel with the Prince of Orange. He was at this time known as an audacious sceptic, and a man of utterly uncontrolled life; and these are said to have so grieved his father, as to have caused his death. On abandoning the army, he took to the study of medicine, partly at the University of Edinburgh, where he gained high honour. He then settled as a physician at Middelburg, where he practised ten years, not, it is said, without some struggle after a higher life, and some concealed anguish as to the eternity before him. It was there that the drowning of his wife and child in the river, while he himself hardly escaped with his life, deeply aroused him—light after light penetrated his soul, until he sank prostrate at the feet of Jesus. In his deep sorrow for the past, and with much inner devotion, he now gave himself to the study of the Bible, and of the Eastern languages, of which it is said, from his astonishing facility, he acquired sixteen. Just at this time a call of the London Missionary Society, then newly formed—to consider the claims of the heathen, fell into his hands. His resolution was at once formed; he offered his services as a Gospel messenger. These were cordially welcomed, and he was appointed to South Africa. Returning from London, on a visit to Holland, before his departure for the scene of his future work, he became the instrument, in the Divine Hand, of rousing the slumbering spirit of his country to the claims of Missions, and to Christian action, and he was the means of there being formed two Missionary Societies, one at Rotterdam, and the other in East Friesland.

After a short stay at the Cape, Van der Kemp left for his Kaffir Mission Field. The time was outwardly unfavourable. The Boers were extremely dissatisfied with the British Government—their Hottentot servants, or rather Serfs, weary of their oppression, were constantly fleeing to the Kaffirs as a refuge—the Kaffirs, too, had suffered wrongs at the hands of the Boers, which they were ready to revenge. The state of the Eastern Border was thus constantly agitated, and there were many raids into the Colony. But Van der Kemp, nothing daunted, pressed onward to meet Gaika, the Kaffir chief. When asked of his mission, he told them very simply that it was to speak to them of things that would make them happier in this life and beyond death. Received coldly at first, he was permitted at last to settle down on the other side of the Keiskamma, then a part of Kaffir territory. The situation of his station he found was pleasant, amid fair meadows, in an amphitheatre of mountains clad with green and flourishing forests, and scattered around were the kraals of the natives. But amid all the fine scenery the life of Van der Kemp was a very hard one. It need not, perhaps, have been so much so—it arose probably from his absorption in higher things, and his want of care for comfort; it was certainly not from an ascetic spirit; but so it was, that in point of fact he seems to have lived chiefly on roots. The salt for his food, he himself prepared from the brine of the ocean. His visits too to the native kraals, to carry to them the message of salvation, were most trying, over thorn bushes and sharp rocks, without hat, or shoes, or stockings, often with bleeding feet. Here he continued for some sixteen months, instructing the Kaffir youth in the Gospel, and seeking also to win the captive Hottentots to the truth. At last he was compelled, as war drew nearer, to abandon Kaffirland. Yet, we may say, that some first fruits of the harvest even then were gathered in. The name of Jesus was spread abroad, and his own, Jinkanna, as he was called, was, as a faithful servant of his Master, long honoured in Kaffraria. One of his converts, too, Sinkanna, touched by the Gospel, composed simple and beautiful hymns, and went about through the country singing them, and offering prayers. After his retirement, too, ultimately to Bethelsdorp, a station near Algoa Bay, a number of the sons of the Kaffir chiefs were sent to him to be educated. The remainder of the life of this remarkable man was a chequered one. It was devoted mainly to his beloved Hottentots, and to the defence of their rights. He was grieved at the oppression they suffered, and stood forth their intrepid champion. Called to the Cape to vindicate his charges against their oppressors, he there received a higher summons, and was called away from his life of noble toil and self-sacrifice to his heavenly rest. Van der Kemp was undoubtedly a man of noblest gifts, and entire consecration to his Master, and he has left behind him a name never to be forgotten. In minor things, however, he was perhaps less judicious, at least honest Mr. Campbell thought and said so. His marrying a native wife, whom he had liberated from slavery, did not certainly conduce, as he himself felt afterwards, to the comfort of his later life, and his conforming himself generally to the rudeness of native usages and living, so much as he did, was not for the furtherance of the Gospel. Civilisation and Christianity, we may say, go hand in hand. The former has in it some leaven of the latter. It is not to the disadvantage of the Gospel, but to its furtherance, that our civilisation has so widely conquered the world. It seems to be, indeed, the narrow edge of the wedge inserted, which shall prepare for something more penetrating to follow. Without expecting rude tribes to adopt all our habits—their assimilation to higher usages of life has its benefit. In this respect, we think the Moravian Brethren in South Africa acted more wisely than Dr. Van der Kemp.*

We have dwelt thus somewhat at large on the life of Van der Kemp—the first great missionary, we may say, of South Africa. It would be, at the same time, quite a work of supererogation were we to enter at large on the history of the London Missionary Society. This was suitable, so far as regards the Rhenish and Moravian Missions, because their history is less known; but the annals of the London Missionary Society are familiar to most, and to attempt

---

* For this hasty sketch of the life of Dr. Van der Kemp I am much indebted to Dr. Grundemann, editor of Dr. Burkhardt's work, "Die Evangelische Missionen unter den befreiten und freien negern, &c." Had I met this before writing the earlier part of this volume, it would have been most serviceable to me. A work so able and carefully written ought to be translated into English.

to compress a narrative which owes so much to its interesting and striking details could have but little general interest. And yet as this Society has occupied so large a place in the Mission history of South Africa, the most honourable we have ventured to say of any, some general thoughts on its Mission polity may, we think, be inserted with advantage in this chapter.

And, first, we would notice as one of its most prominent characteristics, that it has been in South Africa so widely a pioneer in the Mission field. It is with the Moravians that lies the honour of first indeed breaking ground among the Hottentots; but, with this exception, there is scarcely a Mission field in South Africa where the London Missionary Society did not lead the way. There were thus their early Missions to the Bushmen, though these, it must be owned, failed, as those of every other Missionary Society have done, owing to the extraordinary manner of life of this race in its wild state; then there was the approach of their Mission to the Namaquas, and their early entrance into the waste regions of Great Namaqualand. There was their Mission also to the Orlams, where one of their missionaries, Christian Albrecht, was the means of the conversion of Africaner. We have already noticed how Dr. Moffat afterwards, in his Mission work in this tribe, so confirmed and established him in the faith. Then further inland in those regions we now call the Diamond Fields, there was their work among the Griquas, who may be said to have owed to them almost their existence as a race, as well as their conversion to Christianity. It was

Mr. Campbell's wise suggestions that first led to a settled government amongst them and the Korannas. And it was Dr. Moffat at a later time who was the main instrument in setting over them so wise and intrepid a chief as Waterboer. We have already noticed how Waterboer repaid the benefit by saving the Bechuanas from the Mantatees, when they were in danger of ruin. It was the London Missionary Society also which began the work in the East among the Kaffirs—Dr. Van der Kemp gathering the first fruits; but Mr. Brownlee in 1820 permanently occupying the field and holding it indeed until but lately, when the veteran Missionary died at his post.

We cannot doubt that this tentative system, this readiness to sow beside all waters, belongs to the highest ideas of Mission work, and it has thus distinguished this Society in the past, and marks it even now, as in its intrepid resolve to extend its work to Central Africa, and to occupy Lake Tanganyika. It may be said, indeed, that the results of this method, the Mission Society, like the merchant ever alert for some new venture, ready to enter on new Mission enterprises, have not always been successful. As far as the Bushmen are concerned, this is so far true; and it may be added that, in many other directions also, the London Missionary Society, after pressing on for a time, was obliged to recede. This also is true; but it would be erroneous to infer from it that there was failure. When it retired, it was, in almost every instance, because while other fields seemed spread before it, whitening to the harvest, other Societies were prepared at its call, to enter on its initial work, and were fully equipped to do so with success. It may be worth our while to notice here for a moment the position the London Missionary Society occupied, not only in Great Britain, but in the begining of the century, we may add, in relation to all Evangelical Christendom. Its position was peculiarly catholic—it was founded on an idea which in this imperfect state, cannot perhaps be fully carried out, that the Christian Church, however divided and split into fragments at home, should present itself to the heathen as one great unity, one holy Catholic Church. There can be no doubt that the idea is so far just, that it is most unhappy to carry our differences into the Foreign Field, and to display before the heathen the strifes, and rivalries, and jealousies of contending Christian communities at home. Still it may be questioned how far the Christian Churches can thus feel themselves absolved from individual action. May they not profitably apply the organization and equipment and gifts resulting in so many useful consequences at home, in the Mission Field also; so that marching, it may be, as separate tribes, they may take each its place in occupying the great field of the world ? And may it not be possible to do this without sectarianism, and without necessarily obtruding minor differences ? We may say that this is really being accomplished in India, China, South Africa, and other Missions on the part of all the truly loyal-hearted Evangelical Missions. They do not encroach on one another, they are banded together as brethren—they show, amid their diversities, a united front to the heathen. But passing from this, in point of fact from this undenominational character of the London Missionary Society, most other younger Mission Societies, both British and Foreign, rallied around it, willing to accept its counsels as to the positions they should occupy and ready to enter on those the London Missionary Society felt itself unable to hold. Thus it was, for instance, that the London Missionary Society handed over Great Namaqualand, and ultimately its stations in Lesser Namaqualand to the Rhenish Mission—then, too, it resigned the Korannas, another Hottentot race, to the Berlin Mission. So also, while invited itself to occupy Basutoland, it counselled the French Basuto Mission to enter on the work there, and thus also in British Kaffraria, where its missions indeed still flourish, yet Mr. Brownlee gave over, we believe, the first station he occupied to the Scottish Presbyterian Missions. It is an interesting history—the success of these missions which thus entered on the fields first occupied by the London Missionary Society. It is a fine illustration of those deep sayings of our Lord—"One soweth and another reapeth," "both he that soweth and he that reapeth may rejoice together." At the Diamond Fields or the Gold Fields of South Africa, the first searcher, however enriched, often leaves behind him greater wealth than that he had gained, others follow him in fields abandoned as almost hopeless and find there unexpected treasures. So is it in the kingdom of God, so has it been with these Missions among the Namaquas, Korannas, Kaffirs, and other tribes. These Mission fields have yielded and are yielding greater wealth than ever, and in the future, even richer results may be anticipated.

Before passing from this it may be taken as an interesting instance, showing that the Divine Seed of the Word is not lost, to recall the story of the Makololo tribe. Those who have read the narrative of the London Missionary Society in South Africa, will recall Livingstone's intercourse with them— the Mission expedition to Linyanti—its unhappy failure, with the loss of valuable Mission lives from fever—the collapse or rather seeming destruction of the tribe. And yet Livingstone's Christian work had not, it was found, been without its fruits—fragments of the Makololos still survived. Mr. Young, for instance, the able conductor of the Livingstonia Mission expedition, found some of them on the banks of the Shiré, rising by their European knowledge and learning to the rank of chiefs, and to them the Free Church was mainly indebted for the safe transport of its steamer—the Ilala—which it has lately launched on the waters of the Lake Nyassa.

There are other characteristics of the London Missionary Society's labours, which, as connected with the whole polity of Missions, are worthy of note here. It is in harmony with what as have we already indicated—the Society holds it as a great principle that Mission work is evangelisation or the plantation of Churches, not their permanent building up and consolidation. We quote on this subject some excellent sentences from their last Report— "Delay in the readjustment of such positions"—the reference is to older churches—" was for a long period a weak point in the arrangements of the Society, and even now it is not found always easy to determine when the pastoral oversight of converts shall be given up."—" But in the judgment of the Directors it is only right and wise that the old state of things should pass away, not only on the ground of the resolutions passed by their predecessors, but because the policy in itself is perfectly sound, and is the course most beneficent to the native Churches themselves."—" Throughout civil and religious society, young men, young churches, young communities will grow into perfect manhood, only as circumstances require them to manage their own affairs, to maintain themselves by their own efforts, to bear their own burden of duty or privilege, and to fight their own battles against temptation and wrong."—" All real growth is from within. No human instrumentality from without can impart or promote it—it depends upon an inner life, an inner organism. That growth will usually occupy a long period, and it will require a variety of influences."—" The gradual process—the fruit of the Word accepted and professed is evidently not the work of the Evangelistic Society, whose functions it is to bring the Gospel to a people for the first time. A Missionary Society has to plant acorns and care for saplings. Only the storms of centuries, and native growth under God's sun and air, will make them oaks of which a land is proud." *—It is in carrying out this important principle that the London Missionary Society latterly has " thrown to a large extent upon their own resources the twenty Churches of the Society within the Cape Colony."

* London Missionary Society's Report, 1878, p. 38.

These are by no means going back, "on the contrary growing out of their transition state, united in a practical and well managed union, anxious to fill some of their vacancies by new men from England, and to train their best native teachers at Lovedale, and the Kuruman, they are endeavouring to render their position more secure, and to maintain Church ordinances more firmly than ever." We may notice here a crucial instance, if we may call it, of this their later system. They were recently called to "consider their relation to the well-known Mission among the Griquas." In Eastern Griqualand the chief town is Kokstad; the claims of the Griquas for Missionary help were pressed upon them, and a Missionary was sent in 1870. He lately accepted the pastorate of this Griqua Church, and asked the sanction of the London Missionary Society to remain there. They were anxious, however, believing that his evangelistic work was done there, that he should go to Tanganyika. The result has been that holding their Missionary "in high personal regard, and respecting his conscientious convictions of duty, they are prepared to place him in his charge in comfort, and they offer him their best wishes for his prosperity and usefulness, but with this arrangement their care of the Griqua Church and people comes to an end."—The London Missionary Society has thus acted on similar principles to those of the Rhenish Society. We believe with it indeed was the initiative, and from its older establishment and more developed progress, it has been able to carry out thus vigorously a decision which will relieve its funds considerably. They will be thus set free for aggressive work. We may hope that even more than this will be accomplished, and that their native Churches in the Cape will be not only self-supporting but evangelistic, contributing their share in men and means to the great work to be carried on in Central Africa.

The Evangelistic progress of the Society has ever been in one direction. It has been earnestly, we might almost have added instinctively, turned northwards; but that we see in this, rather the hand and providence of God, and a simple earnest faith. A wide door and effectual of entrance had been opened in this direction, and the Missionaries felt pressed to go in by it, scarcely knowing, it may be, like the patriarch, whither they went. First, crossing the Orange River, there were the Griqua and Koranna settlements established by them—then passing the Vaal, they took possession of Bechuanaland—then onwards to the Matabeles, and lastly, now they have formed a station close to the Lake Ngami, near the Chief Moremi. It is but a step onwards to reach the Zambesi, and using it as a base to press into Central Africa. It is remarkable, we may observe, the advances that are now being made northwards. It is but a few years ago, since Livingstone pioneered the way, and now we read, in a South African Journal,* that a famous elephant hunter and his companions have just returned from their wanderings—their journeys having extended far north of the Zambesi.

* The *Natal Mercury*, one of the leading South African Journals, where much valuable information may be often found on South African progress and colonisation.

In this Mission progress, one feature especially prominent is concentration of Mission effort. The Society has still, indeed, its important stations among the Kaffirs, and in the Cape Colony generally; but it is evidently now devoting its highest energies and strength to the Mission fields of Bechuanaland, the Matabeles, and the adjacent tribes. Most of the South African Missions, indeed, while open to every Mission call the Master may address to them, find it best to devote themselves to one field—as the Rhenish Mission, for instance, the Berlin, the French, the Presbyterian, the Wesleyan, &c. We need not say that Bechuanaland has not been chosen by the London Missionary Society, because it is a pleasanter or less laborious field of work than others. On the contrary, its arid hot climate is often very trying to the European, nor is the work itself so promising perhaps as among the Basutos, the Fingoes, the Kaffirs, or the natives of the Transvaal. Nor has it the great advantage of Colonial rule. It has had many trials indeed, to endure from the arbitrariness of native rule, and the brutality and cruelty of native chiefs. Still this has not deterred it from entering resolutely on the work to which the Master plainly had called it, and its efforts among the Barolongs, the Batlapins, the Bakwens, the Bamangwatos, the Matabeles, are being crowned with ever increasing success. Its stations are in various stages of progress. Kuruman, the chief scene of Dr. Moffat's labours, with its eleven out-stations, has become an important centre of work, and its Mission College is now established on a broad and satisfactory basis. All the stations of the Mission still, however, largely partake of an Evangelistic character. Those longest established have still many heathen towns and villages within their influence, while the latest founded deal with heathenism in almost undiminished strength. Among the Bamangwato and Matebele tribes, the Missionary brethren have found a hard field of labour, and have had to endure long patience. But " called as this Society has been to occupy the field, the hardness of the people has been no argument for neglecting or quitting the field." It has "simply led them to make the Mission strong, and to send to it some of the best qualified men they can find." "They have broken up the fallow ground—they have gathered in the stones—they have laid bare the soil to rain, and sun, and air, they have steadily sowed the seed, and they have had abundant proof that their teaching, their example, their kindness to the sick, their counsels have had a powerful and steady influence."*

In even so rapid an outline as this of the work of the London Missionary Society in South Africa, it would be to overlook a signal feature did we not notice the many men highly gifted and qualified for Mission labours whom the great Master has graciously bestowed on this Society. There is Van der Kemp, the gifted heroic self-denying Missionary to the Hottentots; there is John Campbell, the first visitor of the Mission, not a man perhaps of great natural gifts but possessed of a sagacity and holy energy which did much to consolidate the early Mission

* Report of London Missionary Society, 1877.

work, and whose fervid, and at the same time humorous, sketches* of South Africa and its natives helped to inspire British audiences with an interest in the work.

Then the Society had Dr. Philip, another able and energetic Mission administrator, who did so much also to inspire Continental Christians with a zeal for Missions, and who so greatly aided the young Continental Societies, such as the " Societé des Missions Evangeliques " of Paris, with the Rhenish and Berlin Missions, in seeking out appropriate spheres for their Mission work. His manly, earnest, and able championship of the Hottentot, following in this in the steps of Van der Kemp, but with more success, for it was he who mainly won for them their freedom, will make his name ever to be honoured by the philanthropist, and especially to be endeared to the race he rescued. Later still there is Moffat, with all his remarkable combination of Missionary gifts, his sagacity in penetrating native character, his power to influence and control it by his Christian eloquence and by his moral energy, his long laborious study of the Bechuana tongue, and his successful translation of the Bible into this language, his interest in geographical enterprise, in which for the gospel's sake he so aided Livingstone, and his highly poetic oratory, which, on his first visit to England in his prime, so impressed

---

* As regards humour some of his sketches still live in the memory of old auditors and even yet stir to laughter. Especially his account of his arrival at Lattakoo—his question pronounced in his broad Scottish Doric, " Whaur is Lattakoo ? " and his astonishment to find the great African City lying with its huts at his feet like so many ant hills, burrowed in the ground.

and electrified his audiences.* Then above all there is Livingstone, the incomparable Missionary traveller, with his amazing energy and patience, his indomitable courage, and his great observational powers, whose method of travel is so superior to any other, if, in our quest of knowledge we seek to win it not by intimidating or killing the poor ignorant wretched savage, but by seeking to conciliate and win him to the cause of civilization and Christianity. Dr. Livingstone's Mission polity here is, if we may so describe it, the Divine method of the Gospel, enforced and illustrated by the example of the great Master and Evangelist of the Church.

Besides these distinguished Christian agents in the Mission work of the Society, we might have noticed, had our limits allowed, the many interesting instances of native conversion to be found in the records of the Society; but these are too generally known to need to be related. We shall refer only to one native Christian chief, whose life and character merit our honour. Khame is the chief of the Bamangwato tribe. His life is one of singular romantic decision, as with Joshua, to serve the Lord. Dr. Fritsch, the learned German traveller, who is, I may observe, in general, far from being a friend of Missions, says of him in language we translate, "The eldest son of Sekhome (Khame's father was then alive,) is a bright exception to the character of the Bechuanas, and does honour to the efforts of

* In the Martyr of Erromanga, if we recollect aright, the late Dr. Campbell gives a very vivid impression of the powerful effect of these addresses, and the zeal they inspired in the cause of Missions.

these pious Missionaries. I rejoice to have had the opportunity of making Khame's acquaintance, and to name a black whom I should in no circumstances be ashamed to regard as a friend. The simple, modest, yet noble bearing of the chieftain's son awoke in me a feeling of satisfaction such as I have never experienced in the society of blacks." The Rev. Mr. M'Kenzie, of the London Missionary Society, says of him at a later date, "Instead of a heathen chief" (Sekhome, his father) " and community as in 1862, there are now a Christian chief and community, almost all the young people of which are learners of Christianity. There is now no rain-making, and the Missionary teaches them instead to pray to God for daily bread all the year round. Heathenism no longer presides now either at seed time or harvest, but these seasons are graced by Christian prayer and thanksgiving."

The statistics of the London Missionary Society for this year 1878, are the following :*—It has in South Africa, apart from the Tanganyika Mission in Central Africa, 17 principal stations, with 52 out-stations. There are of these 5 principal stations in the old Cape Colony with 8 out-stations ; then 3 in British Kaffraria with 14 out-stations, 7 in Bechuanaland with 30 out-stations, 1 in Matabeleland with, let us notice, a staff of no less than 4 missionaries. We must add to this the proposed station at Lake Ngami, but regarding it we have no statistics. The total number of English Missionaries in South Africa, apart from 3 engaged in the Tanganyika Mission, is 22, with 113 native preachers. There

* Eighty-fourth Report of the London Missionary Society, 1878.

are in all 4615 members of the church, with 24,022 native adherents. The schools number in all 42, and there are 2052 scholars. We have already noticed that at Kuruman is the Central Higher Educational Institute. From last accounts, the buildings comprising the Moffat Institution now in course of erection at Kuruman, are progressing rapidly, and their completion may be looked forward to at an early period. Mr. M'Kenzie, a highly accomplished missionary, has been appointed Resident Tutor. The site of the College is excellent, and it is being excellently and substantially built. We are informed, too, on good authority, that the industrial element will occupy a considerable place in its system. The Bechuanas are not indeed so far advanced in agriculture as the Fingoes or Tambookies or Basutos, and such an Institution cannot thus rival in extent Lovedale; still its efforts will be directed to promote the same cause of agricultural progress.

CHAPTER XV.

THE DUTCH CHURCH OF SOUTH AFRICA.

WE may notice here the Dutch Church of South Africa. Its centre is the Cape, and it is not only the largest Colonial Church, but it has also latterly been doing good service in the South African Mission cause. We have already observed with what warmth of heart, Christian Bos, a Dutch minister, welcomed Van der Kemp and his fellow missionaries to the Cape. The South African Missionary Society which was then formed, exerted soon a happy influence—exciting far and wide in the Colony an interest in the Christianisation of the native races. While the attitude of the Boers in general still continued repulsive, yet there were also sincerely Christian men and ministers in the Dutch Church who sympathised with this new movement, and readily consented to place their slaves or their Hottentot servants under Missionary care and instruction. The South African Society cannot indeed be said to have done much for a long period in direct Mission work—this it rather handed over to the Mission Societies from abroad, still, as in the case of the Rhenish Mission, to which we have already referred, and the French and Berlin, we may

K

add also, it gave liberally and heartily to promote the Mission cause. Latterly it has assumed a far more earnest Evangelistic attitude than before, and has formed a number of Mission stations. As this Colonial Church is so intimately bound up with the destinies of South Africa, and as the new life and vigour infused into it give promise that it may yet occupy a leading Evangelistic position in Africa, my readers will permit me shortly to glance generally at its history.

The Church is old as the Cape Colony itself. It is a seedling of the old Evangelical Dutch Church transplanted to the Cape. "It has proved," says a recent writer, " a merciful providence for South Africa, that though Popish Portugal was the means of its discovery, its colonisation was reserved for Protestant Holland. Had it been otherwise, the religious condition of half a continent, as regards both the white and coloured population, would have been very different from what it is. Instead of peaceful, thriving communities, with numerous and varied circles of Christian activity, we should have expected to find countries analogous, socially and religiously, to Mexico or Brazil."* The arrival of the Huguenots in South Africa brought with it, as we have already said, the infusion of a deeper life into the Church, and the vigorous impulse it gave is felt still. Many of the best of the Dutch pastors have now in their veins, the blood of those heroic men who abandoned all for the truth's sake. Another

* We quote from an unpretending, yet interesting sketch of the South African Dutch Church, by the Rev. John M'Carter— "The Dutch Reformed Church in South Africa," &c. Edinburgh, W. & C. Inglis.

feature, we may add, has been impressed on the Dutch South African Church by the accession of a number of Scottish Evangelical Presbyterian ministers in this century, eleven arriving in 1822 and following years, and eight in 1860. To this, for instance, the Dutch Church owes the Murrays, whose names, from their valuable Christian services, are almost household words in the Dutch homes of South Africa. The Church of South Africa has thus many affinities. "From the Church of Holland," writes one of its ministers,* "it has its general framework, with its Confession, its Liturgies, and its form of service. To it it owes its use of organs and hymns, the celebration of the holidays of the Christian Feasts, the systematic preaching on the Heidelberg Confession, &c. To the Church of France it owes much of its best spiritual life, still markedly visible among the descendants of the French refugees. The influence of Scotland may be traced in its theology, its view of the relations to the State, its pastoral work, as well as its religious life, as seen in Sabbath observance, prayer meetings, and missions." In its external history, the following are the most important points. For more than a century the Cape Church was under the rule of the Church in Holland. In 1803 it received a Constitution, then an Ecclesiastical Commission sent out from Holland. In 1843 the Dutch Constitution was displaced by an English ordinance, intended to give the Church more liberty of action. In 1862 the Church of the Colony was separated from its three

* The Rev. Dr. Andrew Murray—The Presbyterian Churches throughout the World, p. 59. T. & A. Constable.

smaller branches in Natal, and the two Republics, owing to its having been found that a Synod with a Colonial ordinance could not allow ministers from beyond its boundaries to take part in its legislation. In the same year commenced its battle with Liberalism introduced from Holland, resulting in a collision with the law courts, and latterly in the withdrawal of the most advanced of the Rationalist ministers. In 1875 a Bill in the Cape Parliament made an end of the State support, which up to that period, the congregations of the Church had received." It will be seen from this, that the Dutch Church is now disestablished. We may add, that with every movement toward its liberty, it has been shown more clearly how firmly it stands on the basis of the Dutch Church of the Reformation— a Church which made so noble a confession and endured such martyrdoms for the cause of the gospel, and of Christian liberty. The Dutch Synod of the Cape is an earnest evangelical body. Having been present at its Synodical gatherings, on first touching South African ground, I may say how much they impressed me. Perhaps there was something more of the stiffness of older times and of the formalism of older ecclesiasticism, than is generally found in these less ceremonious days. The Ministers were all attired with strict ecclesiastical etiquette in their Dutch gowns and bands, and with a little stretch of fancy, one might have supposed they were present at some old Dutch Assembly, or even let us say at the Synod of Dort. But behind all these forms there was manifestly all the Christian life of the nineteenth century. We have seldom, indeed, witnessed more earnest gatherings, or listened to debates conducted with sounder wisdom, or more evangelical fervour. There is a great deal that is sterling about many of the Boers, even although, like the Southern Planters of the United States, there still remains too much prejudice as to race. You rarely enter a Boer home where there is not stated family worship—and however scanty the Library may be, it seldom wants the Hall Bible.* Few are the households too, that, even at a great sacrifice of time, do not travel to their quarterly "Nacht Maal," or Lord's Supper. Many families even build for themselves a dwelling near their church, only used by them on the occasion of these solemnities. The large expenditure, too, of the Dutch South African Churches in the erection of suitable and handsome ecclesiastical edifices, in which they vie, indeed, with our home churches, is some indication of their interest in religion. In South Africa there are now three distinct Dutch denominations. There is first the Dutch Reformed Church of the Cape, which is by far the most numerous, the most influential, and the most energetic. There is, again, the Reformed Free Church, sometimes called the Church of the Doppers. It adheres with great tenacity to the early standards of the Dutch Church, and strongly objects to hymns in public worship, as being unscriptural. Then, there is, also, the Dutch Reformed Church of the South African Republic, the Transvaal, "which owes its existence to the with-

* I do not know what Mr. Froude, our distinguished historian, has written on this subject regarding the Boers, or if, indeed, he has published any observations. But it is scarcely, I think, betraying any confidence to say, that from his remarks, in conversation on South African life, this was a trait which struck and interested him.

drawal, under the influence of ministers from Holland, in 1858, from the Cape Church of some of its members in the Transvaal, owing to the wish to be free from anything like British influence, and to be more closely connected with the Church in Holland."* This last has only some four Ministers, and is understood to be neological in its views. As regards Mission work, ever since the Reformed Cape Synod, in 1848, took this into its own hands, the zeal for it, and the active organisation for carrying it out, has been increasing. The South African Dutch Missionary Society has quite given its adhesion to this, and its work is being now carried on far more efficiently than at an earlier time under the guidance of the Church itself. There are now, within and beyond the Cape Colony, eleven Mission Stations, with as many ordained Missionaries, labouring among the native population. Such a Mission, for instance, as that of Mr. Hofmeyer, in Zoutpansberg in the north of the Transvaal, is one that may compare in zeal and piety with the best stations in South Africa.

As regards numbers, if we include all the Dutch Churches of Africa, the number of Colonial adherents is some 238,863; there are probably also about 26,000 Mission adherents in all, and about 4,500 Mission members.†

May I, before leaving the Dutch Church, suggest how invaluable it would be if in South Africa a

* Presbyterian Churches, Dr. A. Murray's Report, p. 60.
† Neither the Dutch Church, the Propagation Society, nor the Wesleyans distinguish betwixt their colonial and native adherents. Our calculation is based to a considerable extent on the last Church statistics given in the Cape Census. It can only claim thus to be an approximation.

Church Union or Federation could be formed betwixt the Dutch and the Anglo-Saxon Evangelical Churches, which are in doctrine and spirit so closely allied? Union is strength, and strength is needed to resist the aggressions of traditional sacerdotal ecclesiasticism. As regards the Dutch, the French Basuto and the Anglo-Saxon Churches, there is nothing to hinder such a union being speedily formed. In point of fact, in Natal the Dutch Reformed Synod has made overtures to the Presbyterian Churches to form as speedily as may be such an incorporation, and the Presbyterian Churches are on their side equally prepared for such a union. The difference of language need not form an obstacle. In Scotland, for instance, there are English-speaking and Gaelic ministers labouring side by side, and forming one united Church. There might be a similar arrangement in South Africa. Where the Dutch language and population receded, the English might be adopted, in place of the young being handed over to Anglican Ritualism; while with an ever-increasing Dutch population, new spheres would be constantly opening up for the Dutch ministry.

CHAPTER XVI.

WESLEYAN MISSIONS IN SOUTH AFRICA.

THE Wesleyan Missions are the next which claim our attention. Their strength, it may be said, still lies in the Cape Colony, although their stations stretch widely beyond. With its usual Christian zeal and enterprise, the Wesleyan body was early in the field in South Africa. In 1814, they sought to begin a Mission at Cape Town, but permission was at first refused by the Cape authorities. This led them to enter on Mission work in Lesser Namaqualand, which is still continued with success. At last, the Rev. Barnabas Shaw obtained permission to open Services in Cape Town itself, and one of his colleagues, the Rev. Mr. Edwards, began to preach there. It was at first the day of small things with the Mission. The first place where worship was held, was an empty wine shop—where service was held in the Dutch and English languages—later two churches were built in the town. Now, by the last Wesleyan returns there are seven chapels. The work of the Society gradually from this centre spread over the Western Colony, where now there are many chapels, and the attendants number nearly 10,000.

But it is in the East Cape Colony that Wesleyanism has struck its deepest roots. It is, we may say, since 1820, and its settlement of British emigrants in the Eastern districts, that the Wesleyan body has achieved its most remarkable successes. This plan of colonisation was doubtless intended by the Government mainly as a defence of the Colony against Kaffir aggressions. But it has issued in nobler results in the extension of the gospel among these warlike tribes. It is one of the finest instances we know of colonisation speeding the cause of Christianity. The East Cape Colony, now the most thriving, populous, and enterprising province of South Africa, owes a great deal, as we have already said, to the Wesleyans, not only religiously, but materially and morally. It has had a number of eminent and successful Missionaries. The Rev. William Shaw, who is not to be confounded with the Rev. Barnabas Shaw, of the West Cape, who came out as one of the Colonial pastors, was in every way fitted to be a Christian pioneer, distinguished by his great ability and sagacity, his power of organising, his deep Christian interest in his work, and his sincere piety. He has left his mark in the district, especially, we may say, in Graham's Town, the very centre we may call it of the Eastern life of the Colony. The story he has himself written of his Mission is a work full of much interest. The Rev. Mr. Shepstone, the father of Sir Theophilus Shepstone, now the governor of the Transvaal, occupied here also an honourable place with Mr. Ayliff, whose family have since taken distinguished positions in the Colony and Natal.

Nor should Alison be overlooked, to whom we have already referred, first as a Wesleyan Missionary, and then as joining the Free Church of Scotland. His earnest Mission work will ever merit honour in Natal.

The Wesleyan body has taken a large part in promoting Colonial Christianity in South Africa, This, I may say, is in part owing to its organisation, which has so far a certain analogy to that of the S.P.G. Its missionaries are in many instances also Colonial ministers, or, we might express it *vice versa*—its Colonial ministry is also missionary. This is a question of Mission polity which is not unworthy of serious consideration. For my own part I should think preferable that the Missionary should be mainly a Missionary, and the Colonial ministry Colonial. They are separate vocations needing different gifts and mental habits, while their work will at the same time meet at many points, and if they are men of a right spirit they will be mutually helpful and valuable coadjutors. In point of fact, it is but rarely that the great Missionary will be found the acceptable colonial or home preacher. And even if he had the gifts it is doubtful, from the whole setting of his habits, if he would find himself quite at home in such work. On the other hand, still more rarely would the brilliant, Christian orator, who wields such power over his audiences be found to possess the gifts which would make him a successful and great missionary. Doubtless, instances of such distinction have been found, but it is as rare as a double first at the University.

At the same time I must own that weighty

opinions are to be found on the other side. The Rev. Mr. Calderwood, an able and experienced Missionary of the London Missionary Society and afterwards a Government Commissioner, writes,— " The Wesleyans have understood this subject better than any of the kindred Societies and have acted accordingly. They have throughout the Colony, especially in its Eastern Province, a large number of European members who take a deep interest in Missions to the heathen." Mr. Shaw, again, the Superintendent of the Mission, whom we have already noticed, observes—" It is a great charity to take the Gospel to our emigrant population. How many professed Christians and their children have thus been saved from degeneracy into heathenism." On the other side, however, it may be reasoned that the course pursued by the London Missionary, the Presbyterian, the American, and the Foreign Societies, has issued in greater Missionary results. This is a matter, of course, of appreciation. But however this may be, may not these words be addressed, if not to the Foreign Missions in South Africa, yet to other British Mission Churches: " This ought ye to have done, and not to leave the other undone." Have not your Colonial fallen countrymen, your kinsmen according to the flesh, a strong claim upon you ? If formed by you into Christian Churches, would not their Colonial aid powerfully help you ? Be this as it may, Wesleyanism thus occupies, colonially, a position of the highest importance, in which we cannot indeed but rejoice. She is, along with the Dutch Church, a stronghold of defence against that Ritualism which threatens

South African Evangelical Christianity. Another valuable result has been that the Wesleyan Colonists are increasingly interested in Christian work. We say increasingly, because it is an interesting fact that some at least of the original Colonists were drawn to South Africa as a Mission field of work. But now they have many of them considerable means at their disposal, and this is their resolution according to a late report: " Our friends will rejoice to hear the evidence of the fact that the African Mission Churches are becoming more and more *missionary* in their spirit and action. Our churches are aware of the danger of Colonial self-sustaining churches settling down into quiet parishes, and their pastors into easy chaplaincies wherein all local resources are consumed within the area of the several churches." "The organisation of a Missionary Society for South Africa was a step in the right direction, a platform on which we may raise broad expectations." " The work is expanding—new ideas are spreading—Christian public sentiment is maturing. The relations which Colonial Churches bear to surrounding heathen populations have of late been more distinctly apprehended, and the numerous obligations arising from these relationships have been more clearly recognised, and more cheerfully responded to."* " If rightly worked, we are persuaded that this will prove one of the most powerful means possible for the evangelisation of the millions of that great Continent."

As regards Mission work more especially, the Wesleyan Missionary Society, like the London, has

* Wesleyan Report, 1877, page 83.

been a pioneer in the field. It is inferior to the latter only in the extent of its exploration, and the only other Mission which is perhaps abreast of it in this, is the Berlin Society. It had, as we have observed, early Missions in Lesser Namaqualand, which were gradually extended to Greater Namaqualand, from which it has since retired. Its work has embraced Orlams, and Bastards, Griquas, and Barolongs, Fingoes, and Galekas, Pondos, and Zulus, &c. Like the London Missionary Society it has indeed wisely receded from some of these extended positions, when other societies were prepared to occupy them, but as regards most of the South African races —the Hottentots, the Kaffirs of Kaffraria, the Zulus, the Barolongs—it has firmly kept its hold on them, gradually but vigorously extending, indeed, its operations. As regards the last race, the Barolongs, we may single out one of their stations, Thaba Nchu, as in extent and evangelistic progress belonging to the first order of South African Mission Stations. Thaba Nchu, is an enclave of the Free State surrounded by it on all sides. To the honour of that Republic it has never made any encroachment on the Barolong territory. This has been doubtless owing to the prudent conduct of Maroko the chief, and the counsels of the Wesleyan Missionaries. The Barolong population amounts to some 20,000,* the number of members is above 1000, and of church attendants 4,500. Mr. Trollope, in his South African Tour, gives an interesting and friendly notice of this station. The Society for the Propagation of the Gospel has since 1863 a station here. It seems

* Wesleyan Report, 1878, p. 130.

strange that they should plant a Mission on ground preoccupied by another Christian Society during so many years. They say indeed that "in the face of the vastness of heathendom the Wesleyan and Church Missions do not clash in any offensive way."* The comment of Grundemann, the able German Mission historian, on the subject is this, (we translate it): "It is to be regretted that there should be such encroachments on the work belonging to others in the Mission sphere." †

The circuits of the Wesleyan Society in South Africa are large and well arranged to support one another. An unbroken chain of stations stretches along the coasts beginning in Lesser Namaqualand in the West, extending over the South and only terminating on the East at the boundaries of Zululand. All the circuits represent very considerable bodies of Church attendants; the Cape circuit which comes first, some 10,000, the district of Grahamstown and Port Elizabeth on the south-east some 23,000, the Queenstown district, including British Kaffraria and most of Kaffraria beyond, 21,000, Natal including the Pondos, but exclusive of the Coolies, nearly 16,000. Then inland there is the vast circuit of the Free State and the Transvaal with some 13,000.

To give a summary of the general statistics for South Africa, there are 240 Wesleyan Chapels, besides other preaching places, 102 Missionaries and assistants, 17,233 members, 83,602 Church attendants, apart from Coolies, 198 Day Schools, and

* S.P.G. Report, 1876, p. 59.
† Die Evangelische Mission, &c., Sud. Afrika, p. 210.

11,552 Day Scholars. I regret that it is impossible to gather from the Wesleyan returns the number separately of native Mission adherents and members. I can only offer as an approximation, partly based on the last Cape Colonial statistics, that its native adherents may amount to some 28,000, and its native members to some 5,500.* In connection with the Day Schools it is to be observed that at Heald Town there is a Collegiate Institute of a high character for the education of the native ministry and for educating native teachers.

As regards Central Africa, the Wesleyan body is not yet prepared to follow in the course indicated by the Free Church Mission† and the London Missionary Society. "The Committee," the Wesleyan Report says, "rejoice in the Mission of other Churches to the Central Lakes, but while there are such dense masses in the North-Eastern frontier of the Colony, easy of access, the Committee feel it is their paramount duty, in the first instance, to care for them." ‡ It is satisfactory to gather from this that the Society intend to pursue an evangelistic and advancing work in the North-East. We may add that they have given still more definite expression to this in their Report for this year. They propose that a strong and effective Mission should be commenced in the Transvaal without delay, and that the South African districts should take an

* Adding its Colonial adherents, the total may amount to 93,062. These statistics, as regards the Cape, differ widely from those given in Silver & Co.'s South Africa.
† We may add that the Established Church of Scotland, although it has no Missions in South Africa, has also enlisted in the cause, and the U. P. Church is usefully aiding the Free Church at Livingstonia.
‡ Wesleyan Report, 1877, pp., 4, 5.

active part in this. Arrangements are suggested also for practically carrying this into effect. With its usual catholicity of spirit we have no doubt that this purpose of the Wesleyan Society will be accomplished without, in any way, trenching on the work of other Missions, which now occupy in part the Transvaal. There is wide room for all. May we regard this resolution of so important a Missionary Society as the Wesleyan, as some pledge, that speedily all the native tribes south of the Zambesi will be brought within the joyful sound of the Gospel.

CHAPTER XVII.

THE SOCIETY FOR THE PROPAGATION OF THE GOSPEL.

THE Society for the Propagation of the Gospel has devoted considerable attention and energy of late years to Christian work in South Africa. It entered, indeed, comparatively late into the field. Its oldest station, according to the date given in its Report, is Stellenbosch, founded in 1838. It is thus a younger Mission Society in South Africa not only than the Moravian and London Missionary Societies, but than the Wesleyan, Presbyterian, French, Rhenish, and Berlin Missions. Most of its stations, nearly all date from a period subsequent to the appointment of Dr. Gray as first South African Bishop. Dr. Gray is one who has left his mark in South Africa as one of its ablest, most energetic, and devoted Christian ministers. Though not called to all the privations and trials of Missionary life, his was a career of untiring and exhausting toil—of able episcopal administration, and of high Christian enthusiasm. From the period of his arrival in South Africa, the Missions of the S.P.G., and the stations occupied generally by the South African Church have gone on over more widely extending. The stations now occupied by the S.P.G. exceed 100, and the Colonial and Missionary adherents of the South African Church cannot, probably, be reckoned as less than 50,000.* Like the Wesleyan Missionary Society, the aims of the S.P.G. embrace both Colonial and Mission evangelisation, and like it, very considerable success has been achieved in the former field. Nearly three-fourths of the stations are Colonial, and somewhat more than a fourth, devoted to the heathen. Their Colonial progress is, we may gather from the Reports of the S.P.G., a source of great satisfaction to the Society. "The position which the Church holds there," (in South Africa) " is a subject of even more than usual interest, and it may be added, of more than usual satisfaction. It is the offspring of the English Church, planted and reared by Englishmen; but it is the untiring and consistent exponent of that faith, which before all things proclaims, that both in the kingdom of nature, and in the kingdom of grace, we are members one of another, and that all the members of the Church, let their nationality be what it may, have common interests, and a fellow feeling with each other, whether of suffering or rejoicing."† " The Church, by her position and influence, will surely do very much towards producing peace and good-will throughout the country." I am sure all the other Missions of South Africa will heartily bid the S.P.G. God-speed, in carrying out such an aim as this, to be a "bond of peace and good-will throughout the country." The Bishop of Maritzburg, Dr. Macrorie, we observe, in a letter to the Society, shares in the impression of the rising

* This we must say, is only an approximation.
† Report, S.P.G., 1876, page 46.

prosperity of the South African Church—at the same time, expressing his views, in a form less conciliatory. He writes thus regarding Natal: "There is, I thankfully report, progress almost everywhere, and had I the means for placing a few more clergy in the districts which are yet without the regular ministrations of the Church, there would be good hope that our communion may take the place, which we should all desire, and be regarded by the rising generation, both of Colonists and natives, as the Church of the Colony." * I shall not venture to say how far this may be true, as regards the rival Episcopate of Bishop Colenso, although, even in this relation, the statement may be open to some question. There is, in point of fact, as is very well known, in Natal a considerable body of estimable English Churchmen, who, while repudiating Dr Colenso's theological opinions, refuse to admit that they compromise themselves, in clinging to their old communion as members of the Church of England. They feel, in fact, safer to remain where they are, than to entrust themselves and their families to the spiritual care of a Church with such ritualistic proclivities as the Anglican South African Church. As regards Christianity in Natal generally, and the hope of the Bishop, that his will be the future Church of the Colony, it certainly rests on no basis whatever of existing facts. Colonially viewed, the position of the Wesleyan, Presbyterian, Independent, and Dutch Churches, quite excludes the idea of the Anglican South African Church being in any sense the Church of the Colony, as

* S.P.G. Report, 1875, p. 54.

their membership very far exceeds those under the care of Dr. Macrorie. In reference to Missions, again, the hope is still more baseless. In fact, when one contrasts the feeble success of the S.P.G. Missions in Natal with that which has been attained by the American, the Presbyterian, Wesleyan, Berlin and Hermannsburg Societies, any one knowing the facts, cannot but be surprised at such a statement made on such authority.*

Whatever views we may form of such aspirations as those of Dr. Macrorie and of "their tendency to be a bond of peace and goodwill," it is pleasant to turn from them to such a statement as the following of Bishop Callaway of St. John's, regarding his position to other Churches. Bishop Callaway is, we may say, pre-eminently in his whole spirit and life, the Missionary Bishop of South Africa, full of zeal and yet of charity. Even in this early stage of his Episcopal work, the native members of his diocese are probably more numerous than in any other.† The statement of Bishop Callaway is from an address to his Synod—" In conclusion, I would just say one word on the existence in this country of other Missionaries. Our own position is distinct and well defined, neither need we have any hesitation in asserting it with becoming meekness and gentle-

* Looking over the returns of the various Societies, I should estimate the Mission-members of these Churches in comparison with the S P.G., as three to one, as regards communicants the proportion is more, nearly as four to one. It deserves also, to be noticed here, that about half the S.P.G. Mission members and communicants in Natal, as given in the returns, belong to one Church of which a Berlin missionary, who has gone over to the S.P.G., is minister.

† The last S.P.G. Report gives no statistics of members in the Diocese of Bloemfontein.

ness towards others. At the same time, we must allow the principle that wherever we see the fruits of the Spirit, we must refer them to the works of the Spirit, and acknowledge, not only theoretically, but practically, that from Him, and Him alone, proceed all holy desires, all good counsels, and all just works. On this principle we shall be able to rejoice at any good work done, though not done by ourselves, and outside our own Church, and it may be even in ways we do not think desirable, and of which we cannot approve, because of the good work that has been done by the grace of our Father in heaven, by the help and blessing of our Lord." "We may not be able to agree with these Christian communities who hold a separate position, either as regards Church government, or as regards some doctrines, or as to the best mode of bringing the truth of Christ home to individual souls, and keeping alive the Divine life quickened in them by the grace of the Holy Spirit; but there is one subject in which we can all agree, that it is the duty we owe to God and to man, to do all the good we can to all within the circle of our influence, and to endeavour to help all, whether of our Church or not, to the utmost of our ability."* Such statements as these, while marked by catholicity, involve no compromise. There is not one of our Evangelical Missionaries who would not heartily subscribe to them. They are valuable also as suggesting a *modus vivendi* betwixt the Missions, and if carried out, would be highly advantageous, not only to the comfort, but to the progress of Mission work.

* S.P.G. Report for 1875, pp. 65, 66.

In no branch of the Christian Church have these principles been more fully carried out than in the Church of England itself. I quote on this subject a pleasing testimony borne by the London Missionary Society. It relates to the cordial aid offered both by the Church Missionary Society and the Free Church Mission in support of the proposed Mission of the London Missionary Society to the Lake Tanganyika. "The Directors cannot help observing, however, that co-operation like this is nothing new among Missionary Societies. Friendly union and mutual help have been from the outset the rule among the committees, and to a larger and more practical extent among the Missionaries of these Societies, all over the world. Not only have personal friendships, frequent intercourse, and common service prevailed among them, but mutual consideration has been shown in the establishment of stations; and invasion and interference have not only been rare but have proceeded almost entirely from sacerdotal quarters and from those who believe that only through sacramental channels does complete grace descend upon the Church and the world. In the present instance no such disturbing element enters to hinder complete co-operation." "The Missionary brethren who have gone thither are prepared to work together in perfect harmony, though it may be in somewhat different ways, to assist each other in every way, to preach to those neglected races the unsearchable riches of Christ." *

I have made this quotation as indicating the position which the Church of England Missions

* London Missionary Report, 1877, pp. 118, 119.

may occupy, which, in point of fact, those of the Church Missionary Society do hold, to other Evangelical Missions. In South Africa, we must say it with regret, the S.P.G. alone represents the Church of England, and while in the case of Bishop Callaway, we find a generous and catholic spirit, this is by no means the rule. In other parts of South Africa, these principles have not been followed out. As the subject is one of common and deep interest to all the Evangelical Missions it is necessary for me to give some proof of our averment. Polemics have not certainly been the design of this volume, but in the interests of Christian unity peace and progress, it is necessary to notice some unhappy incidents which expose it to the greatest peril.

I shall first refer to the Berlin Mission in the Cape. It complains that its old Station Zoar has been interfered with. Its German pastor had been called to another important Mission station, belonging to the South African Dutch Missionary Society, and he accepted it. Some opponents of the Berlin Mission at the station "used the occasion to address themselves to the Episcopal Church, and to ask them to undertake the charge of this station. The English preacher Hewitt, at Riversdale, immediately seized the opportunity to inquire of us if we were disposed to hand over the Station of Zoar to the English Church." We have read the story of the Mission of Zoar, to which the Berlin Mission devoted so many labours, from a period earlier indeed than the beginning of the work of the S.P.G. in South Africa, and we can well conceive the wounded feelings with which such a proposal was received. " We, on our side," the Berlin Society writes, "are naturally not inclined to surrender this field of our tears and of our arduous labour into strange hands. At the same time we see that if the Anglicans gain the lead of the opposing party, we shall have a hard battle." * The Berlin Committee have, we find, in consequence of this raised the Cape Colony district into a Synod, and placed at its head Pastor Schmidt as superintendent to resist this aggressive action.

But it is the French Basuto Mission which has especially reason to complain of this aggressive system. The Report of the S.P.G. Society says of this Mission in seemingly friendly terms: "The French Colonists have had Missions among the Basutos for many years. The Missionaries live simple lives, and are earnest and devoted men. When Mr. Barrow visited their stations at Berea, Meryale, and Hermon, he was received by them with the greatest kindness." † I shall have occasion afterwards to notice more especially this interesting and flourishing French Basuto Mission, here so justly, though somewhat inadequately described. But what I wish to notice, is the aggressive policy pursued toward them by Bishop Webb. The question is one of considerable inportance for the future in South Africa. We are not prepared to regard the Propagation Society as responsible for the action of Bishop Webb, until it has deliberately expressed its approval of it. We would rather give them credit

* Jahresbericht Berlin Mission, 1876, p. 9.
† S.P.G. Report, 1876, p. 59.

for supporting such views as Dr. Callaway's, but it would seem to us the two cannot very well be reconciled.

But in justice to Dr. Webb, it is necessary here to notice what are the grounds of complaint of the Société Evangelique de Paris against him. Their statement, in regard to their position to the S.P.G., or rather to the Bishop, is the following—" In what related to us, it concerned us first to assure ourselves of the dispositions of the Bishop of Bloemfontein towards us." They commissioned thus M. Mabille, one of the French Missionaries who had occasion to speak with Dr. Webb, to inquire in what attitude he stood to their Mission, and they learned from the mouth of the Bishop, that, according to him, " Lessouto (Basutoland) is not yet a Christian country; besides your teaching is incomplete, the doctrine of the apostolical succession is put aside by you, and that of the sacraments enfeebled.* From the moment," the Report adds, the bishop " thus entrenching himself behind a non-possumus, discussion was no longer possible." " Things being thus there is no other remedy than to be in advance of the Ritualists in doing more than them, and better than them." It is thus to be observed that the Paris Society, to guard its own Christian convictions and principles, is driven, like the Berlin Society, to occupy a firm, defensive position; a course that none of the Evangelical Missions would willingly adopt, in regard to a Society professing to represent the Church of England, unless by necessity. The

* I translate from the Journal des Missions Evangeliques Paris. Octobre, 1877, pp. 374. &c.

Paris Mission, like the Berlin, is aware that, as a Foreign Society, it engages in such a struggle under considerable disadvantages. " It is not to be dissembled," it says of the South African Anglican Church, " that they have great advantages. They can count upon abundant resources in money and in persons. Let our Basutos see near their villages a school well kept, well furnished materially, directed by English ladies, who, if they speak Basuto badly, teach at least, and above all, that English language so ardently desired because it is supposed to be the key of all knowledge, and to put them in the way of arriving at greatness. It would be more than surprising if our people did not turn away from following the modest instructions of the French Missionaries, however loved and respected they may be." " Let it be added to this that there are a certain number of lukewarm Christians disposed to think our discipline too severe, the foundation of a rival Church will thus respond to their wishes, the Ritualists will not put before them embarrassing questions, but will fling their doors open to receive them."

The Paris Committee has thus determined to resist this aggression by decisive action, rather than by remonstrance. The subject is one of so great importance for the future of Missions in South Africa, that I make no apology for translating further from a letter written by M. Casalis, the Secretary of the Basuto Mission, to the Committee of the Presbyterian General Council which met recently in Edinburgh: " You are not ignorant, dear and honoured brethren, that our Society is at this moment under the threat of a menace, and of the beginning of plans aggressive on our rights. Up to this time the Basuto Mission which God entrusted to us more than forty years ago, in ways of providence universally known and wondered at, has been disputed by no one. Anglican Ritualism, represented by Bishop Webb of Bloemfontein, tries now to enter the country, and does not conceal its intentions of proselytism. There must necessarily follow a struggle. Flocks which consist generally of portions of the same families, will be urged in opposite directions, in what relates on the one hand to ecclesiastical rule, and on the other, to those doctrinal views to which salvation belongs. Disquiet, dissatisfaction, rivalry will enfeeble the faith of the converts; doubts, discussions, controversies will dull in the hearts of the heathen the appeals to repentance, and the invitations to accept the grace of Christ. This is a struggle all the more arduous for us, that our adversaries present themselves to the Basutos with the prestige of a nationality, which has become to them a guarantee of preservation and of earthly prosperity.

"The intrusion has been already begun. It has appeared in the immediate neighbourhood of two of our principal stations, Leribe and Bethesda. In point of fact, the two points chosen are the residences of English magistrates, but the whole population is composed of Basutos, and already some of them have acceded to the proposal made to them to enter the new Church.

"Having obtained nothing by protests, to which Bishop Webb and his subordinates oppose a non-possumus, we shall be forced to save our missions at the expense of great sacrifices. We encourage our agents to occupy the positions, the most in danger, by erecting buildings intended for the catechists and teachers of schools. According to us, the only efficacious *modus vivendi* is to abstain from placing ritualistic pastors near our stations, and their annexes, and we are persuaded that this concession will not be made, with whatever urgency we may press it, and whatever may be the force of the arguments to which we may have recourse.*

Such a statement made on the authority of a Society of so high a character as that of the Société des Missions Evangeliques cannot fail to awaken the deepest feeling on the part of all who have at heart the Evangelisation of South Africa. They seem to suggest the expediency as a last effort in behalf of peace, to ascertain what is really the mind of the S.P.G. on this subject.

If the Society is unable to accept these principles of careful forbearance in approaching the fold of other Missions, which have been to the honour of all the Evangelical Societies adopted and scrupulously enforced, and which Bishop Webb has plainly violated, have they any proposals of their own to make as to a *modus vivendi*? It was a good service we believe the Archbishop of Canterbury rendered in defending the American Missionaries against the intolerance of the eastern Bishops, but this is even a higher question, or at least it has as great a bearing on the future of Christianity, what are to be the relations of the Mission Churches? The Basuto

* The Weekly Review, London, 9th February 1878, contains this correspondence at length.

Mission Conference in its appeal justly says: "This is a question touching not merely the honour of the Paris Mission Society, but of all the Presbyterian Churches unitedly." This it certainly does, and it has awakened a deep sympathy which will, we trust, be followed by important practical results, but it goes far beyond the Presbyterian Churches. It embraces all the Evangelical Churches. Bishop Webb writes thus on the subject, as given in the Report of the S.P.G.* This seems to have been just when he had entered on or was about to enter on the Basuto Field, "Basutoland Missions.— *We have*† a large country and population here, and we are late in the field; French Roman Catholics and French Calvinists are there already." In reference to such a statement, it may be asked, does Bishop Webb place French Roman Catholics and French Calvinists, as he calls them, on the same level. This is not the course which the Evangelical Missions generally have followed, as regards the Church of England; they have always treated it with respect and honour as a sister Church. Bishop Webb states also that he is late in the field. Has not the French Mission thus a legitimate priority which the Missions have always as a rule recognised? The whole manner in which he writes, and in which he has acted, seems to us very inconsistent with the course which not only English Bishops but the English Crown and England itself, have ever followed in regard to the noble Martyr Church of the Huguenots, and, I think, it is scarcely worthy of him, knowing, as he must very well do, what admirable results have

* Report, S.P.G. 1875. † The Italics are ours.

followed this Basuto Mission. If he had adopted Bishop Callaways wise and catholic test, or rather let us call it the ordinance of the Great Master Himself, "By their fruits ye shall know them," he would surely have been led to act differently. The position of matters demands some solution. The Evangelical Societies know definitely their relation to Roman Catholic Missions.* There cannot, from the opposition of great religious principles, be co-operation with them. Are they to be forced to the same conclusion as regards the South African Church and the S.P.G. ? I am aware that many to whom struggles in the Mission Field are deeply distasteful, have come to the conclusion that nothing remains now save vigorous united defensive action. We trust, however, for the honour of our common Christianity, that some solution may yet be found.

The aggressions of the South African Church Missions on the French Mission, somewhat painfully recall those of the French Roman Catholic Missions on the stations of the London Missionary Society in Tahiti. Religiously, the causes in the two instances were not perhaps very dissimilar. In each it was the sacramental, sacerdotal form of religion as opposed to the simplicity of Evangelical Christianity. The warm indignation of British Christians against French Roman Catholic aggression, may be taken as some measure of the deep feeling which the South

* May I say here that the differences with Roman Catholicism being fundamental, there must be everywhere the same division, yet my intercourse with South African Roman Catholics led me to esteem many of them as men of culture, excellent colonists, and ready to cultivate a friendly spirit towards their neighbours.

African Ritualistic action has caused now among French Protestants. There may not be, indeed, the same political feeling as in the instance of Tahiti, leading almost to a breach between England and France; but the French government with a Protestant minister of State like M. Waddington, will scarcely regard it as just to France that Anglicanism should seek to use a prestige, to which it has rightly no claim in South Africa, to damage a Mission, based on the purest and noblest principles, and which does high honour to France and to French Christianity. Our own Colonial Cape government has borne testimony to this, as we have already stated elsewhere. I have never read any British Colonial Blue Books bearing so strong a witness to the advantages, educational, industrial, moral, and religious of Missions as those which relate to the Basuto Missions.

Lately another African Bishop has been consecrated as Bishop of the Transvaal. The *Times*, in its notice of this event, states that there are only five clergymen [*] there and adds, that there are many who think that the sending out of a dozen extra Missionaries would have been a more useful measure, leaving a bishop to be supplied some twenty years later. However this may be, it is to be hoped that Dr. Bousfield will not follow in the aggressive course of Bishop Webb. He will find in the Transvaal a noble, and tried and most successful Berlin Mission, with so able, learned, and earnest a Missionary at the head of it as superintendent Herr Merensky. There is also the Hermannsburg Society doing a noble work, with the South African

[*] The S.P.G. Report for the year 1877 gives only four, p. 39.

Dutch, and Swiss Missions also.* We may say of
the Berlin Mission, that, like the Rhenish, it represents the United Prussian Church. Any intrusion
of Anglicanism into the Mission fields, while there
are such mighty masses of the heathen still in
gross darkness, will be a dishonour to catholicity
and to the Church of England. I may add,
from some acquaintance with German Potestant
Christianity, that any such aggressions will excite
even deeper feelings in Germany than those in
Basutoland have done in France. It will be indeed
a poor return for all the valuable help the
Berlin and Hermannsburg Missions have rendered,
in promoting civilisation, education, and Christianity in the Transvaal; and let me add, for the magnanimity of the German Emperor, in declining the
protectorate the Boers would have so willingly
bestowed, were the German Missions tampered with
in any way, either in their religious interests or as
regards the property they have obtained to help
them in Mission Colonisation.

But apart from the justice and Christian courtesy
due in South Africa, to Foreign Missions nobly
helping us in Christian work, there is, we think, a
special ground deserving the consideration of the
Society for the Propagation of the Gospel in regard
to the polity to be pursued in the Mission fields of
South Africa, and the liberty it will allow to
aggressive Bishops to encroach on other Missions.
The events that have just happened and are now
happening in South Africa very plainly show how

* The justice of this will be more apparent when we add that if we judge by the S.P.G.'s report, the clergymen in the Trans-vaal are all employed in Colonial, not Mission work.

wide is still the gulf betwixt the Colonists and the native races. There are no other British Colonies, indeed, where the danger likely to arise from this is so great. How is this chasm to be bridged? It has not been British policy in South Africa to follow the Boer in his enslaving or exterminating courses. It has rather been the aim of the Colonial statesman to conciliate and civilise the native, and to develop industrial habits, so that he may be fitted to be incorporated in the same society. Now Colonial statesmen, apart from any special interest in Missions, readily own, that Christianity is by far the most powerful mediating influence, industriously, educationally, and morally. And the results of Missions prove this, in the progress of the Basutos, the Fingoes, the Tambookies, the Hottentots, the Namaquas, the Bechuanas, all in fact, of the races it has reached. How wide are these great and enlarging fields of Mission work, and what need that, in place of turning a good Wesleyan Barolong Christian, or one of the French Basuto Church, or a Berlin Hottentot Christian, or a Kaffir Presbyterian, into a member of the South African Church, all such unhappy and paralysing rivalry were abandoned, and all the Missions in their allotted spheres should hasten on, the work of reaching the native heathen tribes; a work on which depends the peace, the progress, the salvation, we may say, of the South African Colonies. Let Bishop Webb employ as many brotherhoods and sisterhoods as he pleases, and let him furnish all the attractions of ritualistic services to captivate and convert the heathen, and I have little doubt he may obtain some success; but

M

let him not venture on other Mission fields—the fruit of long laborious work—where they, who, at the first, sowed in many tears, begin now, in some measure, to reap in joy.

The South African Anglican Church seems to cherish as its ideal the Cyprianic Christianity of North Africa. It would aspire to subjugate South Africa to the same forms of religion which once prevailed there. But the history of Christianity in North Africa is, in some aspects at least, rather a beacon to warn than a light to mark out the path of the Church on its onward way. Bishop Wilberforce, in one of his Mission addresses, has very eloquently shown that North African Christianity failed in a Missionary spirit. It hugged its northern shores, and did little with the leaven of Christianity to spread its influence among the inner tribes of Africa. Hence its decline. We should rather attribute its failure to the effete superstitious religious forms which took possession of it, eating away as a canker worm its early evangelical Christianity. These forms were very fashionable in Rome just before the advent of the barbarian, and in North Africa they also prevailed. How in their feebleness they were swept away in the former instance before the violence of the Goth, and in the latter by the fierce Moslem hosts! Their miserable end may well inspire the hope and prayer that such a system may never gain the ascendency in South Africa. It were injurious to its higher Christianity, and disastrous in relation to that great Mission work in Central Africa, to which South African Christianity seems to be especially called.

As regards the statistics of the S.P.G. and the South African Anglican Church, we may notice that as the Wesleyan charges are divided into five circuits, so there have been, until the recent appointment of a Bishop of the Transvaal, five dioceses. One of these is Zululand—which is at present greatly reduced, and suffering like the other Missions planted there, from the tyranny and violence of Cetywayo. We have already observed that the S.P.G. does not distinguish betwixt its colonial and native adherents, and membership. Nor does it, of course, go beyond its Mission and Colonial work, to give us the statistics of the South African Church. Only an approximation can thus, as we have already said, be offered. It is probable that the adherents of the South African Church may amount to some 50,000, of which its native adherents may be 16,000. The native communicants do not probably exceed 4,000. The S.P.G. does not furnish us with the statistics of its schools. Its higher Kaffir Institution at Grahamstown, is, we believe, of a very efficient character.

CHAPTER XVIII.

THE SCOTTISH PRESBYTERIAN MISSIONS OF SOUTH AFRICA.

As we ascend the East Coast of the Cape Colony, we find in British Kaffraria and Kaffraria itself, the principal seats of the Scottish Presbyterian Missions. These stations are connected with the Free and United Presbyterian Churches of Scotland. As these Missions had a common catholic origin, as, although now separated, they are animated by a common spirit, and thoroughly united in fraternal affection, and as they are likely to be incorporated at no distant day, into one common Church, we shall view them together.* These Missions were first established in British Kaffraria at a period, indeed, before its annexation under that name to the Colony. They date from 1821, and they were thus somewhat later in the field than the London Missionary Society, and somewhat earlier than the Wesleyans. We may say here that the Scottish

---

* I am not here referring so much to the union of the Free and U. P. Churches in Scotland, as primarily to a South African movement of the Presbyteries of the two Churches towards incorporation. Presbyterians are generally united abroad, even though in Scotland obstacles still intervene.

South African Missions, begun by the Glasgow Missionary Society, were originally based on principles, analogous to those of the London Missionary Society. They did not represent Churches individually, but rather the union of the Scottish Presbyterian Churches, or rather Christians. This common basis led to an early cordial fraternal feeling betwixt the London and Glasgow Missionary Societies, and, we may add, there still exists in South Africa the same hearty Christian friendship. The division into two Presbyterian Societies originated, we need scarcely say, not with the Missionaries, but with the home Churches, and that growing alienation some forty years ago, in consequence of the Voluntary question. The feeling ran so high, as to issue in an unnecessary and unhappy separation, which we could only deplore, were it not that it has in the end probably strengthened the Mission cause in South Africa, by impressing into the work, the zeal, energies, and Christian resources of two Presbyterian Churches, marked by their earnest evangelistic spirit. At the time, the result of the controversy was, that one section of the South African Missionaries clung to the Scottish Established Church, and when the Disruption came, rallied to the Free Church, while the other ultimately joined the Church now known as the United Presbyterian. These Missions, like those of the Wesleyans, the London Missionary Society, the S.P.G., and others, have had to pass through many hardships, and trials, during the long succession of Kaffir raids. At times there was so great discouragement, that some of the supporters were almost ready to abandon South Africa for more

promising Mission-fields. But the great Head of the
Church has ordained it far otherwise, and the stations
of these societies have since attained to such a position
of Mission and educational importance, that their
withdrawal now would be deplored as a serious loss
to the Colony, and to the cause of Christianity.
This last war, we may say, has inflicted very serious
losses, especially on the United Presbyterian Mission
Stations, several of which were planted near the
centres of the late severe struggles. All the experience of the past, however, warrants the hope
that not only the losses will be repaired, but that
the United Presbyterian Church will probably obtain in the future a still more influential place among
the frontier tribes. Before noticing these Presbyterian Missions in their individual work, I may say
that they have been one signally in this. They
have aimed at a high ideal—a very high ideal,
indeed, we may say, in their plantation of native
Churches. They would have their converts abreast
in moral and religious character of the home
Churches. They are endeavouring to give a sound
Christian education to the young—they are seeking to raise up a native ministry, thoroughly well
educated in higher literary studies, and in theology;
and there is found in many of the older Churches,
especially, a tone of piety, and a zeal for evangelistic
work, scarcely less than in our home congregations.
It is cheering, on this subject, to have such a
decided testimony as that of so excellent and earnest
an evangelist as Major Malan, not only to the
growing extent of these stations, but to the Christian devotedness of the Mission labourers, and the

living piety to be found among the native converts.*

The Free Church Mission has under its care a number of Mission Stations. Several of these are very considerable. The largest congregation is at Lovedale, and numbers 560 communicants. Its ordained pastor, called by the congregation itself, is a native, the Rev. Mpambani J. Mzimba. He is the first instance of a fully qualified pastor being appointed, who has received his whole education in South Africa."† The well-known and greatly esteemed Tyo Soga was indeed the first ordained Kaffir pastor; but his higher education was obtained in Scotland. We shall have further occasion to refer to him. There are other congregations numbering so many communicants‡ as 478, 371, 257, with other later charges having fewer converts. There are now seven principal Free Church stations, with thirty-five Branch stations, three of the principal being on the other side of the Kei in Kaffraria.

But the most prominent aspect in which the Free Church Mission presents itself in South Africa, is in the attention and care it has devoted with so great success to higher Christian, educational, and indus-

* I shall not attempt any sketch of the history of these Missions. To those interested in the subject, Mr. Theal's work on South Africa may be recommended. It is the best compendium we possess. I do not happen to have it with me in writing this book, but I have read it with much interest. Both its authorship and its press publication, do honour to Lovedale. It has been, I believe, lately published also by a London publisher.

† Free Church Report, May, 1876, p. 30.

‡ Members and communicants are to be distinguished in South African statistics. By members are generally understood all the baptized infants and adults. Their number is usually two or three fold as many as the communicants.

trial training. We may say that Lovedale, its great central institution, with its large and thoroughly trained staff of ordained Missionaries, of male and female European and native teachers, and of European masters of industrial departments, and with its numerous European and native students, numbering some 450, occupies a position almost unique in South Africa, as a model establishment. Mr. Trollope's opinion of it we have already stated. Sir Bartle Frere, in a recent speech, has singled out Lovedale with its affiliated institution at Blythswood, as model establishments for educating and elevating the native races, and training them for agricultural industrial pursuits. "Lovedale," writes Major Malan, "is quite a collegiate establishment, both architecturally and otherwise. After going over the whole establishment during the time I stayed there, I cannot sufficiently express my admiration of everything connected with it, and the excellent way in which it is managed." Lovedale is an institution which has a right to support from all who desire the advancement and Christian civilisation of the natives of South Africa. It is an honour to the British nation."*

The Lovedale Institution mainly owes its origin and character to two causes. In the first place, it was an attempt to follow out that higher educational Mission system initiated with such remarkable success by Dr. Duff in Calcutta. Lovedale had for its basis similar principles, only modified to meet the different circumstances of South Africa. The plan was first introduced with considerable

* Rides in the Mission Fields, pp. 134-141.

success by the Rev. Mr. Govan, long a laborious and successful Missionary. In its present developed form, however, it is also indebted to the Great Indian Educationist and Missionary, whose recent loss the Churches deplore—the Rev. Dr. Duff. He visited, at the request of the Free Church, the South African Missions of the Free Church, before occupying the position of its Convener of Foreign Missions, and his visit, observations and suggestions gave an impulse which has never since been lost.* It was he who, from his personal knowledge of the Rev. Dr. Stewart, saw his high qualifications for such a position as Lovedale, and who induced him to enter on a work for which his gifts, Christian energy and sagacity so remarkably qualify him.

I have referred to the Industrial character of Lovedale, in which it so markedly differs from Indian Mission Institutions. It has its industrial masters who educate and train blacksmiths, carpenters, waggon-makers, printers, bookbinders, telegraphists even, and farmers. "The boys are taught manual labour, as well as letters. Every day they are told off in fatigue parties and regularly marched to their work in various parts of the extensive College grounds." "Dr. Stewart told me," Major Malan writes, " that in early life he studied farming and could never understand why, until he came here. Now he finds his knowledge invaluable." It is in this way, by its industrial and agricultural work that Lovedale earns so deservedly the large

---

* I may say that some months before the death of Dr. Duff, I heard from his own lips privately the interesting history of his connection with Lovedale.

supplementary government aid it receives of £2000 annually. Even this, however, with all the liberal support of the Free Church, and with the College fees, is scarcely adequate to the support of the Institution. "Nothing but the best management and Dr. Stewart's knowledge of farming and unusual capacity for superintendence could keep it going."

The support which industrial and agricultural education has received from the Cape Government is honourable to it—we have already had occasion to refer to it. It was Sir George Grey who first carried out effectually this policy. He was allowed by Parliament some £40,000, to help in the elevation of the Kaffirs, and he wisely regarded industrial education as one of the most useful ways in which to expend the money. Quite a new mode of agriculture has been gradually introduced by this action among the Kaffirs, especially among those tribes under British protection, such as the Fingoes and Basutos, and in some less measure the Gaikas and Tambookies. The Fingoes have indeed felt the benefit to be so great to them that they offered Dr. Stewart £3,000 if he would establish for them at Blythswood an Institution similar to that at Lovedale. This has been accomplished. The Blythswood Institution has been formally opened, the £3,000 have been given, and the Free Church has supplemented this by £1,500. Still, however, there was a deficit of £2,000, but to meet this the leading men among the Fingoes nobly and readily promised to raise at least £1,000 more. Such a history as this—such liberality on the part of a tribe sunk but recently in slavery and degradation—

deserves to be noted. Blythswood has already its resident Missionary and European Missionary teacher, but its staff will doubtless be enlarged, according to its needs. It began with classes which rose to 36, and would have advanced much further; unfortunately the late hostilities broke out, and for a time, in place of being a Mission Institution, the necessity of war turned it into a garrison. So it was with Lovedale also, in 1846 ; but the tide of war has now receded, and we trust this is the alone warlike episode in the annals of this interesting Institution.* I may notice here how popular these industrial educational efforts of the Free Church in South Africa have been. In one year alone, apart from the government grant, £3,960 were raised from school fees, Colonial and native subscriptions.

I shall have occasion, before I close this South African sketch, to notice how important it is to introduce a better system of land tenure if we are to improve and elevate the native races. There must be a personal system of land tenure, in place of that tribal one which exists so extensively. We shall never get the natives to interest themselves as they ought in agricultural improvements till this change is made. The reason, for instance, that the Fingoes make so much progress, is that under our rule they have personal tenure of land. But I do not enter on this wide subject here. I may, however, remark that the advance making among the Fingoes or Basutos in the increasing use of ploughs has been valuable, not only industrially but in relieving

* Free Church Report of Foreign Missions, May, 1878, p. 45.

woman from her grinding servitude, and assigning agricultural labour more to male labourers.

The present equipment of the Lovedale Institution for its work is the following:— There are 4 ordained European Missionaries; 7 European Missionary teachers, male and female; 4 native teachers; 9 European Missionary artizans. In all, the staff of Christian agents amounts to 24.* The native male boarders in the institution are 184. There are 53 native female boarders; there are also 62 apprentices, and 30 European boarders; and 14 in the Native Work Department. These, with the addition of 37 day pupils, and 50 in the elementary school, make a total of 430. The previous year the number was 499; the difference may be accounted for partly from the war, partly also from the absence of Dr. Stewart, the vigorous head of this noble missionary institution.

I may add here that the Free Church has also 3 mission stations in Natal. At Maritzburg, the capital of Natal, there is the largest of these. It was established by Mr. Alison, to whose labours we have already had occasion to refer. There is a considerable native congregation, but the chief mission aim, I may say, is here also to establish a first class English Educational Institution for the Zulus. From the growth of the Zulus in wealth there is a growing desire to know the English tongue, and such an education is in the highest degree important to civilisation, the spread of the Gospel, and the training of a higher native Christian agency. The staff of labourers is here still too limited, but the

* F. C. Report, 1878, page 63.

missionary at the head of it, who is a well-trained Christian educationist, is making good progress. The Gordon Memorial Mission is another of these Natal stations, under the superintendence of the Free Church. It owes its origin to the large liberality of the Gordon family, who founded it *in memoriam* of a pious son of the late Earl of Aberdeen, who had intended to devote himself, I believe, to South African Mission work, but was unhappily and prematurely taken away. The Gordon Mission is excellently equipped for its work, and its position is good for mission work. Situated as it is, near a great native location, important results, we trust, will accrue from it. If we add the mission communicants in Natal to those in British Kaffraria and Kaffraria, the total will be 1,969. The number taught again in the schools amounts unitedly to 2,497.

The United Presbyterian Mission in the Cape Colony forms a part only of its many labours among the blacks. It has stations, for instance, on the West Coast of Central Africa, in Old Calabar; and it has Missions also in Jamaica and Trinidad. It has also lately lent to the Free Church Dr. Laws, an able medical Missionary, who is now at Livingstonia, and whose salary it pays. It devoted also to the same work, and with the same liberality, Shadrach Inquinana—a young and promising Catechist—who has, unhappily, too soon been taken by death from the post he had so earnestly longed to occupy. The United Presbyterian South African Mission is, we may say, exclusively Kaffir; its stations being planted among the Galekas, Gaikas,

and Fingoes. Both as regards the Gaikas and
Galekas it occupies an influential position. Sandilli,
the late Gaika chief, looked up thus with great
respect to Mr. Cumming, the venerable Missionary
stationed not far from him at Emgwali. Kreli
treated in the same way, as specially his Missionary
and friend, a truly able, gifted, and devoted
Missionary, the Rev. Mr. Leslie, whose loss the
U.P. Church and the Mission cause has recently had
reason to deplore—worn out, we fear, at the last
by the anxieties, fatigues, and griefs of the war.
It need not be said that both these Missionaries exerted their utmost influence to prevent the outbreak. After the first meeting of the tribe to
consider war or peace, Sandilli came to Mr. Cumming when confined to bed as an invalid, and
declared that he was for peace. "I thanked him,"
writes Mr. Cumming, "for the word, but it was like
the early cloud and morning dew. He no sooner
entered among his bad counsellors than he was
carried away with them."* In reference again to
the collision with Kreli, Mr. Leslie wrote some time
ago :—"I believe there was a possibility of its being
avoided, if the Government had had any system in
its administration. When I think of the weakness
shown by this government, their want of firmness,
and the incapacity of some of the officials, it does
seem a marvel that the peace should have remained
so long unbroken."† As regards the actual outbreak it
is stated in the United Presbyterian Missionary Record: "Had Mr. Leslie been consulted by the authori-

* U.P. Annual Report, 1878, p. 36.
† U.P. Annual Report 1878, p. 39.

ties at the very beginning when Fingoes and Galekas began to show fight and had his influence with Kreli, the result of his wise and faithful friendship with that wise chief, been made use of when Kreli was summoned to Butterworth, when he refused to put himself at the mercy of British military power, the war might have been averted. But Kreli, who loved and trusted the missionaries, dreaded British Government soldiers, remembering as he did the end of his father's (Hintza) death and capture at the hands of Sir Harry Smith. But Mr. Leslie had not the opportunity of interposing at the right time in the interests of peace. He and Mr. Dewar had all the wisdom and courage needful, to go between the assegais of Kreli and his people, and the swords and rifles of British soldiers and police, had their services been asked; but the fatal blow was soon struck, the signal of war raised, and from that moment, no white man has seen the face of Kreli."*

As regards the former of these statements, it will, I think, be generally conceded that the policy of the Cape Government was weak and without firmness, as Mr. Leslie wrote. The Blue Books lately published, abundantly prove this. Firmness based on justice, and tempered with clemency, is the only way of dealing with such chiefs as Sandilli and Kreli, and it was awanting as regards both, especially, we think, the former. As regards the last statement of the Missionary Record, referring to the effect which Mr. Leslie's influence might have had in staying hostilities, by inducing Kreli to comply with the summons to meet Sir Bartle Frere at

* U.P. Missionary Record, August, 1878, p. 260.

Butterworth, we confess we have grave doubts.
The apology that his father, Hintza, was killed in
attempting to escape from the British, would be
more just if it had been an act of treachery on the
part of the British, which it was not, and if Kreli
had not had so many proofs since of British loyalty
and even of British generosity. A somewhat similar
attempt was made by Bishop Colenso to apologise
for the refusal of Langalibalele to obey a similar
summons. The British public are scarcely perhaps
in circumstances to judge of the real meaning
among the Kaffir tribes of refusing to obey the
summons of the paramount chief. They may fancy
that it is scarcely to be supposed an ignorant chief
should understand that such an act of disobedience
was a heinous offence. Those, on the contrary, who
are acquainted with Kaffir laws, and the chiefs, who,
however little else they may know, are thoroughly
versant in them, are aware, that to disobey a summons from the paramount chief is an offence somewhat analogous to that of a soldier refusing to
appear before his commanding-officer. It is more
than that; indeed, with the Kaffirs it is an act of
high treason, and had Sir Bartle Frere tolerated it,
he would have brought his government into con-
tempt. My impression is, in regard to both cases,
Langalibalele's and Kreli's, that the refusal is to
be understood as an act of open defiance. Had
Kreli been really a Christian convert, Mr. Leslie's
judgment would have deserved very great weight,
but he was not. What he was, the calm, yet penetrating judgment of a Christian soldier may help
us to decide. Major Malan says of him—" Kreli is

a fine-looking man, there is something noble in his face. But the working of a mind, filled as his is, with all sorts of designs, soon writes traces of such thoughts on the countenance; cunning, doubt, and restlessness are plainly written there. He was once lord of a large country, of which now he only has a strip. No wonder, as a heathen, he is always thinking how he may regain his land." I submit my opinion on this subject with great deference—I am very far from wishing for a moment to support any Colonial injustice to the native races or the native chiefs. But it seems to me, from the high character Sir Bartle Frere holds as a humane ruler, from his position as Lord Commissioner, which is to rule the native races justly, and from the clemency he has shown already, in the conduct of this war, that he would not have proceeded to extremities with Kreli, unless, in his judgment, he had been convinced that justice, and the interests of British South Africa, both Colonial and native, demanded it.

The late Kaffir war has for a time seriously crippled the work of the U.P. Missions. Out of nine principal stations, "three," it is stated in the Mission Report " of our Missions have been destroyed,"* and for a time in others, the work has been arrested. Situated as some of these stations were, near the very centres of the struggles with the Gaika and Galeka tribes, it can be readily understood how they have borne the brunt of the battle. Many of the Christian converts have been also widely scattered abroad. This is a very marked change indeed. It is but a short time ago when, if there was nothing perhaps

* U.P. Annual Report, 1878, page 34.

so salient in the progress of these stations, as in some other Mission fields, there was yet much quiet progress and advancing spiritual life. The earnest evangelical preaching, the faithful discipline, the evangelistic work carried on by the elders and other members of the Churches, the efforts successfully made to battle with the evil of intemperance and other besetting sins, the work the Gospel achieved in winning the hearts of the converts, and in disciplining them to the habits of a Christian life, were conspicious in these Missions. Major Malan in his "Rides in the Mission Fields," has given us a pleasing impression of this. We believe it might have been said of many of these Churches, that having rest they were edified, and walking in the fear of the Lord, and in the comfort of the Holy Ghost, were multiplied. But if it is otherwise, apparently for the present, the hope may yet be cherished that these stations will come forth from the fiery furnace purified, fitted to exercise an ever-increasing influence on all the tribes, more especially may we trust on the Gaikas and Galekas, with whom the U.P. Missions have been so closely and honourably identified.

It will ever be to the honour of the U.P. Missions that the first thoroughly educated and ordained Kaffir minister, Tyo Soga, was gathered from their ranks. An eminent German Mission historian says of him, "A remarkable example of the height of Christian culture, to which the Kaffir is capable of rising, this Mission, (the U.P.) has shown in Tyo Soga, too early fallen asleep. His thorough culture, as well as his pure Christian character, deserve all recognition. He laboured in his Mission office with great self-denial, and was till his end occupied with translations in which a blessed memorial of him remains to the Mission." * Major Malan writes, on visiting Tyo Soga's place of burial at Teduka: "Here Tyo Soga, the first Kaffir minister of Christ, preached the Gospel to his heathen fellow-country-men. Here his body rests until the coming of the Lord. The Mission House built by Tyo Soga is the most roomy and comfortable house I have seen in the Trans Kei, his church the prettiest. I could not but remark this, for it showed to me the mind of the man. Tyo Soga often told Kreli of the Lord Jesus. May he believe before it be too late."† The father of Tyo Soga was killed during the late Insurrection. The story is a somewhat striking one—the contrast in the deaths of the father and the son—" Soga was a hereditary and influential counsellor of Sandilli, and a Kaffir in all his instincts, but he was opposed to the insurrection and resisted it so far as he could." "It is to be feared," says the Report, "for the best part of his life that he halted between two opinions." He was killed at a cave whither he had fled by the Colonial forces who "did not know who he was, nor did he tell them, and so he did not escape."‡ It is a mournful contrast—the happy departure of him whose life was decided for Christ, and the unhappy end of one, like Balaam, halting between Moab and the Lord's people.

I have already noticed that Shadrach Inquinana,

* Burkhardt's Mission Bibliothek, Sud. Afrika, p. 266.
† Rides in the Mission Field, &c.
‡ U.P. Annual Report, 1878, p. 39.

the Catechist who gave himself to the work of Livingstonia, belonged also to this Mission. The words of his mother, on hearing of his purpose of consecration, are spoken like a true mother in Israel, "Shadrach is not my child, I gave him to the Lord at baptism, if He has called him to engage in this work, who am I that I should say no? He is His. Let Him do with him as seemeth good in His sight." "Such a testimony," the Missionary adds, "I never heard coming from the lips of a Kaffir mother before."* As regards ordinary evangelistic work, it is also prosecuted with diligence. One of the Missionaries observes, that "he has fifteen native elders, who are not paid for the work, but who may be seen every Sabbath morning mounted on their horses, carrying the everlasting gospel to their benighted brethren."

This related to a period a year back. In the Report of the present year, we read of the elders of the same station, (Paterson,) that they are now thus occupied. "It will be pleasing for you to know, that all our elders being called out to the war, embraced every opportunity of preaching, and exhorting their countrymen. Several of the English commanders have told me of this saying, Those Fingoes make us ashamed. In the morning, before day-break, they are on their knees before God, and often march out of camp singing the praises of the God of battles, who is also the God of salvation. Therefore shall we not fear since God is our refuge and our strength. The Lord Omnipotent reigneth."†

* U.P. Annual Report, 1878, p. 40.
† U.P. Record, June, 1877, p. 542.

The statistics of the United Presbyterian Missions are the following. There are 9 European Missionaries, 1 European female teacher, 24 native evangelists, 18 native teachers, 9 principal stations,* 24 out-stations, 1038 members, 2485 in attendance at the services, 683 week day scholars, &c. It may be interesting before leaving these Presbyterian Missions, to observe, that, taken unitedly, belonging to the Free and United Presbyterian Missions, there are 3007 members, 22 ordained European Missionaries, 2813 in the schools, and the number of adherents may be stated approximately at 9000.

* U.P. Report, 1878, page 34. In the summary the number of stations is given as 10, but in the detailed account, only as 9.

CHAPTER XIX.

THE FRENCH MISSIONS IN BASUTOLAND.

WE pass on to the Société des Missions Evangéliques, or to give it a name by which it is better known in South Africa, the French Evangelical Basuto Mission. Although these Mission fields do not lie on the coast which we have been, as it were, skirting, yet they are not far distant from those Kaffir stations we have noticed. They extend beyond the Drachenberg, chiefly on the flanks and spurs of the parallel Maluti range. These mountains rise in parts to the height of 7000 feet. This Mission field has its special interest for Evangelical Christianity, as planted, sown, and cultivated by the labours of Missionaries of the old persecuted Huguenot Church, to which, both directly and indirectly, most Protestant lands owe so much.* We may observe, that, like the Rhenish and other Missions, the Paris Evangelical Society does not limit its work to South Africa. It has its Missions also in Senegal and in Tahiti, and in the latter, it has done a good work, in aiding in the defence of the Protestant cause. Still South Africa was its first

---

* Mr. Smiles's interesting work on the Huguenots has opened quite a new view of our obligations to these, religiously, socially, and industrially.

field—its operations have been most extensive there, and in this field it has won its noblest triumphs. The sedulous care it has given to this Mission, the pious and earnest labours expended on it, the long patience with which it bore heavy trials, and the rich harvest that has been gathered, entitle this branch of the work of the Société Evangélique to rank very high indeed among missions. We may say that Basutoland was a virgin field, it was ground untrodden before by the missionary. It was the French missionaries who broke up the fallow ground and who gathered up the stones; and, we may add, that in fulfilment of the gracious promise, righteousness has been rained down upon their mission fields. Their work, we would add, has been more concentrated than that of any other South African mission, and it owes it to this perhaps, that it has won such success as to make Christianity if not universal—which it is not as yet—still the predominating power in the country. Heathenism will not be able long to resist its progress, nor the alienation of ambitious chiefs, if the good cause be not damaged by unjust aggression, and unhappy religious controversy and discussion.

The Society may be said to date, as regards active work in the Mission Field, from a visit of Dr. Philip to Paris, in 1828. As he persuaded the Rhenish Mission Society to begin their work in South Africa, so he won over the Société Evangélique of Paris to the same course. It had before aided only as an auxiliary to other Missions, now it resolved itself to put its hand to the mission plough. The setting apart by ordination of the three first

French Missionaries in Paris, in 1829, was, as in the instance of the Rhenish Missionaries, a touching and impressive scene, thrilling the hearts of the French Evangelical community; and the words of self-sacrifice and self-consecration spoken by M. Lemue, one of the departing Missionaries, in their name, were a noble expression of humble faith and high Christian resolve.* On the arrival of the three Missionaries in South Africa, they received a very cordial welcome, especially, as it may be supposed from the descendants of the old French refugees. If these are now members of the Dutch Church, and have forgotten, many of them, in their long exile, their native tongue; yet the names they bear, the memories of the past they deeply cherish, their culture, their tone of piety, all recall that they are Huguenots by blood. They were very desirous, not only to speed the Missionaries in their work, but that one of them should remain to preach the gospel to them, and to teach the slaves, of whom there were some 700 or 800, the truths of Christianity. This was in 1829, before the Emancipation. The request was granted at first, only for a time, but the permission was ultimately extended. M. Bisseux, first called to this sphere of work, is still a labourer in the same field. His station has been, indeed, removed since to some distance—it is now at Wellington, a pretty town not far from Capetown, situated in a lovely cultivated valley.

* This and many other incidents in connection with the Basuto Mission are told with great pathos, and I should add, Christian eloquence, by Major Malan, in his "South African Missions." (Nisbet & Co.) I am indebted to him for some interesting information on these Missions, and I refer my readers to his earnest pages.

The other brethren Rolland and Lemue travelled on to seek out a mission field. They visited the Kaffir districts, but decided, as these were occupied, to seek out some new sphere of mission work. They travelled on to Lattakoo, at no great distance from which Dr. Moffat was labouring at Kuruman. From the advice given them they resolved to seek out a new mission field among the Baharutse, a tribe situated in the West of what is now called the Transvaal. But these were the days of Moselikatze's power, before he had been driven by the Boers beyond the Limpopo into what is now called Matabeleland. He saw with a jealous eye this new mission station among the Baharutse, an inferior tribe, and they were thus compelled to abandon their first station at Mosiga. Strangely enough, the Basuto Mission, in a new and interesting evangelistic effort it has been making to reach the Banyai, has met with similar opposition from Lo Bengula, the son of Moselikatze, and has been compelled also to retire. But we shall have occasion later to refer to this. The French Missionaries then, by the advice of Dr. Moffat, occupied a station at Motito, not very far from his own, and long held it under the missionary charge of M. Lemue. Later they resolved to concentrate their work in Basutoland, and Motito was, in the end, handed over to the London Missionary Society, of which it is now a station.

But eaving these first brethren, we notice a later arrival at the Cape of M. Arbousset, Casalis, and Gosselin. They learned that their brethren had been driven from Mosiga, and undecided as yet as to the course they should follow, they visited Dr. Philip at Philipolis. From him they learned that the chief of Basutoland, Moshesh, had sent eagerly desiring to obtain missionaries for his country. The Brethren saw in this unexpected call the bidding of their Divine Master, and they hastened to meet the chief at Thaba Bosio in Basutoland, his mountain fortress and home. I shall have occasion afterwards to say more regarding this really great native chief; meanwhile, these remarks may form a sufficient introduction. Basutoland has only been latterly occupied by the Basutos, probably betwixt the second and third decades of the century. The same race is found farther north in the Transvaal, and are there called the Bapedis. The Berlin Mission has especially devoted itself to this race, and has accomplished an important work among them. But their chief is a man awanting in all those high qualities of bravery and sagacity which distinguished Moshesh. Sekukuni, with whom we are now at war, but who is a very different opponent from what Moshesh was, is the chief of these northern tribes. It is likely that the home of the Basutos was originally farther to the north than Basutoland. Probably the tribe was considerably dispersed during Chaka's bloody reign. We know that for a time the Bapedis were subjugated to his sway, and Cetywayo yet makes claims on their allegiance as the superior chief. Probably at this period the part of the tribe to which Moshesh belonged was driven further south. It is about this time the young chief Moshesh comes to the front, beginning his career in troublous times. He had a hard battle to fight at first for existence, being first assailed by the Zulus and then by the Matabeles, the two conquering races. He was thus driven back in self-defence on the strongholds of the Maluti mountains. These are, as we have said, lofty ranges only a little inferior to the Drachenberg. Here he selected, as the central fortress of his tribe, Thaba Bosio. It is a very strong position indeed, impregnable almost if occupied by disciplined forces. It has never in fact been taken. Matabeles, Korannas, Boers, the British even have failed in their assaults to scale its rocky precipitous heights. Moshesh became by his defence of it in time a powerful chief to whom other tribes gradually rallied for relief, and who won even important victories over the Tambookie Kaffirs. Moshesh was now in the prime of life, some 32 or 33 years of age. He had heard of the white missionaries, such as Moffat, and of what they had accomplished for the natives. He felt anxious to obtain such men for his own tribe, and to show his sincerity and his appreciation of their value he sent to the white chief 200 oxen, praying that in return they would send him missionaries to instruct his blacks. His embassy, however, was attacked and the cattle were taken, but the message, as we have already seen, reached the missionaries, and brought them to Basutoland to meet the chief, and to offer to him and his tribe their mission services.

The Basuto Mission began thus favourably—Moshesh helped to choose a site for their first station Morija, at the base of the mountain, where his fortress Thaba Bosio is situated. He gave them also in their work his loyal and hearty support, and he was long wont to descend from his mountain home on the Lord's day to listen to the preaching of the Gospel. This he gradually understood so well that he would often explain the message he had heard to others. Not that he became a Christian then. There were two obstacles in the way; not only the aims of his ambition as a chief, but also the fetters of polygamy, which he would not break. His views, as regards Christianity, were in great part politic. One of his chiefs afterwards, indeed, when converted reminded him of this, "You told me, he said, when you bade me take care of the Missionary, that I was only to put one foot into the Church, and keep the other out; that I was only to listen with one ear, and keep the other closed; I put one foot into the Church, but I could not keep the other out. The love of Jesus drew me in."*

We cannot follow the history of the Mission. At the first, it was but the day of small things. After a five years residence, not a single convert seemed to have been gained, but the Gospel was earnestly, affectionately, and faithfully preached, as it is by the Evangelical ministry of the French Church at home. At last the hearts of some were reached and the Missionaries began to reap in joy. Pains had been taken from the beginning to educate the natives. Some of the Gospels with other portions of the Scripture, and a book of hymns had been translated, and there were now eager learners and readers of the Word. The baptism of the converts was regarded with deepest interest by the natives,

* Malan's South African Missions, p. 56.

and the simple confessions of faith by the converts, with their fidelity in refusing all adhesion to heathen customs, compelled the respect of the heathen, even though it might not disarm their hostility. Thus it may be said the work went on for nearly twenty years in comparative peace, the stations being gradually increased, churches and schools being built, with all the other tokens of Mission prosperity. The only dark cloud that gathered over Basutoland was Sir George Cathcart's attack on the tribe in 1852. One of the Kaffir wars had just been finished by him—Moshesh seemed to have been represented to him as an intriguing crafty aggressive chief, and it was resolved to intimidate him into a more submissive spirit. The result was an attack by British forces on Thaba Bosio—in which Sir George, though a gallant soldier and an excellent general, suffered a severe repulse—an unusual event to British forces. But what was perhaps more unusual was the magnanimity of a savage chief, subduing, as it did on this occasion, the resentment of a British officer at such a defeat. "O my master," was the message of Moshesh to Sir George the following morning, "I am still your man—I am still the child of the queen. Sometimes a man beats his dog and the dog puts his teeth into his hand and gives him a bite; nevertheless the dog loves the master, and the master loves the dog, and will not kill it. I am ashamed of what happened yesterday, let it be forgotten." It was thus peace was made. Sir George Cathcart was just the gallant soldier to appreciate so fine an action, and to respond to it. He wrote of him after this battle—"Another advantage I gained was in the acquaintance with the chief Moshesh, whom I found not only to be the most enlightened, but the most upright chief in South Africa, and one in whose good faith I put the most perfect confidence, and for whom, therefore, I have a sincere respect and regard." Sir George Cathcart learned in this way also to know the French Missionaries, and to appreciate the good work in which they were engaged. But for them, indeed, and the influence of their intelligence and Christian teaching, the action of Moshesh might have been far different. " A third advantage," writes Sir George Cathcart, "among many resulting from my visit to Platberg, was that of making the acquaintance of M. Casalis, and the other gentlemen of the French Mission, who, from their conversation as well as good works, I have learnt to know, are loyally disposed toward the British Government, and are sincere wellwishers to, and promoters of, the cause of peace."

There was another event, we may add, that even before this last, caused great anxiety to the Basuto Mission. Even from 1845, the funds of the Société Evangélique had been severely taxed to carry on all their enlarging Mission work; then there came the Revolution of 1848, quite paralysing them. "The Mission House in Paris had to be closed, the pupils dismissed to their homes, no more missionaries, in the meanwhile, were to be sent out—all costly undertakings were to be given up, and the Mission was to count in the future on a limited contribution only from the Society."* The Missionaries were thus in great straits, very much as the

* Burkhardt, Sud. Afrika, p 195.

Americans were during their civil war. But in both instances, we may say, the cause was so good, and so commended itself to the Christian sympathy of the Churches, that aid was supplied enough to carry the missions successfully through their difficulties. A host of friends was raised up to help the French missions. M. Casalis made an earnest appeal to the Cape Colony for help, and £900 were raised —other friends in Holland, India, the Continent generally took part, and £2000 in all, were contributed.

But greater trials than these were coming on the Basutos, and their beloved French Mission. The recognition by Great Britain in 1854, of Boer independence, in the Free or Orange State, was an event justly occasioning alarm, not only to the French missionaries, but also to the British, and, we believe, the latter warmly remonstrated against it. It turned out as in fact is not unusual, that unwillingness to undertake a responsibility may entail in the end more disastrous results than a courageous policy. It was an unworthy attempt to get rid of a burthen from which we cannot be freed with honour, if we are to hold South Africa. But at the time, few, save the Missionaries, and the unhappy tribes, the victims of this arrangement, saw this. They were left to the mercies of the Boer. The general attitude of the Boers to the natives, we have already described. They had now an opportunity of carrying out their policy as they had not dared, since the arrival of British Forces in South Africa, and they speedily used it. The difference between Boer and British policy, may be seen generally in the fact that in Natal the Zulus are probably 15 to 1 to the European Colonists. In the Orange State the natives are said by some to number only half the Colonists—reckoned at the most, they are probably inferior; but as there has never been an exact return, the numbers cannot be given definitely. The feelings of the Boers towards the Basutos were perhaps the more inflamed, as in the east toward the Caledon, the latter were possessed of exceptionally rich lands. For a time things went smoothly, and there seemed to be a tolerable understanding with the Boer; but this peace did not last, and soon there succeeded border difficulties with border feuds and raids. Basutoland was invaded, and Moshesh besieged, the commanders of the Boers, however, being repulsed again and again. At last the times grew even darker. The Boers were enraged at these defeats, and they resolved in 1866 that the French Missionaries must abandon their stations and leave the country. Compensation was to be given them indeed, for their buildings and property, but their presence was no longer to be tolerated. Thus, for instance, M. Daumas, a much esteemed Missionary, was driven to Natal, where he died, and others shared the same exile. The British and French and Dutch Governments remonstrated, but it was of no avail. Four of the French stations were torn from the Mission, and it seemed as if the supreme agony of the tribe had arrived. Many of the Christian converts had to flee for their lives, and some hundreds of them were preserved in the caves and dens of Thaba Bosio for more than three years. The Cape Colonial Government refused long to interfere.

At last in the eleventh hour it accepted the Protectorate which Moshesh craved—who thus by his sagacious resolve, in which he was strengthened by the counsels of the French Missionaries, saved his people from destruction. The Basutos had, indeed, still to surrender some of their best lands to the Boers, and the four French stations were lost to the Mission, but they were now under the British Protectorate, and it is surprising the prosperity and increase the Basutos have since attained. We may add here, that the temporal adversities of the Churches seem to have issued in higher good. The fugitive converts came out of the furnace, not only purified, but strengthened. Philemon, the schoolmaster of Morija, watched over the large number of converts hidden in the dens and the rocks. At the end of the war all the Churches were increased, and a revival took place, which lasted for two years. Philemon brought 100 converts to the Missionary at the close of the war, and there were 436 candidates for admission to the Church of Morija.* Elsewhere also among the stations, evangelists were raised up, and the result was, " that at the end of the war all the Churches had largely increased."

It was just as the Basutos had emerged out of their trials, that Moshesh their great chief died, 11th March, 1870. His had been a chequered career, but ere he departed he could see that a brighter future was before his people. There is also reason to hope that with himself personally, "at eventide there was light." We may be pardoned if we glance for a moment at his career.

* Malan's South African Missions, p. 132.

His life began in troublous, revolutionary times if we may so express it, for South Africa. At eighteen he begins to assert his place as a bold and warlike chief. As his life advances it develops not only these qualities, but his power of rule, and his great sagacity. He was evidently one of nature's nobles, in his original character, with the views doubtless of a savage, but of a higher mould than the Chakas or Moselikatzes or Cetywayos. We have already said that he did not at first become a Christian even with all the missionary teaching he had received, but we may think that its leaven was leavening the lump—raising him to something purer, loftier than he had originally been. We should infer this from such a testimony as we gave of Sir George Cathcart. Here is another from Mr. Orpen, a colonial magistrate. "The most original, able, enlightened, and upright barbarian chief that South Africa has ever beheld. His humanity, his mildness, his love of peace and justice, his horror of war, are conspicuous on every occasion; his forbearance under extreme provocation; his steadfast fidelity and devotion through evil report and good; his patience under false suspicions and accusations; his magnanimity and generosity; the possession of these and many more good qualities would almost lead us to believe that our faithful and long-suffering 'ally' as he calls himself was a Christian." Moshesh was ill for some months before he died. One of the missionaries saw him privately and reminded him of the Judgment-seat where he must soon appear, where the blood of Christ alone could save him. He wept bitterly all the time, saying, "I know it is all true; what am I to do?

What is it that still holds me back? Later, when dying, he wished to see his missionaries, to one of whom he said, "I hear that your wife has a baby, how old is it?" "Three months old." "Then," said the chief, "he is just my age, I have only just been born." Afterwards he met the missionary's wife, who held out the child to him. He looked at it for a moment, his eyes full of tears. "My child," he said to her, "your baby is my age, he is my thaka," (one of the same age) then pressing her hand,—"You have shown me the road and I shall get to Jesus." His last instructions were, "Let my missionaries not be weary to teach my people and especially my sons."*

The Basutos and the French Mission, since this period in the enjoyment of peace, have continued rapidly to advance in prosperity. We cannot note the history of this interesting progress. We would give here the last leading statistics of the Mission† The adults baptized during the last year have been 348: the children 356. The adults on probation and in preparation for baptism are 1772: the day school pupils are 3120. In the Normal school at Morijah there are 43 pupils. In the girls Normal school there are 53 pupils. In the preparatory Normal school the number is 78. There are 20 catechists and students. The principal stations are 14. The out-stations or annexes are 66. The native assistants, including catechists and school-

* We must refer our readers for a fuller notice of the deathbed of Moshesh to Major Malan's book, pp. 145-147.
† These do not appear in the Report of the Société Evangelique this year, having arrived too late. I am indebted for them to the courtesy of M. Casalis, Director of the Mission House at Paris.

masters, number 115. The native collections in aid of the Paris Society during the year have been £868, 19s. 3d. The sum contributed by the natives for the Banyai mission has been £76, 13s. 6d. For other charitable purposes, the contributions have been £43, 4s. 6d.* The total number of adherents and hearers belonging to the Basuto Mission may amount to 20,000. The total number, of members by the last published report, were 3449. We may add that to establish an industrial and agricultural Institute the Paris Mission has contributed £1000.

These statistics are highly suggestive. In the first place, the large number of adults baptized during the year, nearly 350, almost as numerous as that of the infants, indicates that the evangelistic work of the Society is still advancing. The Missionaries are not settled on their lees—they would utterly avoid becoming, as one of the Reports says, a number of white priests directing vast parishes of blacks. The number of day-scholars is also encouraging, being more than 3000. We are interested to learn that M. Rolland, son of the venerable French missionary belonging to the first band who reached Africa, " has now the place and the title of director-general of primary education for all Basutoland."† This is a gratifying proof of the confidence of the Cape Colonial Government in the Mission and its work. The higher Normal School on which so much of the future of the native Pastorate and the native schools de-

* The statistics that follow are furnished from older reports of the Société Evangelique.
† Report Société des Missions Evangelique, 1877, p. 29.

ponds, is also steadily advancing. It will be observed, that if we add to the Normal scholars 43, those in the preparatory Normal School, there are in all, 121. This is a large agency full of promise for the Christian life of Basutoland in the future. The teaching staff is here strong, including M. Mabille, M. Dyke—M. H Dyke his son who has just arrived in South Africa, having completed his studies in Paris and in Scotland—and Dr. Casalis. Mr. Henry Dyke writes, that the impulse and progress of the pupils "leads to the anticipation that it must be sought soon to teach higher branches of study, such as theology and medicine."* M. Mabille has already indeed begun, what may be called, a theological class, although he gives it only the modest name of a "class of biblical studies." It is to prepare a certain number of young persons of approved piety for preaching and the cure of souls. A school of medicine, such as Mr. H. Dyke suggests, were it even elementary, would be of great value in exposing the witch doctors, who have been and are so great a curse to the superstitious Kaffir tribes. With this Normal Mission, we presume, will also be associated the proposed Industrial Institution. We trust that, with the young, energetic, cultivated French missionaries now entering on the field, Basutoland will speedily possess, if on a more limited scale, yet in essential character, a second Lovedale—devoted to the elevation and Christianisation of the tribe. The Female Normal Institution at Thaba Bosio is also doing an excellent work, educating those who may be the future Christian mothers of families and also

* Report Société des Missions Evangelique, pages 30, 31.

female teachers thoroughly furnished for their work. Mr Griffith, the resident commissioner, whose testimony regarding the Mission in general we have already given, writes on the subject of Basuto education: "The Missionaries, themselves educated men, appreciate the value of education as an antidote for the darkness of superstition, and make it a regular practice to devote several hours a-day to the instruction of both young and old." "Besides this, there are also two important training institutions established at Morija and Thaba Bosio—one for boys and the other for girls—which occupy the attention of some of the most able and experienced of the Missionaries. In these training schools the standard of education attained is the highest to which the Basutos have yet been introduced, while the physical and moral improvement of the pupils is insured by the residentiary system, under which they acquire habits of neatness, order, and cleanliness. Their mental and moral condition is proportionately elevated and developed by constant contact with European teachers, by a superior course of studies, and by a complete withdrawal, during the most critical period of youthful life, from the evil association and debasing influence of heathenism."

There are other interesting facts connected with the Mission at present, but which we can barely notice. In the old stations from which they were driven out, by the Boers, their memory is still cherished. The natives who remain there cling to their old simple form of worship, and desire the Christian education of their children. They lately built a chapel, and invited a French Pastor to be present at its dedication, and to give his Christian benediction to their civil marriages. The Boers seem also to retain no longer their old hostility. Another fact which strikes us, in looking over the names of the French Missionaries, is to find among the younger members such names as Casalis, Prochet, Dyke, Rolland—the last, the educational inspector, who, if not of the Mission, is so nearly associated with it. The sons are thus following in the steps of their worthy fathers. They are bringing the culture and accomplishments they have mainly acquired in Europe, to devote them to this remote Mission field. We may add, that they are not only good and simple-minded men, as some represent them, but fully abreast in all the highest ministerial gifts and accomplishments, of those of any of the Societies, the S.P.G., the Presbyterian, or any other.

Lastly, these statistics, taken as a whole, show us that we have here a complete well-equipped Mission, holding a clear, well-defined position, and able to do so with success, from its many and energetic agencies, and from the piety and zeal with which these are animated. It is a painful thought that the sacerdotal party should attempt, by its aggressions, to introduce dissension and discord, where there has reigned unity and peace. The Church of England has long held an honoured place among the Protestant Churches, for the breadth and catholicity of her spirit. Perhaps, for the honour of that Church, the legitimate conclusion is that the South African Anglican Church, however she may seek to lean upon the influence and authority of the mother Church, in no way represents her, either in her learning, her breadth, or her catholicity. It is the Church of Laud, with its narrowness, with its repudiation even of Protestantism, which it seems to represent mainly, not the Church of the Cranmers and Latimers and Ridleys.

But a statistical account of a Mission can give us, after all, but an imperfect impression of its Mission fields, with their Christian life and work, their successes and trials, their lights and shadows. We are indebted thus to Major Malan for his genial Christian sketch of the Basuto Missions. We may say that all Major Malan's visits were received with cordiality and sympathy, and everywhere he met with living, true hearted, Christian brethren. But we must content ourselves with noticing his visit to the oldest, and still the chief of all the stations— Morija. "After about six hours ride," he writes, " the turn of a fine mountain, which I had had before me for a time, brought me in sight of Morija. The Mission station looked bright and invitingly homely, set by the Lord's hand in a beautiful valley, and under a large mountain. The large, substantial house of prayer, standing in its centre, is a testimony that the Lord has owned and blessed the labours of his servants. I had now reached the oldest station of the Church of France, in South Africa. With what joy, I beheld the power and glory of the Lord, in the scene before me. This Mission stands alone among the Missions to the heathen. It is the faithful effort of a long persecuted and very poor Church, and the Lord has signally guarded and blessed it." " How can I describe the welcome of one, whom I had long loved and prayed for, and who had loved and prayed for me, and of others who had loved me for the Lord's sake. It was, indeed, a joy too deep for words, when I met MM. Dyke, Mabille and Casalis, and we at once knelt and praised the Lord." "The Church at Morija holds many hundreds. It was quite full. I praised the Lord for permitting me to testify to such an assembly." "The communion of the Lord's Supper was observed at the afternoon service. I greatly enjoyed joining in this most sacred ordinance with these dear French and Basuto brethren. On Tuesday, I enjoyed a long conversation with M. Mabille, whose whole heart and soul, like mine, are filled with a burning desire to see the Gospel carried on and on, until *it reaches the tribes* under the Equator."*

Major Malan on his tour, visited Letsie, a son of Moshesh, and the paramount chief. "His kraal is built under a magnificent kloof, in the Morija mountain. He is a heathen, who has long resisted the Word of God." Letsie is, we fear, no very contented subject. The old spirit of the chieftain rises against the new institution of a Colonial magistracy. This, indeed, utterly paralyses any attempt to restore the old arbitrary cruel rule. To maintain this new constitution in all its controlling power, is essential to the progress of the Basutos, and, indeed, of all the native tribes. The ignorance, dissoluteness, and tyranny of the chief, is at the bottom of the risings and mutinies of the Kaffir tribes.

And now to notice the fruits of mission work in Basutoland. And first, as regards the generation

* The Italics are mine.

now passing away, with the older Missionaries themselves who began the work, a late Report of the Société Evangélique says * " The first generation of converts disappears little by little, following to the tomb the old and noble chief, Moshesh, and sending us from year to year as farewells the touching testimony of their perseverance in the faith, " crying out at the moment of the great departure with the old Madeleine of Thaba Bosio—Kia tsela —I cross, I cross; or with Mampoï the sister of Moshesh, I have been engaged speaking with Jesus, and we have made, He and I, a covenant firm and sure, in which he promised to care for my children, and to convert them; or, again, there is the old Johanne Moséleng. When asked by the missionary what portion of the Word nourished him, his reply was, ' Let not your hearts be troubled. In my Father's house are many mansions.' Before he died, being asked how it stood with him and God, he replied, ' There is peace, great peace.' "

The Church of the present gives also fair promise. The careful Christian education it is receiving— nearly equal intellectually, and far superior religiously, to primary education in France—must, with God's blessing on the seed sown, be followed by a rich harvest. " That which rejoices us the most," says the last French Report, " is that the conversions have still that freshness, that stamp of simplicity and joyous faith, which has so often moved us, and has done us so much good."† " Others which have been indicated to us, tell of deep convictions long suppressed. This shows us that it is necessary to

* 1877, pp. 23, 24. † Report, 1878, p. 29.

guard against seeing in the numbers annually sent to us, a complete and rigidly true enumeration of the souls in whom the Holy Spirit is acting." It is a satisfactory indication that the work is genuine, to find that the Basutos, when they leave their country, do not leave behind them their Christianity. At the Diamond Fields they have built two chapels, and they gather together under the teaching and guidance of two Evangelists. There are some 5,000 of them, it is supposed, also engaged at the Grahamstown Railway; these are followed by superintendents, chosen by the Missionaries, paid by the Government, and the Christian labourers cling to their religious profession. I may say here that I think the action of the Basuto Mission, in following the railway labourers, deserves to be followed. The South African railways, from the high rates at which they pay labour, may do much to stimulate the natives to systematic work. I so far agree with Mr. Trollope that steady labour is civilising, and, if the Missions watch over it, I trust it may be also Christianizing.

As regards the material advancement of the Basutos, it is incontestable. The number of the tribe given in 1875, was 140,000, an immense increase on the past, and it is steadily growing—the imports alone amount to some £150,000, and the articles thus obtained are chiefly of British or other foreign manufacture.* The exports of wool and grain are also very considerable. Larger areas of land are brought every year under cultivation, and the de-

* These details are official. They are taken from a Cape Blue Book, published so far back as 1874. These are the statements of Mr. Griffiths, the Government Agent.

mand for ploughs to supersede inferior implements, goes on unabated. Last year the number purchased was 600. What has been to me the most interesting testimony to this progress is, that the Basutos themselves express their satisfaction. Blue Books are certainly not always interesting, but the account given in one of the Cape Blue Books, of a Pitso or great Basuto tribal gathering is one of the most instructive documents regarding South Africa we have met with. The meeting of the tribe was presided over by Mr. Griffith, the representative of the Government, but the native speakers evidently felt under little restraint. They very frankly told of their hunger for land, which, with their increasing numbers, is scarcely to be wondered at. They hinted that they would much rather stand in direct relation to the British Crown than be subordinate to a Colonial Government—a fact of which we must take note; and Letsie evidently took a far from popular part in absenting himself from the Assembly. The whole tone of the Pitso was quite loyal, and such a gathering, with the expression of its feeling, could not but afford to a sagacious governor an admirable means of gathering the mind of the tribe, and also provide an excellent safety-valve for suppressed feeling. The truth is, the Kaffir tribes are fond of speaking, and on tribal questions of law and order they can do so with great ability, judgment, and even eloquence. As the village system of India may be said to be the basis of its civilisation, which must be, therefore, ever taken into account in its rule, so the Pitso is a genuine South

African institution. If Sir Bartle Frere could generalise these gatherings they would do more meanwhile, perhaps, than a black suffrage to aid us in the native rule of South Africa.

We have marked in other missions their movements northwards towards Central Africa, and the great results likely to accrue from this. Perhaps in none of the missions has the evangelistic effort b:en more conspicuous than in the French Basuto Mission. Their means did not indeed enable them to contemplate such costly expeditions as those of the London Missionary Society or the Free Church into Central Africa; but there was the same heart; as events have turned out in Divine Providence, it is now not unlikely, although they did not contemplate it, that their enterprise may bring them speedily to the great river Zambesi; but we are anticipating. The story of the whole evangelistic enterprise of the French Mission has something almost romantic in it. A native brother Aser passes into the Transvaal to explore the country, with a view to the preaching of the gospel. He reaches the station in the far north at Zoutpansberg, where Mr. Hoffmeyer carries on his valuable mission work. He passes it with other companions, whose faith and courage is ready to fail, but Aser perseveres. He reaches a tribe beyond the Limpopo, called the Banyai, meets with their chiefs, and receives from them the assurance of a welcome to missionaries, and a promise to give places for mission stations. He then returns south, a long laborious journey of many hundred miles to the Basutos, tells of his pioneer journey, and appeals to the native Basuto Churches to aid in sending the gospel to this distant tribe. The Basuto Churches respond, the French missionaries gladly aid, for it is they, in fact, who had inspired at first the enterprise. Some £280 is contributed by the natives, with twenty-four oxen, and the Société des Missions Evangeliques, not only concurs in this, but gives its aid and liberal support. We may note here, that the Banyai chiefs do not seem to have told Aser of their relations to Lo Bengula, the son of Moselikatse, the great chief to whom we have so often referred. The Banyais are the subjects of Lo Bengula. To this ignorance may be traced, in some measure, the later mishaps of the mission.

We can notice but briefly the events that have followed, although they have been such as to have stirred up the deepest feelings among French Christians. An expedition, headed by M. Dieterlen, an experienced Basuto missionary, was sent out to pioneer the way to this new mission field; a mission band accompanying him of 23 persons, with 2 horses, 37 oxen, and 2 waggons. They were arrested, however, on their way through the Transvaal by the Boers, who have no love for the French missionaries and their support of the Basuto people. Two of the Catechists were thrown by the Boer Government into prison, and M. Dieterlen was obliged to return. In the Providence of God this obstacle has, however, been taken out of the way. Our readers may recall Dr. Livingstone's resolution when the Boers had burnt Kolobeng, destroyed his medical stores, and sold his furniture by auction. The Boers had decided, he said, to close the entry to him to the continent of Africa. He had resolved, for his part, to open it, and the future would show which of the two would succeed. It was in this spirit the French Mission went on. The last French expedition, headed by M. Coillard, found all things reversed in the Transvaal; the Boer Government had disappeared, and in place of it Sir Theophilus Shepstone, a friend of the missionary cause, was installed as British Administrator. "We went," says M. Coillard, "to pay our respects to Sir Theophilus Shepstone, whom I had frequently seen in Natal. He seemed pleased to see us again, and showed, as well as the members of his suite, the greatest interest in our enterprise. He gave us all the information and counsels that he could, and asked us to visit him as regularly and frequently as we could. He asked us to remain till the 24th, the Queen's Birthday, so that our Catechists, to whom he spoke with affection, should realize that they had no longer to dread the prison of Pretoria, but rather to trust in a Government the friend of missions, and the protector of the blacks."

The progress of M. Coillard and his party, after passing the Limpopo, was one encompassed with perils. They had dangers of the flood, to which travellers in South Africa are so often exposed—they had to traverse vast forests, and had often as pioneers to cut their way through the thicket, for their waggons, by the axe. Then, on their arrival, the chiefs of the Banyai, Masondo and Maliankope, seemed to have acted treacherously toward them. They had hoped, perhaps, to obtain ammunition and guns, which the native chiefs so covet, and when these were refused, they were so enraged, that the lives of

the missionary band were in imminent peril.
Happily, they escaped, and reached Inyati, the
capital of Lo Bengula. They had there the society
and support of such Christian brethren, as Messrs.
Sykes and Holm, of the London Missionary Society.
Lo Bengula's opposition to their evangelistic efforts
were by no means, however, to be overcome. He seems
to have suspected treachery, not only on the part of
the Banyai chiefs, but of Letsie, the Basuto chief, the
son of Moshesh, to whom Moselikatze, his father,
had ever borne so deadly a hatred. It is strangely
enough, as we have said before, the repetition of
the old story of Mosiga, in the early history of the
French Missions. Like MM. Rolland and Lemue
summoned before Moselikatze, M. Coillard and his
company must appear before Lo Bengula. The
chief has continued inexorable, and the French
Mission has been compelled to leave the Matabele
country—yet their Christian courage in their straits
has not failed them. M. Coillard bravely writes
thus—" Look not only on the waves. We could
not, in regarding them, but lose all hope and sink.
A look fixed on Jesus, and then a word on His part,
and the tempest will be stilled. I have the deep
conviction that God will open to us some way, and
that all the sacrifices made by the poor Churches of
Basutoland, all the prayers that have been offered,
and are offered still, all will not be in vain. Let
not discouragement take possession of the Churches.
We are ready for everything, but for everything
less than to return to Basutoland. We are in the
field, and we think not of returning to our homes.
You will pray for us when you receive these lines,

for the Lord has said, 'Before they call I will answer them, and while they are yet speaking, I will hear.' Sustain us, do not weaken us. We count on you." These are noble and heroic words—surely these clouds will break. Meanwhile the latest information we have received is, that the French Mission is on its way to the Zambesi, contemplating a mission to the Barotse tribes, far up the Zambesi, on the east. If so, it would seem as if Providence, beyond their own intentions, is directing the French Mission onward to the great mission field of Central Africa.

CHAPTER XX.

THE AMERICAN BOARD MISSION IN NATAL.

THE American Mission in Natal is but a limited part of that great work the American Board is carrying on in the world amid decaying Churches, ancient worn-out civilisations, and savage tribes. The Natal Mission is, I may say, marked by all those admirable features which so distinguish everywhere the work of the Board, the piety of the missionaries, the valuable female agencies they possess, the excellence of their schools, the care they devote to the training of native teachers, catechists, and preachers, the watchfulness of their discipline, and the thoroughness of all their Christian work. They have in Natal rendered valuable linguistic services also as regards the translation of the Scriptures into the Zulu tongue. Their work, I may add, is in Natal highly appreciated alike by the Government, the Colonists, and the natives.

It was Dr. Philip, I believe, who originally, as in the case of the Basuto and Rhenish Missions, directed the thoughts of American Christians to the South African field. The period when the American Board instituted this mission was a little later than the arrival of the French and Rhenish missionaries. Six American missionaries, with their wives, sailed from Boston to the Cape in 1834, reaching the Cape in 1835. Three of these were destined for the interior, three again for Natal. I may refer first to the former, as their story is shorter. They, passing by Griquatown, received from Moselikatze permission to occupy the station of Mosija, from which the French missionaries had been expelled. They were not long there, however, before they were attacked by severe fever ; and then the Boers, to avenge themselves on Moselikatze, attacked Mosiga, and the missionaries were forced to flee. The issue was that they, too, arrived in Natal in 1836 ; and thus the American Mission is as concentrated in Natal as the French in Basutoland. This has, doubtless, been an advantage to the mission cause.

Meanwhile the three missionaries destined for Natal, after being detained by the Kaffir rising of 1835 for some time in the Cape, reached Natal in 1836, during the reign of Dingaan, Chaka's bloody successor. Neither the Boers nor the British were yet in possession of the country. Dingaan, on the arrival of the missionaries, consented to their remaining, but stipulated that their station should be in the neighbourhood of Port Durban. This was established at the Umlazi to the south of Durban. Here Dr. Adams began the work, and founded with success a mission school, where, in addition to Zulu, the English language was also successfully taught. It was soon after this, that the other missionary brethren, who had first gone to the interior, arrived. Among them was Mr. Lindley, whose name is still held in high honour in Natal among British Colonists, Boers, and Zulus, and who belongs indeed, to the very first rank of South African missionaries. It was soon after this, and after the arrival of the Boers with their waggons, crossing the Drachenberg and seeking a home in Natal, that there occurred the sad tragedy of the assassination of Pieter Retief, and a number of other Boers at the kraal of the ferocious Dingaan. Mr. Venable, one of the American missionaries, arrived at the kraal soon after the event. "He saw the luggage of the Boers at the gate of the kraal, but all about was still as in the hour of death. Dingaan afterwards told him, that he had killed the Boers, but that the missionaries had nothing to fear." He also met here with a missionary of the Church of England, living in sight of the Zulu capital. Both anticipated the fierce war to which this act of treachery must give rise, and fled, and the missionaries were all obliged to leave the country."* This massacre was a severe blow to the Boers—many of their families suffering cruel losses, the memory of which is not yet obliterated. A Natal county which chiefly suffered, still recalls this event and its mournful consequences, in its name "Weenen," or weeping. There is a certain parallel here again, betwixt the story of the French and the American Missions. In both instances, the fierce struggles of the Boers and of the natives, inflicted deep injury on the missions; but in the case of the French, there was the more chivalrous rule of Moshesh, who never condescended to such cowardly treason and treachery—in the

* Malan, p. 191.

other, there was the brutality of the Zulu chief, educated in the savage school of Chaka. Some of the missionaries now returned to America, or died in other foreign fields. In 1839, however, Dr. Adams again intrepidly returned to his post at the Umlazi, while Mr. Lindley devoted himself for a time to labour as Dutch pastor at Maritzburg, where he won for himself the deep affection and reverence of his people. In 1847 he returned, however, to his mission work, and founded the valuable station of Inanda, near the coast. In 1841, Panda, who had, with the aid of the Boers, forced the blood-thirsty Dingaan into exile, where he ignominiously perished, invited the American missionaries to establish a station in Zululand. This they did, and for a time their mission was in high favour; but in the end, Panda showed himself ferocious as his predecessors had been. His jealousy was excited, by the fear, that the converts would no longer remain his submissive subjects—his soldiers were sent to assail the station—all the huts of the converts were burnt, they, themselves, were put to the sword, and the American missionaries, shaking the dust from off their feet, fled to Natal. Since that period, there have been no more American missionaries in Zululand. May we trust that the day is not far distant, when, with brighter hopes and prospects, they may again occupy this field!

In 1843 Natal was wrested from the Boers, and declared a British colony. Since that period all the Christian Missions of Natal have not only enjoyed security, but have received friendly support from the Government, both in allocations of land, and in educational grants. Still Mission progress sometimes continues slow, even in the most favourable circumstances. " For ten years the gospel had been preached among the Zulus, without one convert being made. But in 1846, the hearts of the Missionaries were rejoiced by one, and then by others, joining the Church."* From this period, the progress of the American Missions, which we cannot more fully notice here, has gone on ever advancing, until there is now a number of flourishing stations, a considerable membership, a vigorous staff of native pastors, and preachers, and teachers. The last statistics of the Mission are the following—There are 8 principal stations, with 11 out-stations. There are in all 28 preaching places, with average congregations, numbering in all, 1780. There are 14 churches, 9 missionaries, 16 female assistant missionaries, 3 native preachers, 25 teachers, 19 other helpers. The number of members or communicants in all, is 593. 17 Sabbath Schools report 865 scholars.†

One of the most pleasing facts connected with this Mission, is the number of native pastors and preachers it possesses. This is a branch of work to which the American Missionaries always devote themselves with great care, and in which they have gained great success. This is seen in many of their native preachers and catechists. They seek that in place of the missionary who must ultimately leave for other fields, there shall be a pious and well-instructed native pastorate. Major Malan observes, for instance, of the native pastor at Inanda, " I had

* Malan's South African Missions, p. 194.
† Annual Report, American Board, 1877, p. 12.

some converse with the native pastor at Inanda, a man who I do not hesitate to say, is in every particular fully equal in intellect, ability, manner, and all that man needs to fit him for the duties of life, to any European. I have made this remark simply because it is due to the Missionaries to testify to these things. Their enemies charge them with doing nothing. If, as has been done in many cases, they have taken wild Kaffirs, taught them God's Word and Christ's Gospel, civilised them, and then educated their children up to the standard of an educated English gentleman, they have done something." The American Missionaries, we may add here, have done much unobtrusively yet effectively in introducing the arts of life. The square cottage of the Christian Zulu is a very different habitation from the heathen kraal. "I was much struck," writes Major Malan, "in entering Natal with the very superior way in which the Zulu Christians build their houses, especially those of the American Missions. There are no such houses built by heathen natives in the Colony, and in fact many of them I saw would be an ornament to the Colonial towns in preference to the low iron-roofed sheds in which most of the white population live. I can only account for it by the peace which has prevailed in Natal, since the occupation by the English, by the superiority of the Zulu Kaffir when converted, and the energy of the American Missionaries."

The American Mission has devoted great care to its higher educational Institutions. In its Normal Seminary there are ten theological pupils, forty in the normal department. The female boarding schools are, as is usually the case where American Christian Ladies preside, most excellent. The Missionary examiner writes of one of them, "I look on this seminary as a great auxiliary to our Mission, and an eminent blessing to the Zulus, and trust that no pains will be spared to make it a still greater blessing. I love to think of the future of these bright and intelligent girls, and contrast it with what it would have been, had no seminary been established for them." Of another similar Institution it is written, "It is delightful to see how the school is appreciated. Some of these girls have become hopefully pious, all have been wonderfully improved. Soon the girls will be scattered to their homes north, south, east, and west, and they will go preaching in more ways than one, mothers will rejoice, and brothers will put their hands on their mouths in mute astonishment at the improvement, the happy looks, the cleanly ways, the quiet intelligence and obedience of these sisters. So the expansive work goes on, not in one, but in many places."*

What has especially interested me is their kraal visiting. It is a department of mission work somewhat new. It is something akin to Zenana work in India, in which so many American ladies are engaged, but it has its special difficulties and trials in Africa as well as its successes. As I have not met with much on this subject in connection with other South African Missions, I shall quote here from the experiences of Miss Hance, a mission lady at Umvoti. "I do not know but that you

* American Board Report, 1877, p. 14.

would like to hear more about my work in the kraals. I began it more than 4 years ago. It was then such a new thing, and I felt so uncertain about its success, that I did not find courage about it until God brought me more and more to see that He was ready to bless my efforts for those poor degraded kraal women. One day, I shall never forget it, I started with my Bible woman to walk to a place two miles away, where we were to have a meeting. The day was very warm. I became so wearied that we sat down near the road in the hot sun. I felt very tired, yes and discouraged. What will it avail if I go on, I speak the language so imperfectly, and then to-day what could I say that would reach their hearts? While I sat there with such thoughts a woman came up with a pot of food on her head. She said as she ran along, 'I am hastening home with this food that I may be in time for the meeting.' At once we went on, and when we reached the kraal we found one of the houses made clean and nice for us, with mats spread down to sit upon. Soon the house began to be filled with women. I think, this time there may have been as many as thirty. After we had sung I said to the Bible woman, I do not feel as if I could speak at all to-day, ask God to help us; and she prayed. In her prayer she seemed to bring God very near, and I felt such a flood of light break in upon me, such peace and strength in God's love through His Son, that when she closed I began to tell them about this love. I forgot that I was not speaking in my native tongue, I forgot my fatigue, I forgot almost everything but that I had their quiet, fixed attention, and that God was giving me words to speak. As the meeting closed we all went out. The setting sun, with its golden rays, made beautiful the whole landscape before us, and seemed like an earnest of the time when the Sun of Righteousness should lighten every dark corner of the earth. The women were standing hushed, in twos or threes." How pleasing and elevating such converse of the privileged daughters of Japhet with their poorer sisters of Ham.

A Church that is earnest and evangelical, we can scarcely suppose, will not be also evangelistic, and it is so with this interesting American mission. Like M. Mabille, and M. Coillard of the French mission—Mr. Tyler, and others of his brethren are inspired with the longing to use those gifts and resources God has conferred on them and to dispense them to the heathen of the north. The Prudential Committee of the American Board, have not, however, seen their way to this, though earnestly desirous of taking a part in the evangelisation of Central Africa. The state of their funds did not seem to warrant it. The missionaries had thought of moving in the direction of Sofala, on the east coast. This would have brought them into Umzila's kingdom, where no missionary has yet found a place. The languages needed, would be probably the Zulu, Swazi, or Amatonga—and for such, the American missionary would be readily equipped. Then they have an admirable staff of native evangelists to accompany them when they move. The last report of the American Board on the subject, seems to me more favourable than the previous one. The

Prudential Committee will, we trust, find that the highest prudence is often the boldest venture—that such an object as this Mission extension will gather around it the warm, or it may be rather the enthusiastic, support of American Christianity, and that if it has been the high distinction of an American traveller for the ends of science and progress to achieve the noble enterprise of penetrating Central Africa—it will no less redound to the honour of American missionaries, to aid in opening up these vast benighted regions to the light of the gospel, and to the blessings of Christianity.

I quote the last report on the Zulu Mission. The committee express " their great satisfaction with the cheering signs of progress which the exhibit of last year affords. The movement into the interior, and the establishment of a new station, the increase in the number of Church members, the large aggregate of Sabbath school scholars, and of attendance upon public worship, are, of themselves, facts full of encouragement, but still more hopeful is the record of the girls' school, and the roll of theological students. Between Mr. Champion's first school,—his shelter,* the shade of a tree, his book the sand on which he traced the letters, his pupils, the curious few that gathered to watch him—and the present eagerly sought facilities for imparting instruction, a whole continent of mental and moral betterment intervenes." " In the judgment of the committee it would be gratifying to all friends of missions to see a vigorous prosecution of the work, looking more

* Mr. Champion was one of the first Missionaries in Natal.

especially to the *evangelization of Central Africa*,*
and we would ask the question, Whether after forty
years of labour on the borders, the word of the Lord
to-day is not, Ye have compassed this mountain
long enough. Speak to the children of Israel, that
they go forward."†

* The Italics are ours.
† American Board Report, 1877, page 33.

CHAPTER XXI.

THE HERMANNSBURG MISSION.

MANY of my readers have, I doubt not, read of the Hermannsburg Mission and its work.* It belongs to the same noble category of Christian enterprise as the Rauhe Haus at Hamburg, Dr. Fliedner's Institution at Kaiserswerth, or George Müller's work at Bristol. One striking feature of all these has been the greatness of the achievements compared with the seeming scantiness of resources. It has been the earnest Christian life, and the heroic Christian faith, that has accomplished such wonders. The Hermannsburg Mission now extends its labours to Africa, India, New Zealand, Australia—its last mission station is Japan. The work has not yet indeed, been entered upon there, but a missionary has been appointed, and is preparing for it. To us, it has an interest that the first mission field of the Hermannsburg Society having now so extended a work, was South Africa, and its first mission station indeed, among the heathen was New Hermannsburg in Natal.

I glance at the history of this mission. Harms, its founder, was what is called in Germany a Volks

---

* The Rev. Fleming Stevenson's "Praying and Working" gives an excellent outline of the work of Pastor Harms.

Prediger,* (Scotice, a folks' preacher) whose gift it was to bring the gospel home in its life and power to the rural masses. This is very far from meaning that Harms was an illiterate man. On the contrary, he fought a hard and successful intellectual battle at the University with rationalistic speculations and doubts, and he sounded there, to a remarkable degree, learning, theological, philosophical, and philological. Still there remained an aching void in his heart, until the Divine intuitions of the Gospel of St. John, especially its seventeenth chapter, laid hold on his whole soul. Harms was in theology a strict Lutheran—perhaps as much baptized into the spirit of Luther as any man of his age, and his missions bear the same type. There is a considerable amount of sacramentalism, more, indeed, than the Evangelical Churches would generally care for, but there is still no sacerdotalism, and there is all prominence given to the great Reformation doctrine of justification by faith. There is also a catholic spirit, as regards other Churches. Such a creed, however we may differ from it, is Protestant—it has achieved a great work in our day in reviving German Christianity, and it has not the exclusiveness of Ritualism and Romanism.

The chief scene of Harms's labours, was Hermannsburg, under the oaks of Lüneburg, and amidst

* Büchsel, the well-known Berlin preacher and superintendent, belonged originally to the same class of Volks Prediger, although he has now the most fashionable and aristocratic congregation in Berlin. It has often struck me that the late Dr. Guthrie of Edinburgh might have been enrolled in the same class. His preaching delighted alike the high and low, the country people, the townsmen—the higher classes. His pulpit success and Büchsel's, teach us that in the gospel, "the rich and the poor meet together ; the Lord is the Maker of them all."

its substantial Bauers, or peasant farmers, who speak the old Platt Deutsch. The language is not used colloquially only, the peasants delight also in religious services conducted in their homely vigorous tongue. The foundation of the success of Harms was laid in his simple, earnest, powerful preaching of the Word. As set forth by him, it was not only highly evangelical in its doctrine, but evangelistic in its tendencies; many of the peasants and hand-workers were stirred up with a desire to enlist in Mission work to which Harms himself looked, as that which was to revive the German Churches. Harms eagerly sought places for his converts in the German Missions, but such were not always readily to be found, and Harms at last decided to form himself a Mission Training Institute, and then, leaning in simple faith on the Master, to send them forth to form Christian communities among the heathen. No Mission committee was formed, no subscription books were opened. It was one of his familiar sayings which he worked out in practice, "The Lord Christ needs not to beg." As his mission band was chiefly gathered from among the peasant farmers, or the handicraftsmen around, this we may say, gave a particular character to the Mission which it still retains at Hermannsburg, and in the foreign field. One very leading aspect of all its missions is their industrial and agricultural character—the ideal, is in fact, somewhat akin to Lovedale. Whether in the mission field it is always wise to carry out the idea of a ministry detached from all other work, save the preaching of the gospel, may be made a question. Harms had before his mind a system rather like that of those earnest

Anglo-Saxon missionaries who first carried the gospel to heathen Germany, and who trained their converts alike in temporal and spiritual things. In point of fact, it may be said of the missions in South Africa generally, that the successful missionary is usually not merely the teacher and preacher among his people, but that he sets them the example, too, in the various departments of rural industry. This comes, however, into especial prominence in the Hermannsburg Missions, and in the Institution which trains them for their work. Along with the four years of preparatory biblical, educational, and religious training of the young men who devote themselves to mission work, there is at Hermannsburg, as at Lovedale, the daily work of the students in the fields. These young men, indeed accustomed mostly from their youth to field work, or to manual employment, would speedily lose their health and vigour if confined to study alone. A bond of connection is thus kept up also betwixt the Bauers and handicraftsmen and the Mission, so that recruits are never awanting to supply the place of those who go forth in the Mission enterprise. In the Mission field, also, it does not lessen the respect of the natives, but often enhances it, that the missionary goes before them, not only in teaching, but in working, in building a house, or constructing a waggon, or ploughing the fields, or practising the healing art. In the Hermannsburg Missions also, besides the missionaries, who are more especially, though not exclusively, called to the work of teaching, there are also the colonists specially intended to devote themselves to skilled labour. We have attempted to point out generally, how Colonial and mission work may happily aid each other. But this idea is far more specially worked out in the Hermannsburg stations; each is at once a Christian Colony and a Christian Mission. I shall have occasion to see how far this plan has worked practically. Meanwhile I observe, that so far as it can be effected, it is valuable in raising up a Christian Colonial influence to aid in elevating the natives, and especially in affording a defence against the injurious influences which so often follow the contact and intercourse of the Aborigines with European Colonists.

I can only briefly glance at the history of the Hermannsburg Mission in South Africa. The first idea of Harms was a mission to the Gallas, a brave North African race, near Abyssinia. In the small mission brig, the Candace, belonging to the Society, there embarked six Missionaries, with eight Christian Colonial brethren, designed to form a Christian community among these tribes. The voyage was by the Cape and Natal, then Zanzibar and Mombas were finally reached in May, 1854. But the permission of the Imaum of Muscat, who was also the ruler of Zanzibar, could not be obtained for the journey onward to the Galla tribes, and with heavy hearts the brethren were thus compelled to return to Natal. There they received a most hearty Christian welcome from the Rev. Mr. Posselt, an able and greatly esteemed veteran missionary of the Berlin Society. Their aim was now Zululand in the North, but they were wisely advised first to found a station in Natal, where they would enjoy British protection, and prepare themselves for their new field of Mission work. Like other Colonists, they purchased land where they could form a settlement. They paid for this, £600, and they resolved to make this station the basis of their work. To associate it with their old Mission Home, they called it New Hermannsburg, and pleasingly situated as it is, it does no discredit to their original German Mission Home. They industriously built there a large structure to be the home of all the Missionaries and Colonists, where they should live in common, and they began their Mission educational and industrial work. I shall give here a sketch of the station as it is described by Herr Hahn, an esteemed Rhenish Missionary, who visited it:—" In the middle of a valley, which does not lie very deep, there is the great dwelling surrounded with a broad verandah, situated in a flower garden, close to which, on one side, is a plantation; around it are the farm steadings and workshops, from which there comes the sound of hammering, sawing, &c.; still further are the large stables, close to the fields, which are in good cultivation, the sheaves of the last rich harvest piled up; further, again, are the brethren with a yoke of oxen, ploughing. On the right of the valley below, in a little hollow, there is an inconsiderable looking mill, whose merry klapper shows that God's blessing fills the corn-loft. From the hollow, a little further on, a footpath leads us to a new large building. The first has already become too small, although a couple of families are living at the smithy, and the cartwright's workshop. If we turn the opposite way, there is a row of smaller houses—

the homes of the Makoloa, or converts. These are lightly yet neatly built, and within are suitable, tidy, and in good order. Each native settled here has five acres of land and freedom of pasturage." This sketch was written five years after the founding of New Hermannsburg. It has grown considerably since, and its educational Institution has become valuable not only to the natives, but the Colonists. There has been established an excellent Christian Colonial boarding school.

The disadvantage of New Hermannsburg is that it is not near one of the native locations, and has not thus the access to the natives that it might have. A location in Natal, we may explain, is land that has been set apart for the natives, where the Zulu tribes have their home. Many of these in Natal are of great extent, and swarm with Zulus. Two stations, more favourably situated for the locations, were speedily established by the Hermannsburg Mission with the permission of Government. The mission was also invited to enter Zululand, where they speedily obtained the favour of Panda, the father of Cetywayo, by building for him a waggon house which was the largest building in the country. We translate a short notice of this, as a specimen of the industry of the German Colonists and missionaries, and of the impression they and their work made on the Zulus. "They themselves fetched the wood from the forest, and worked at it with saw and with axe. Our Missionaries did such work gratuitously for six weeks,—preached meanwhile on the Sundays several times, and daily during their bodily work imparted also spiritual gifts. Thus, for instance, they sang their spiritual songs as they stood on the roof which they were covering, so that the heathen, noble and simple together, were astonished at their work, and begged them for their hymns. Their King, Panda, said at the completion of their work, when they would take no payment, 'You are different from the other white people; they always want my oxen and cows, but you want nothing. You are good people.'"* The strength of the Mission gradually increased. After five years there were no less than 100 German Mission labourers in the field. Internal difficulties, it must be owned, however, arose, and a superintendent had to be appointed. Their troubles were connected with the relations of the Colonists and the Missionaries. I may say that in the end the Colonists have gradually separated from the Missions. They are, many of them, worthy Christian people, living near the Missions and maintaining their Christian character; but they are now independent of the mission, and the mission independent of them. Even as regards the missionaries and their families, they do not now live in common, but each missionary receives his own salary. In these respects, while still maintaining markedly its industrial and agricultural character, the Hermannsburg Mission is more assimilated now to the other Societies.

The Hermannsburg Mission in South Africa has gradually extended widely into other fields than Natal. We have already noticed the conflict of the Boers with the London Missionary Society.

* Allgemeine Missionschrift, 1877, p. 69.

Wherever their power prevailed they sought to drive them out, as the Boers of the Free State did the French Basuto missionaries. On the other hand, the Boers had a friendly feeling to the German Missions as in character like those of the Moravian Brethren of the Cape. With the latter, indeed, they had had at one period many feuds, but they had gradually got to like them, as being not so dangerous to them in their native policy as the English missionaries. The Hermannsburg missionaries were thus invited to establish missions among the Bakwens, and even the Bamangwatos, old mission fields of the London Missionary Society. It is not necessary for us to notice their work there in detail. For a time they prospered, but in the end they retired from the field. It was different, however, as regards the positions they had gradually occupied in the Transvaal itself in Rustenburg, in the Magaliesberg, and the other western parts of the country. There their work has been crowned with much and continued blessing. Bethanien, a station near Rustenburg, has now more than 800 members, with some 500 communicants. It is regarded as the pearl of their missions. They have also many other flourishing stations in the Transvaal. In Zululand, on the other hand, the action of Cetywayo has greatly crippled their work; and has led, in many instances, to the abandonment of their stations. I shall notice the state of Zululand in connection with the Norwegian Missions, and I shall not therefore refer to it more at length here.

The latest statistics of the Hermannsburg Mission are the following:—There are in South Africa 47 stations with upwards of 4000 converts. Of the 8 first missionaries two have been taken away, and of the later, 13 have gone to their rest. Of those who survive from the beginning is the Superintendent Hohls, "with his old joyousness and fidelity occupying his difficult post." "Let our missionaries," says Harms, "be poor miserable sinners as they may, this will not be denied them that in love and unity they labour on—faithful, industrious, frugal." During the year 1876, 557 heathen were baptized; and the members of the Church amounted to 1724.* For the third time the Hermannsburg Mission would now again attempt to reach the Gallas. Two missionaries are being trained for this at New Hermannsburg, and an older Natal brother will accompany them. The fact is an interesting one. The Hermannsburg Mission, availing itself of its South African resources, like the other Societies there, desires to press on Northward to the Christian conquest of Central Africa.

The name of Harms is so closely associated with these Hermannsburg Missions, and whatever touches him, must so touch them also, that I may allude here to a painful trial, which has lately befallen the worthy Pastor of Hermannsburg. He has been suspended from his pastoral office, and has indeed retired altogether from the National Church. He is, as we have said, a high Lutheran, and a new marriage formulary having been introduced into the Church, his conscience would not allow him to concur in it. The ground of difference is this, while

* I have not the full returns for a later period.

he admits the validity of civil marriage as regards the State, he is not prepared, as the formulary requires to recognise it, on the part of the Church. This is the sole ground of difference; Harms clings to the old Lutheran formulary, or at all events he cannot acquiesce in this new one. It is to be regretted that there has been thus a disruption of the oldest and dearest ties. While we do not share in the views of Pastor Harms, surely the ecclesiastical authorities might have found some way of relief for tender consciences, as our British Legislature, indeed, recently did in the enactment of a new marriage law. Pastor Harms says with deep sorrow, but at the same time in a good Christian spirit, "Without resentment or hatred, I will separate from my dear office in the State Church (Landes Kirche), from the ancient, dear dear Church, from which streams of blessing have flowed over the world—from the ancient honoured sacristy, where Urban, Regius, Hildebrand, Walther, Johann Arndt prayed, where my father, my brother, and I, for so many a year bent the knee, where the palms and Cyprus garlands hang, which the love of my dear King placed on the bier of my brother, from the beloved parsonage, where my family have lived sixty-one years, where I was born, where I have lived, as pastor eleven years, where my brother now in bliss lived, prayed, wrestled, wrote, suffered and died,* and in which I would so willingly have died."† It is sad that the days of the venerable single-hearted, devoted super-

---

* His brother was the founder of the Mission.
† Hermannsburg Missionsblatt, January 1878, pages 14, 15.

intendent of the Hermannsburg Mission should be thus clouded. It can scarcely be doubted, however, that in his trial he will have the solace of finding his missionary brethren rallying around him.

CHAPTER XXII.

THE NORWEGIAN MISSION.

THE Norwegian Mission Society was founded in 1842. Its principles are not High Church, but Evangelical. The seat of its Home Committee is at Stavanger, where is also its College for the training of Missionaries. The most flourishing stations of this Society, we may say, are not in South Africa, but in Madagascar. Feeling discouraged by the slow progress of the work in Zululand, arising from the arbitrariness and tyranny of its rule, it was led, we believe, to begin the Madagascar Mission, which has since proved so great a success. "It is here," its secretary writes, "it has now its greatest and happiest work."* Its first missionaries were Schreuder, and Thomassen, a helper. Schreuder, not wishing to remain in Natal, applied to King Panda to found a station in his country, but was refused permission. After some stay with the American Missionaries, to learn the Zulu language, he left Natal and South Africa altogether. He went for a short time to China, but there, somewhat strange to say, Gutzlaff regarded his northern blond hair as an insurmount-

* For the information I give here, I am considerably indebted to an interesting communication I have received from the Home Secretary of the Mission at Stavanger.

able obstacle to his mission success among the Chinese. He then returned to Natal, and in 1849, a Mission Station was established not far from Zululand, at Upomulo. While there, King Panda took ill on one occasion—sent for medicine to the station, and attributing his recovery to the use of it, took Schreuder into his favour. He was now permitted to found the station of Empangeni in Zululand, not far from the sea. In 1854, another station Entumeni was opened. The total number of stations occupied by the Mission in Zululand is now 7, with one Natal station.* There are in all, some 270 baptized persons, with 9 Pastors. It may be added that Bishop Schreuder has latterly resigned his connection with the Norwegian Missionary Society, on the ground, we believe, that he felt himself cramped in the exercise of his authority as Bishop by them. That differences should arise, was quite indeed to be expected, as the Home Committee do not share his high Lutheran views. None of the missionaries, we may say, seceded with him—all clung to the Society. Bishop Schreuder has, we believe, established two Mission stations in Natal, and Entumeni, in Zululand, has been retained by him.

The results that have accrued from this Zulu Mission may at first sight seem inadequate when compared with the Christian labour that has been expended on them. But the cause is not far to seek. It arises from the insecurity of missions under such a chief as Cetywayo. The stations of the Society

* I should write lately occupied, as in the present state of Zululand, all Mission work has been in great part arrested.

for the Propagation of the Gospel and of the Hermannsburg Mission, have long languished for the same cause. Latterly, the arbitrariness of Cetywayo's rule has given place to open hostility. In 1873, when crowned, by Mr, now Sir Theophilus Shepstone, he promised that his rule should be one of justice and humanity, and he especially pledged himself that no native subject should be put to death without a trial. All these promises have been utterly violated, as well as his friendly assurances of aid to Christian Missions. The Secretary of the Norwegian Mission writes me—" We have been waiting and hoping in the expectation that the English Government, now that the Zulu King has broken so clearly his promise to Sir Theophilus Shepstone, when he was crowned, would take measures to guarantee religious liberty, without which the Missions will not be able to show greater results." This aid we may say the British Government has declined to give. The grounds of this decision are given by the Earl of Carnarvon in a dispatch of 31st August, 1877. I quote the following extract:—
" I request, therefore, that you will cause the Missionaries to understand distinctly that Her Majesty's Government cannot undertake to compel the King to permit the maintenance of the Mission Stations in Zululand, and that it is desirable for them, if they are of opinion that mission work cannot be carried on in Zululand without the armed support of England, to retire for the present from the country. In a very few years at most, it may be hoped that matters will become more settled, and that the country will be in a more favourable condition for

the resumption of their labours of Christian charity, which no one can desire to see continued and developed more sincerely than I do. I may further observe that, viewing the matter as one of worldly wisdom, they will, I believe, advance their cause much more effectually by a brief and prudent suspension of proceedings, than by risking an open quarrel with Cetywayo at the present moment." As regards this dispatch, one might have desired to know more definitely from his Lordship what moral pressure he had brought to bear on Cetywayo. Apart from hostilities, we should have expected his Lordship to have directed that the strongest remonstrances should have been made as to the murder of Christian natives, and the flagrant violation by Cetywayo of his promise to put no one to death without a fair trial. In point of fact, the missionaries and their converts have been in great part compelled to abandon the country, as Lord Carnarvon suggests may be expedient. As to a more settled state of things to which Lord Carnarvon looks forward in a very few years, it is likely that the crisis is much nearer at hand than he seemed to anticipate. The recent violent aggressions of the Zulus on Natal territory, carrying away from a Natal Police Office, and killing one poor fugitive Zulu woman, and murdering in cold blood another found also on British territory, are violations of international law which demand explanation and redress.

An attempt has been lately made in the British press to show that Cetywayo was not responsible for the murder of the Christian converts, to whom we have previously referred. An article lately appeared entitled : " A Visit to King Kctshwayo by Magema Magwanza, communicated by Bishop Colenso, Macmillan, March, 1878." It may be well on this question to lay before the British public the strong evidence which substantiates Cetywayo's guilt.

The murder of one of their native Christians took place at Ekyowe, an important Norwegian Station under the charge of the Rev. Mr. Oftebro, the superintendent of the Norwegian Mission. He is now, we may say, with his converts, a fugitive in Natal. The Secretary of the Mission writes to me regarding this:—" In the month of April, an old Zulu, at the *command of the king*,* was killed at Ekyowe, he was not yet baptized, but was preparing for baptism, and died at the hands of the executioner, praying and confessing the name of Christ. Some of the baptized were also persecuted by the Impis of the king, but escaped. The reason why the anger of the king fell especially on Ekyowe was, that Christian principles had latterly got great influence there." Another more detailed statement is found in the Hermannsburg Missionary Journal:— " The superintendent Oftebro, had at the wish 'of the old Zulu convert,' just the week before, spoken with the king, and as Oftebro wrote me the king had been quite friendly. Eight days later, he sent an Impi, (a native soldier,) and without anything further caused him to be killed. His end was happy. As the soldier came, he asked why he would kill him. The answer was, Because you are a learner and would be baptized. Well ! he says, let me first

* The Italics are mine.

pray. It was permitted to him. He knelt down and prayed, and then rising up, added, I am now ready, shoot me."*

The other murder was perpetrated at Enyezane, a Hermannsburg Station, near the Zulu coast. It was a Sunday morning when the missionary heard a sudden confused noise of a crowd of natives, gathered around the hut of Joseph, a Zulu convert. Joseph had just been praying with his family when the murderous band drew near to assail him, uttering loud cries, " Umtakati and uteyfu," the one word meaning a witch or sorcerer, the other strychnine. The missionary hastened to the crowd, who were howling, crying, mocking, striking. "Two or three pointed their guns at me, he says, but did not shoot. I hastened to Joseph. What a spectacle, fearfully beaten, his body flowing with blood, he was stretching out his hands to me, which they were in the act of binding. I sought to work my way through to him, but was forcibly pushed back." He was now bound to a tree and beaten. The missionary inquired of the leader, on what account, who told him he had been *sent by the king* to kill this umtakati. He had bought strychnine from Bishop Schreuder, and with it he had poisoned one of the cattle of Usindwangu, a neighbour. The cow had in fact died of lung disease. Usindwangu himself appears a little later on the scene, while Joseph is still alive, but in reply to his prayers, all he says is, "This is not my affair, have you not heard that the king has sent and will kill him." Joseph, after a few hours further torture, was shot,

* Fröhling's letter, **Hermannsburg Missionsblatt,** October, 1877.

and his body flung into a large pond. Later, a kingly official, Umbilwane, came and brought me the king's word. He had little to say which I did not know, only he emphasized this, that I was not guilty. Joseph had bought the poison from Schreuder, and I had known nothing at all regarding it."*

Our readers will, we hope, excuse our inquiring with some care into these cases of undoubted martyrdom. That the men were guilty of any other crime than that they were Christians, none who know their story will affirm. But the question is, Who was the real agent, who was guilty of the blood and death of these two poor Christians? If a Christian bishop regards it as his duty to adduce exculpatory evidence in behalf of a native chief—and it is but right that justice should be done to him—our inquiry is at least equally suitable. "Precious in the sight of the Lord is the death of his saints."

We turn then now to Bishop Colenso's impression. "Such exaggerated accounts," he says, "have been sent to England of the state of things in Zululand, and particularly of the atrocities, which are said to have been committed by orders of the king in respect of numerous native converts, and to have caused a sudden flight of many of the missionaries from the district, that your readers may be interested in a narrative of a visit which has just been made to the Zulu king by a Natal native, written by himself in Zulu, and literally translated into English."

"The writer," he adds, "is the manager of my

* Hermannsburg Missionsblatt, October, 1877.

printing-office, which is wholly carried on by
natives. I have had him with me from a boy—for
more than twenty years—and I am sure his statements are thoroughly to be relied on as accurate
reports of what he has seen and heard in Zululand,
and of what he believes with reference to the condition of that country and the intention and wishes
of its present rulers."*

According to Bishop Colenso, Magema may be
"thoroughly relied on." I have these remarks to
offer on this. It is, of course, not to be supposed
that the British public can be acquainted with the
more obscure incidents that occur in the history of
a small colony like Natal. But the Natal readers
of such a statement as the Bishop's will not forget
Magema's name in connection with a native Christian petition to Sir Garnet Wolsely, when in Natal,
of so offensive a character that, abandoning the
blandness of his usual communications, Sir Garnet
thought it his duty exceptionally to censure it. But
what bears more on the value of Magema's testimony
is the fact, which will not readily be forgotten, that
it was also clearly established on a careful scrutiny
that the petition itself was a forgery, having appended
to it the names of a number of native Christians,
who protested that they had never given authority
to Magema or any other to sign for them. This is
in the recollection of every Natalian, as it made a
considerable sensation, not only as regards the Natal
public, but the Legislative Council of the colony
also. But I pass from these general considerations
to look at Magema's testimony in regard to Zululand

* Macmillan, March, 1878.

and those atrocities which the Bishop regards as exaggerated.

The two murders to which we have referred are, of course, admitted. The question is, Was Cetywayo privy to them? Let me notice here on what evidence Magema rests. It is altogether hearsay. It is the authority of two Christians, whom he meets at Cetywayo's kraal, and who tell him what they had heard on the subject. They were not themselves personal witnesses. It is a somewhat remarkable fact, we may notice, to find these Christian converts so near Zulu royalty at a time when most of the native Christians were flying the country, and Cetywayo's views on missions and missionaries were generally well known.

As regards the murder at the Norwegian Station Ekyowe—these converts insisted that Ketshwayo was not at all to blame for that shedding of blood. Mr. Oftebro had told the king of the conversion, at which he was surprised, as Gaoze, the inferior chief of the convert, had not told him. He was astonished at this, and when Gaoze heard it, fearing that the missionary had informed against him, he sent a man to kill the convert, at once before Ketshwayo knew of it. Ketshwayo stated on this subject, to Magema, "He was killed by our people, without my orders." This evidence is quite contrary to the testimony of the Rev. Mr. Oftebro, who affirms that it was done at the order of the king. It may be also here added— if done contrary to Cetywayo's will, why did he not punish the murderers? *

As regards the murder at Enyezane, the account of

* Macmillan, March, 1878, p. 427.

R

the converts is that he was "killed by Sentwangu's people," but they concede, "Evidently that convert was killed, though perfectly innocent of any fault." Then Cetywayo, whom Magema interviews on the subject, says—"The matter was reported to me after the convert had been killed. I was startled at that when I heard it, and blamed Sentwangu's people very much, for killing a man, without my orders. But they assured me, he privately did that. But that convert did, no doubt, a very bad deed." The testimony here again of the Missionary Fröhling, is quite clear, that the officials sent declared that they killed the man by order of Cetywayo. On the other side, the statement of the converts is mere hearsay, and Cetywayo's declaration must be taken in the circumstances, for what it is worth. Of course, his evidence is more direct than theirs, but is it in any way satisfactory? He blamed, he says, Sentwangu's people, but was there then any inquiry made, or were the murderers punished?

The whole story of the visit of Magema to Cetywayo, as translated by Bishop Colenso, can scarcely fail to occasion a smile to those who know anything of the Zulu character. It is quite characteristic of them that as face answers to face, so the mind of Magema, an old attached follower of the Bishop, should reflect, as in a mirror, all the Bishop's ideas about Natal, Langalibalele, Matshana, Ketshwayo, &c. Still we could scarcely have fancied that one whose position before the world is that of a keen inexorable single-minded critic could have ventured to rest a charge of "exaggerated accounts and atrocities" on such meagre hearsay gossip as Magema retails. It will, I think, overtax even the Bishop's ingenuity to prove to the British public that the persecutions of the Christians in Zululand are a myth. I may add here that the evidence proving Cetywayo's direct part in these murders, given by the Norwegian and Hermannsburg Missionaries, has been also strongly confirmed by some later correspondence of the Rev. R. Robertson, a highly respectable missionary of the S.P.G. I must say here also, that Bishop Colenso, having translated Magema's evidence on the subject, I should have expected that before publishing such a testimony he would have investigated the evidence, so readily to be obtained in Natal from his Missionary brethren, the German, Norwegian and Anglican Missionaries.*

* The narrative of Magema's visit to King Ketshwayo, was communicated to Mr. Trollope when at Maritzburg. He had evidently his doubts as to the value of the testimony. "As the writer of the Journal, he says," "was present, my doubts could only be expressed when he was out of the room." "There is a touch of romance there, I would say when he left us alone." "Wasn't that put in especially for you and your father, I asked as to another passage?"—Trollope's South Africa, voL i. p. 311.

CHAPTER XXIII.

THE BERLIN MISSION.

THE Berlin Mission, like the London and Rhenish Societies, is widely extended in South Africa. Like them, its stations stretch on from the South toward the North, the Rhenish Mission forming the left wing, the London Missionary Society the centre, and the Berlin Mission the right. The London Missionary Society has, indeed, pressed further northwards than either, but the Rhenish and Berlin Societies with the co-operation of other Missions, which begin also to enter on the field, will not, we trust, be long behind in reaching the Zambesi. The Berlin Society has devoted its efforts to South Africa exclusively, and, thus concentrated, it has laboured with success to fulfil its mission.

On the interesting history of the Mission I can say here but little. The subject has quite gathered around it a literature of its own. There are, for instance, Herr Merensky's most interesting lectures, to which we have often had occasion to refer, and which were delivered originally, I believe, to large German audiences of the most intelligent classes, and were received by them with great approval.

Then there is Dr. Wangemann's elaborate and complete history of their South African Mission, containing many graphic sketches of the natives, and of Mission life, with well matured and weighty opinions on Mission progress in general. These enable us to form a very complete idea of the work that has been thus accomplished. I trust that these contributions to the history of South African Mission work, especially as regards the Transvaal, a field with which the British public is little familiar, may yet, in some condensed form at least, be presented to English readers.

The Berlin Missionary Society was founded in 1824, but so far as its operations in South Africa are concerned it dates from 1834. The missionaries originally sent out, were intended to labour in the interior among the Basutos or Bechuanas. This was, we believe, the earnest purpose of General Von Gerlach, a leading member of the Society; but it was not then carried out. Ultimately it has been; and now the most flourishing and growing Mission Stations of the Society are in the Transvaal among the Bapedi and other Basuto tribes. Two of the first missionaries remained for a time in the Cape Colony without much success, and then passed further to the north to labour among the Korannas. The Missions of the Berlin Society have gradually taken deep roots in this tribe, and to no other Mission Society is it now so deeply indebted for Christian ministration. It was first in the year 1837 that the Cape Missions of the Society began to obtain a firm basis of work. This was at the station of Zoar, a Hottentot village picturesquely situated at the foot of the Groote Zwartberge. A Mission had been established there by the South African Missionary Society in 1816 or 1817, and a small church erected, with other buildings; but the Mission had long gone to decay. It was in 1838, with the permission of the South African Society, handed over to the Berlin Mission, but on the condition of being restored if required at a later period. The Berlin Missionary Gregorowsky found it in a very wretched state indeed, drunkenness entailing the deepest misery, murder, too, and adultery prevailing, so that the minds of the people were quite blunted to all impressions of the Gospel. The Berlin Mission eventually overcame these great evils, mainly, through the preaching of the Gospel, but aided, we should add, by a careful system of discipline. I have specially noticed, indeed, this first station of the Society just in reference to the latter fact. It is an important question of Mission economy among such races, if some vigorous system of discipline be not absolutely required to protect the young converts from the besetting sins of the heathen by whom they are surrounded, and to train them into industrious settled habits of life. The Berlin Society has given much careful attention to this subject. In Zoar it gradually organised a staff of deacons and deaconesses for the Church, with a body of general overseers to maintain order and propriety among the people. In Amalienstein, a station near Zoar, which was afterwards established, this was carried out even more fully. The land on which Amalienstein was founded was purchased by the Society with funds in part the legacy of a noble German lady, whose name was given to the village.* As the property, some 20,000 acres (10,000 Morgen) belonged to the Society, they were enabled thus to introduce and enforce regulations as to the conduct of the occupants. The land was not sold, only rented to the natives, so that any unruly and disorderly families could be excluded.† Amalienstein, we may observe, is now the largest of the Berlin Cape stations, having some 780 members, with 501 communicants.

Our readers may recall a previous notice of Zoar and Amalienstein in connection with the S.P.G. We may state here that Zoar was given up, as had been agreed on, to the S.A. Missionary Society in 1854, but again restored to them to their great rejoicing in 1867. This gave rise, however, to unhappy dissensions. A party in Zoar were unwilling that the Mission should be in the hands of the Berlin Society. They did not wish, it is believed, to submit to the stricter discipline it enforces in its stations. Hence the occasion for the unhappy and ill-judged interference of the Rev. Mr. Hewitt, of the Society for the Propagation of the Gospel.

A number of other stations of the Berlin Society exist in the Cape Colony. There are four chief stations. The last of them which has been founded, Riversdale, seems among the most flourishing. Its

* Burkhardt, Sud. Afrika, p. 80.
† The same system has been carried out at other Mission stations. It is established thus, at Impolweni, Natal, where the property was bought by the Free Church, and the land is let at a very moderate rent to the native families. Mr. Allison, the Missionary, informed me that he regarded this as the best system, and regretted that he had not introduced it at Edendale. Whether, even as a Colonial Government measure, it might not be better to rent the land to the natives, than to give it in fee simple, is a question well deserving consideration.

number of members, 772, is nearly equal to Amalienstein, and there are 317 communicants. An excellent Female Boarding School has also been established. All these stations, we may add, possess good schools. We are gratified to learn that in the judgment of the Society these stations are approaching the same position as those of the London Missionary and Rhenish Societies in the Cape. They have reached such a degree of culture that they may be regarded far less as initial missions than as really " parishes of black baptized people."

In British Kaffraria the Berlin Mission has also a number of stations. These are four in number besides out-stations; the oldest was founded in 1837, but the greater number at a much later period. The Society has here, we may say, a Colonial as well as Mission work to carry on. There is a considerable German colony in British Kaffraria, consisting partly of settlers from the German legion which served in the Crimea, and to whom the government offered lands in South Africa, partly also of a body of North Germans, hardy peasants, some 2000 in number. These are sober, steady, industrious, and much better educated than the same class in England, and have proved a valuable addition to the Colony."* The Berlin Society has discharged a useful mission in providing, as it has sought to do, for the spiritual wants of these enlightened colonists. "These attach themselves," the last Report says, "ever more closely to the churches of which our Bethel missionaries form the

* " South Africa," Silver & Co., p. 63.

central point." The missionaries have the happiness of seeing the development of Church and Christian life among them.

The Berlin Society is by no means so satisfied with the progress of Christianity among the Kaffirs here — the reference is more especially to the Amaxosa tribes. It separates from these the Fingoes as more accessible and more church-going. As regards the others the Report says, "Since the gospel has lost the charm of novelty the large mass of the Kaffirs occupy a position to it, which is repulsive — expressed by some in cold civility, in others by mockery and hatred." The missionaries complain, with some justice, of the hindrance placed in the way of missions, and of every means indeed of elevating the natives, by the free sale of spirituous liquors. This is not the case in Natal, and it has helped to save that Colony from trouble, even although the government regulations have been imperfectly carried out. " Among all the heathen Kaffir tribes there is a deep fermentation of evil, an utter despair of the future, urging them to violent and frantic means of defence." † We may add that the free sales of arms in the Cape Colony has largely contributed to the strength of the mutiny. The natives fancy that their possession of arms, apart from military discipline, places them abreast of Europeans. Here, again, the Natal government has acted more wisely, and the limited number of guns held by the natives has contributed not a little to the safety of the colony. In the case,

* Jahresbericht, 1877, p 15.
† Jahresbericht, 1866.

indeed of a struggle with Cetywayo the difficulties will be greater, as he both possesses guns, and his regiments have a certain rude discipline.

In the Cape Colony the Berlin Society has two Synods—one west, the other east, in British Kaffraria. There are 8 chief stations, with the considerable number of 2789 baptized, 1451 communicants, and 273 baptized during the last year.

The Berlin Missions in the Orange State are also flourishing. They are limited for the present to three, but these are considerable—the number of members of the churches amounting to 1133, and 158 have been added to the church during the last year. Openings in Providence have also presented themselves for the planting of new churches. They are about to establish a station thus at Kimberley for the Germans settled there, and also for the natives gathered at the Diamond Fields from so many of their stations in the Transvaal, Natal, and the Orange State. One of their missionaries is also now settled at Bloomfontein, as pastor to the German colonists in that new rising town and sanatarium, and he has also begun a mission among the blacks. What has been, however, a special joy to the Mission has been the resurrection at Saaron of an old church that seemed to have passed away. We have been interested to observe that the Berlin Mission has had a number of such instances to record. Some of these have been, indeed, as in the Transvaal, the re-establishment of stations destroyed by persecution; but this of Saaron is of another kind. "An especial joy," the Report says,* "has

* Jahresbericht, 1877, page 18.

been the restoration to life of our station at Saaron, written among the dead since 1854. At the time of the scattering of the Links Korannas our brother, Johann Schmidt, now in bliss, continued notwithstanding to build up the massive walls of a new church, and he wrote regarding it—' Should, in the most sorrowful case, this people be altogether broken up, the word that has been preached here will remain as a testimony against them, and may this building also do the like, which has been reared in sorrowful times from love and care for the soul-cure of this people.' Such faith and such love has its promise and its blessing. In the first days of March, 1854, the Korannas withdrew; and on the 10th April the faithful missionary followed them —after holding a last service with three families that remained. But his prayers found an inclining ear. The love which they had experienced at Saaron—perhaps also even the walls of the church and dwelling built with his own hands by the faithful brother Schmidt—exercised so attractive a power on these Links Korannas that they gathered together again in thousands at the old place, and last year surprised Brother Kallenberg at Pniel with the intelligence that during the twenty-three previous years they had never ceased to hold there united worship, nor earnestly to pray for a missionary." It is but rarely thus that old churches are rebuilt. The ruins of the apostolic churches of Asia are a memorial of this, yet the grace of God can accomplish such an end; and Saaron is a pleasing instance of His divine love and power.

The Berlin Station at Pniel has of late caused

the Society some anxiety and vexation, as regards its secular affairs. As the question raised is one that has really an important bearing on missions generally, I shall notice it. The title of this Society to the lands it holds has been called in question. I may observe, that many of the South African Missions have obtained, gradually by purchase, or by free grants, tracts of land. The Church of England, I believe, has had quite the lion's share of these. Still, grants have been liberally given to other Societies also. These have been most useful in providing sites for the building of churches, for the plantation of native Christian villages, and for providing land, where the converts may be trained to industry and to a better system of agriculture. At a more advanced stage of progress, such native Christian colonisation, if we may so call it, may not be so much needed; but now, as nurseries for Christian rearing, they are, however some may sneer at them, of the greatest possible value. For native Christian families to continue living in heathen kraals, with their savage usages and immoralities, must be most injurious. Many of these mission settlements in South Africa are now greatly advanced in civilisation—as much so, indeed, as our European villages generally are; and they form a striking contrast in material progress, as well as in moral and religious character, to the heathen kraals. We are quite aware that some will gainsay this; but the evidence in support of it, which can be readily adduced if necessary, is not only weighty but overwhelming. If it be said, regarding these mission lands to which we are referring, that having cost but little, or having been free grants, the fixed rights of property scarcely belong to them, it might be replied with equal justice, that the same applies to the colonists, many of whom have obtained valuable grants, at a mere nominal rate, on the condition of occupying and cultivating the lands, which, I may add, the mission settlements do equally. To charge, as some have done, the Missionaries with allowing or encouraging their people to squat on the land, is an utter calumny. A well-conducted Mission Station is, compared with the kraals of the heathen, a hive of industry. Did my limits allow, I could easily establish this, from the statistics of the Berlin Mission.

And now I shall briefly state the mission grievance of Pniel. In 1857, the Society purchased the land, which was not a grant, with every legal form, "in aller form Rechten." It was sold to the Society by the Griquas, afterwards the Boers, when they occupied Pniel formally, recognised their right, and the Society for a number of years paid the taxes. Pniel was afterwards annexed to the British territory of Griqualand, in 1870. It is since that period, that the titles have been refused. Recognised in the inferior courts, these have been called in question in the Court of Appeal, and the Society feels a difficulty in prosecuting its claims there, at considerable expense, out of funds designed only for benevolent and Christian ends. "We have," says the Society, "nothing else to set against force but our protest before men and our prayer to God. But it will be a remarkable incident if a heathen chief sold us a piece of land so large, and at so moderate a price, that thus the salvation of the Gospel might be preached; and if this destination of it should be withdrawn by Christians who have entered in later,* and we should be injured in our lawful rights." "The officials do not scruple to say that they regard our property as too large, and that they intend to cut down its limits considerably." I may say that I am aware, from the strongest testimony, how deeply this has wounded Christian feeling in Germany. They have thought it but a poor recompense for the disinterested labours of their South African Missionaries. Christian Missions are no national preserves. We ourselves carry the Gospel to other lands than our own. And it is to the benefit of our possessions if foreign missionaries, such as the French or the German or our American brethren aid us in the promotion and extension of the Gospel. Their rights should be as dear to us as those of our own British Churches. For my own part, I cannot doubt that these claims, when brought under the consideration of Sir Bartle Frere, will receive that attention they merit, and that he will do substantial justice to them, which is all that is asked by the Berlin Mission.

The Natal branch of the Berlin Mission belongs to the most efficient and successful in that Colony. None of the Missions in Natal have as yet grown to large numbers, although some individual stations are considerable. But all the Societies there, we may say, American, S.P.G., Berlin, Presbyterian, &c., are marked by devotedness, both to Mission work and to Christian education, from which

*Jabresbericht, 1876. The expression as here translated, "entered in later," is stronger in the original "Eindringlinge." The Society in fact feels extremely aggrieved.

great results may be anticipated with God's blessing in the future. The Berlin Mission in Natal dates from the close of the Kaffir war in 1846-7. The Missionaries then in British Kaffraria had all been driven from their stations. They met together to take counsel as to their future, and the result was, that at the invitation of Mr Shepstone (now Sir Theophilus), they resolved to begin a Mission to the Zulu Kaffirs in Natal. Their first station was at the foot of the Drachenberg range, but they have since extended their settlements over the Colony. Their leading station now is near the Coast at Christianenburg. This is occupied by Mr. Posselt and his son, and has some 440 members. Christianenburg, we may say, combines a thriving young German Colony with a Zulu Mission. These are both under the charge of the Missionaries. The German community has here formed a Missionary auxiliary, and there is an annual festival, the brightest of the year alike for Germans and Zulus, when German and Kaffir hymns are sung, and Mission addresses are given. We should like to see so happy and holy a bond widely extended betwixt the Colonists and Christian natives of South Africa. The Rev. Mr. Posselt occupies, as a Missionary, a place of great esteem from his admirable Mission work; from the place he holds as an experienced Missionary among his brethren and in the Colony generally, and from the Catholic spirit which distinguishes him. There was a signal instance of the last in his cordial reception of the Hermnannsburg Missionaries. His veteran and able services well entitle him to occupy a place in the first rank of South African Missionaries.

The stations of the Mission in Natal are now six in number, extending from the coast to the spurs of the Drachenberg, where Herr Zunkel and Herr Glöckner, a young and energetic Missionary, worthily maintain their outposts. Another station is at Königsberg, near Newcastle, a place where there are valuable coal mines. This position on the Natal frontier, towards the Transvaal, is a bond of connection betwixt the Natal and the Transvaal Berlin Missions. There are in Natal, resident at the various Stations 2371 natives, with 826 members, of whom 302 are communicants, 92 were baptized last year, and there are now 67 catechumens.

We notice now the work of the Berlin Mission in the Transvaal. It deservedly occupies the first place in the history of this Society. The latest in its origin, it holds now the largest and most influential position of any. There are no less than 20 stations now established in the Transvaal territory, with 2478 members—of whom, 400 were baptized last year, including among them 134 adults. The Mission may be said to have been initiated from Natal. Two missionaries, Merensky and Grützner, were sent from that colony, in 1859, to the king of the Swazies, at Hocho, his mountain fortress; but their mission was in vain. The Swazies refused to receive the Gospel. On their return, the Dutch magistrate of Leydenburg, a place which is now the centre of the gold fields, advised them to go to the Basutos, which they resolved to do. The old purpose of General Von Gerlach was thus accomplished, and in honour of him, they called their first station Gerlachshoop.

The site of Gerlachshoop, was obtained from Maleo, the chief of the Bakopas, whose mountain home, recalled to the German visitors the picturesque Lilienstein, which the tourist knows so well in Saxon Switzerland. We notice one or two circumstances of interest, in connection with this station. One is, to do the Boers justice, that they did not oppose themselves to this mission enterprise. On the contrary, it was Piet Nel, a Boer Veld cornet, who, using his influence, induced the chief Maleo to permit the residence of the Missionaries among his people. But what is to us a more interesting circumstance, is to turn for a moment to the interpreter of the Missionaries on this occasion. This was Sekoto, a native convert already. His story, as showing us how the Gospel spreads in South Africa, may be worth notice. We give a mere outline of it, taken from Dr. Wangemann's Mission Narrative:—

"In the middle of the fiftieth year of our century, a Bakopa youth, Sekoto, travelled in the interior to obtain a gun, that ideal aim which every energetic Basuto has in view. He worked a year, and then, having obtained his gun, returned home. He travelled anew, and met this time a Christian Boer near Bloomfontein. The Boer said to him, You travel round the land, but do not know the God who shelters you on your wide path; or do you think that it is by your own strength and skill, that you continue so well? I know it, answered Sekoto, that Modimo* protects us; but I know him not. The goad thus driven in still pricked him. Who was

* Modimo is the Basuto name for God.

this Modimo of the whites? and although he returned home again, this would not suffer him to remain there. With resistless power it urged him to go back to the country of the whites, to learn who Modimo was. This time he took a friend with him, Mäele. On their way another friend met them, who told them, Do not go into the villages, there you find teachers who teach God's Word, and he who learns that Word forgets his fatherland and goes no more back. So was it lately with one of us at Graaf Reinet. Work rather with the Boers where there is no danger."

From that hour the thoughts of Sekoto were on Graaf Reinet, where he hoped to find what he sought. On the way he met a teacher, who, in return for his garden work, taught him to read a little, and also some Bible history. When he came to Graaf Reinet he found the preciousness of God's Word. The missionary would have had him remain till he could baptize him, but he would not be separated from his fatherland; still there were words that sank deep into his heart. The first word was, "Jesus receives sinners." Then there was another word of the missionary—Love the Lord and seek Him; read diligently God's word, and pray, Lord teach me! Lord teach me! Lord teach me! Sekoto returned to his home, and daily prayed "Lord teach me." For the first time then he opened a Dutch hymn-book, and the first words he met with were—Jesus receives sinners. Now he felt certain this must be the truth, and so he proclaimed, in common with his friend Mäele, who had also learned the truth, what he knew of God's word, taught the natives also to read as well as he could, and ceased not daily with Mäele to pray, Lord teach me Lord teach me! The joy of these two in meeting with the missionaries can be supposed. They became faithful servants of the Lord, were wonderfully saved when their tribe was overthrown, and then at the last joined the Berlin Mission Station at Botshabelo.

The tribe of the Bakopas, of which Maleo was chief, was not destined, however, long to survive. They were assailed and overthrown by the Swazies, and what remained of their possessions was plundered or destroyed by their neighbours. Maleo himself did not receive the gospel, but became at the last its open enemy. Fragments of the tribe, however, survived and found their refuge in the Berlin Station at Botshabelo. While thus one door was closing, another, however, and still wider, was thrown open. Sekwati, the powerful chief of the Bapedis, invited the missionaries to his territories. He was probably induced to do so by motives of policy on account of the services they might render to him as interpreters and mediators in his transactions with the Dutch; but, from whatever reasons, he remained their firm friend till his death. Merensky and Nachtigal visited him at Thaba Mosegu and obtained permission to found their station not far from his fortress at Khalatlolu. May we here venture to introduce another incident illustrative of mission work in South Africa? While the missionaries were in the capital of the Bapedis, two men met them with eyes that beamed with joy. Masadi was the one, Mantladi the other.

Masadi had under his arm a book, the Pentateuch in the Kaffir tongue, and a tin box which contained a well preserved paper. This was the certificate of his baptism, which had taken place in a Methodist church, at Port Elizabeth. He could read tolerably in his book, and told them that his companion, though not baptized, was also a believer. The Mission brethren were astonished, and thanked the Lord with their whole heart that in this distant corner of South Africa, which they had thought was so buried in night and darkness, streams had penetrated from the sun of the Gospel. The brethren were soon afterwards on their return journey when one of the company, a bearer of some of their luggage, asked, Whence do you come, from the Colony or England? They replied, We come from a country further than England—Germany, and we have made the journey to proclaim to you Jesus Christ. Then the natives both smiled with joy, and one of them cried, That is good. Then the Missionaries marked them, and recognised that they were Masadi and Mantladi whom they had met before. They had secretly, indeed, followed them, that they might be with the brethren. Can, said Masadi, the baptized native, Mantladi receive baptism after being two weeks with you? No, the Missionary replied, the Lord above would be angry with us, were we to baptize those whom we do not sufficiently know. Oh, said Mantladi, it is indeed a great thing baptism. But, said Masadi, you do not know him, he believes much, he has long loved the Lord, and everywhere he goes about and preaches and confesses Him. He has already spoken to Sekwati of Modimo. He has also exhorted the other chiefs, but they have replied, that he is out of his mind, and that he must be silent or they would chase him away. But Mantladi is not silent. Already, through him, two men of Sekwati's town have been won, who pray there, who will soon come to you. "Have you then prayed the Lord," said the Missionaries, "for a teacher?" Yes, they answered, every day, for our land is still so dark. Now we see that the Lord has heard our prayers. Then the brethren knew why there had been no rest to them at Gerlachshoop, and were the more rejoiced when the two pious Bapedi told them that they had during the two years since their return from the Cape observed the Lord's day. They never worked on that day, but came together to speak of God's Word, and to pray."* Both these converts continued faithful to the end. One of them died a solder's death, fighting for his chief, in his last moments praying to the Lord; the other's end was in peace with his family at Botshabelo, with his dying words expressing his faith and trust in God.

The successor of Sekwati was Sekukuni, a name familiar to all in the later annals of the Transvaal; first, as the enemy of the Boers, and now of our own Colonial Government. Sekukuni seems at one time to have been on the verge of the kingdom of God, but his impressions passed away; a dissolute life, drunkenness, pride, and evil counsels, gradually alienated him from the Christian faith. His own brother, Dinkoanyani, was baptized, but this, so far from influencing him towards the gospel, seems to have aroused all his jealous fears. The baptism of

* Lebensbilder aus Sud. Africa, Wangemann. Berlin, 1876.

three of his wives stirred this feeling into fury, and led to cruel persecutions, the sad story of which has never yet, so far as we know, been related in English. We cannot enter on it here. Sekukuni felt, as probably Cetywayo now does, that with Christianity a new power had arisen in the tribe, the power of conscience ; and that there was an inner province now, in which the chief no longer wielded absolute supremacy. Hence, in many instances where the chief remains a heathen, he becomes either an uncertain and treacherous friend, or an open and avowed enemy. Sekukuni became ultimately the latter. The Christian converts and Merensky their missionary, were at last compelled to flee for their lives. Dinkoanyani, the brother of Sekukuni, was compelled to do so also. Happily, this has turned out for the furtherance of the Gospel. The Boers allowed the missionaries to establish a station at Botshabelo, where the converts were safe, and they were permitted also to strengthen their position by building a fort, where, if attacked, they might find safety. Botshabelo, though never assailed by an enemy since its foundation, has yet had its trials. Dinkoanyani, who joined the Mission with his followers, still retained, as a Bapedi, his dislike to the Boers, and they on their side imposed on him heavy taxes. The result was, his resolution, to the great regret of the missionaries, to leave Botshabelo and to establish himself nearer his brother in an independent position in a part of the country lying close to what are now called the Gold Fields. To this resolution, Sekukuni, who had been latterly reconciled to his brother, gave his support, and engaged to aid him against the Boers, a promise he did not, however, in the end fulfil. Those who have read in the Press the late history of the campaign of the Boers against Sekukuni, may recall the tragic end of this chief, the attack of the Boer artillery on Dinkoanyani's fortress—the hand to hand fight with the Swazies, and the issue that while the fortress was not taken, in consequence of the cowardliness of the Boers, Dinkoanyani received his death-blow in the fight. It is said, that he died professing his faith in the Bible, and in the Gospel, but with his old warrior national hostility, expressing his thanks that he owed his death, not to the cowardly Boers, but to a brave black race. By this withdrawal of Dinkoanyani and his followers, we may add, that the ranks of the Mission adherents at Botshabelo were, for a time, considerably thinned; but the station has now far more than regained its strength. At the end of last year, 1877, the station had 1295 residents, 1029 members, and 491 communicants. We believe there is scarcely any Colonial village or town in the Transvaal, which can compare with it, in its roads, defences, and walls, with its church and schools, with its various Mission Institutions, and with its well organised rule and discipline.

The other stations of the Berlin Society are widely scattered, but they are all so planted after careful mission exploration—(Recognoscirungen und Reisen) as to support one another. They include Pretoria, the capital, Potschefstroom, one of the most important Colonial towns in the Colony, Leydenburg, Heidelberg, and other stations. In the last year no less than four stations were added. These are not indeed, all new, but in some instances, as we have already noticed, the restoration of Mission settlements, which had been crushed by persecution. We are interested to notice that Sekukuni's territories are being again so nearly approached, and we trust the day is not distant when in this field the Berlin Mission will have regained all its Christian influence. The chief efforts of the Society are still northwards. It is there harder work, for it is breaking up fallow ground; but the Society enters bravely on it. The last word of Dr. Wangemann in his interesting history of the Transvaal Mission is, "Forward," (Vorwarts). "The mountains which one sees" he says, "from the northern slopes of the Drachenberg, are inhabited by numerous peoples. Thither often eagerly turn the eyes of our brethren, and their heart measures the time when the feet of the Missionaries of peace will bring to the heathen the message of light." We regret to notice, from a recent earnest appeal of Dr. Wangemann, the mission director of the society, that the resources of the Berlin Mission are so crippled that they can scarcely hold the positions they occupy, far less advance into these wide mission fields thus opening before them.* They have been obliged to draw largely, of late, on their reserve funds.† It seems to us a subject worthy of consideration if some Mission Aid Society might not be formed to help those Missions of South Africa, which are straitened in their resources, to pass on northward to Central Africa. The design of this would not be to aid

* Wangemann, Die Berliner Mission im Bassuto Lande, page 789.
‡ Berliner Missions Berichte, No. 7, 8.

them in the maintenance of existing stations, but to help in occupying new fields. The French Basuto, the Berlin, the Rhenish and the Swiss Societies would be strengthened by such help. The question of the evangelisation and progress of Central Africa is one of such magnitude and deep Christian interest as to rally to its support all Christians, even if their own Churches have no special missions devoted to South Africa. Many, we think, would heartily contribute to so noble an enterprise.

The last Berlin Mission Report ends with these words: "We close our account with thanks for the fruit the year has brought, and with joyous hopes for the future, and with thanks especially for the 934 baptized during the year,—a number exceeding those of previous years. Through these the total of our members has been raised to 7224. We give thanks also for the 1006 catechumens who remain under instruction, and for more than 2000 children instructed in God's Word and in useful knowledge in our 37 stations. We have the joyous hope that, through the many dispensations of Providence which have passed over the people of South Africa, the ground will be so prepared that we, in the coming years, may rejoice in rich harvests."*

* Jahres Bericht, 1877.

CHAPTER XXIV.

THE MISSION OF THE FREE CHURCH OF THE CANTON DE VAUD.

THE Mission of the Free Church of the Canton de Vaud in South Africa may be regarded as yet in its infancy; and yet, although but some three years old, its growth has been such as to be full of promise for the future. It is a study, often not without deep interest, to mark the early history of a Mission; the fresh zeal with which the Mission labourers are inspired; the interest that belongs to occupying new unbroken ground; the hopes that are inspired; the deep sympathies of the Home Churches; the prayers that encompass the Mission; and then with these its first trials—its labours, its patience, and the first fruits that it gathers in. The first step taken towards the formation of this society was in 1869, when MM. Creux and Berthoud, now the missionaries of the society in South Africa, offered themselves as missionaries to the Free Church of the Canton. They were at the time theological students. The Vaudois Free Church, after prayerful deliberation, accepted their offers; and sent MM. Creux and Berthoud to Scotland to complete their studies—to learn English, which was thought indispensable, and to acquire some knowledge of medicine. One of them, M. Berthoud, in point of fact, has since, by his studies at Edinburgh and Paris, fully qualified himself to act as a medical missionary. The question was then to select a mission field, and in this the Free Swiss Church was naturally influenced by its friends of the Société Évangélique. They had lost some valuable missionaries, and they invited the Swiss Church to give them some temporary aid, by sending out their missionaries to labour, at least for a time, in the Basuto field. This was agreed to with great advantage to both societies. The Swiss brethren were found most useful there. Those who have read Major Malan's tour will remember his very friendly notice of them; they were placed here in an admirable position for training for their ultimate work. An exploring tour was then made in the Transvaal to find some suitable sphere, and as Sekukuni and the Bapedis are closely allied to the Basutos, it was thought that an opening might be found in his tribe. Sekukuni, however, refused utterly to allow them to remain in his territories. A station further north was then sought out, and it was ultimately decided to establish one at the Spelunken, not far from Zoutpansberg, in a position where there seemed important openings for the preaching of the gospel to the native tribes. The locality had also its attractions for the missionaries, as the beautiful undulating country, with the wooded mountains in the distance, and the Zoutpansberg, with its picturesque peaks, recalled to them some of the scenery of their own romantic Swiss canton. The Mission was ultimately established here in 1875, and the station was appropriately named Valdézia. The tribes in the neighbourhood of the Mission partly belong to the Basuto race, partly to the Makwamba or Amatonga, or as the Portuguese have named them "Knobnosed Kaffirs." They are a tribe akin to the Zulus.

Short as has been the history of this Mission, hardly three years, it has already had its baptism of trial and persecution. The feelings of hostility are well known which the Boers have ever cherished towards Moshesh, the sagacious chief who, to save his country from invasion invoked the English Protectorate against them. The fact that these Swiss brethren had been labouring with the French Basuto Missionaries, whom next to Moshesh the Boers detest, naturally awakened their jealousy and anger, and on the ground of certain formalities not having been gone through, the missionaries were summoned to Marabastad, a northern provincial town or village, and there placed under arrest. This forced absence did not, however, impede the cause of the mission; on the contrary, it deepened the sympathies of the home Church and stimulated its prayers, while in the district itself it excited the indignation both of the white and black populations. The work of the faithful and earnest native evangelists, whom they had left behind, was so blessed also that on their return they found their little Christian society doubled. Their being allowed to return to resume their work was associated by the Boers with some vexatious limitations, but it is unnecessary to notice these as they have been all swept away by the annexation of the Transvaal to the British Empire. The Swiss Mission of Valdézia can thus in quiet resume its interesting and earnest work.

The exact number of mission members of Valdézia I cannot gather from its records. It must be, however, growing, as in one year there is the record of 30 baptisms. It has 3 out stations, and 5 native catechists, who all seem devoted Christian men— one of them is Bethuel, the brave evangelist, who, when the Basuto missionaries were prevented from crossing the Transvaal to reach the Banyai, went from Valdézia to explain this to the Banyai, and to preach to them the Gospel. We may notice here that the Swiss Mission has come to an arrangement with the Berlin Society, that leaving to the latter the Basuto tribes, it will devote itself to the Magwamba. They are a people considerable in numbers. They supply in part, for instance, the Natal demand for native labourers. The tribe stretches far away to the north in Umzila's kingdom, especially betwixt Delagoa Bay and Sofala. We heartily wish the Swiss Mission success in this interesting enterprise that lies before them. May they yet possess the east, as the Rhenish Mission so nobly occupies the west of South Africa. And may Sofala itself yet render to them its tribute, if not in the gold of Solomon, in that better treasure—the gold of the Gospel tried in the fire.

Let me here, before leaving this young but most interesting mission, quote from a mission sketch given by M. Creux. It is an account of his first reading to the converts of one of the most deeply touching stories of the gospel. This had been translated by him, and it was the first time it had ever been rehearsed in the Magwamba tongue. "The Sunday before Christmas we celebrated," he writes, {" the Supper. There were about thirty communicants. I read to them the story of the agony of Jesus in Gethsemane which I had translated into Magwamba, and gave some remarks and exhortations. I cannot say with what joy I read a portion, newly translated of the Word of God ; my joy was great that evening in seeing the profound impression made by the recital. Not a tear, but bright looks, intense attention, a profound emotion, which let itself be perceived rather than seen." The next day a young Motsuethla, who has followed diligently the services at Bethuels station, came to say to me, that he was now decided to follow the Lord Jesus. "I have heard," he said, "yesterday evening things that have touched my heart; Jesus the Son of God has suffered so much to save me. Although he saw death before Him, He accepted it to atone for my sins. I would not delay further then to be his disciple."

Later, at Christmas, 12 catechumens came to receive baptism, "after having had, as we believe, the baptism of the Spirit. There was first a missionary address, then an opportunity was given to the neophytes to speak, so that the church on the one side, and strangers on the other, might hear from their own mouth the testimony they were called to give. Their movi ig words may be thus rendered :—' We were darkness, we are now light—we were blind, we now see—we were as sheep without a shepherd, we have returned to the Bishop of our souls—Glory to God for His Love to poor sinners.'—" In the afternoon there was another fête. It was ten couples upon whom we were to implore the blessing of the Lord. For us the ceremony offered an interest, deeply moving. Here is a new Christian and civilising Society, destined to conquer and to transform this people. Here is the Christian family with its joys and griefs sanctified, here the woman is put into her place, and her children are no longer treated as cattle, but as heirs of life everlasting,— here, I might add, are so many churches that will be founded, so many houses and villages, where the name of the Lord shall be adored and His grace proclaimed." *

A magistrate in the Spelunken, not far from the Mission, gives the following testimony regarding Valdézia, " I am astonished to see the progress of the Gospel among the Magwamba, I could not have believed it possible. Near me, I know a number of young persons, who have renounced idolatry and drunkenness. They are persecuted and expelled by their parents, but they hold fast." †

* Bulletin Missionaire, 1878, pp. 236-239.
† Bulletin Missionaire, 1878, page 234.

CHAPTER XXV.

THE ROMAN CATHOLIC MISSIONS IN SOUTH AFRICA.

"As to the Roman Catholic Missions in South Africa," Dr. Grundemann, the missionary historian, writes, "we have learned very little. The only source of information is the Annals of the Propagation of the Faith, which, during the last five years, contain only a very general statistical statement of the western circuit of the Cape, according to which this includes 7000 Catholics and 12 churches."* The only native Mission, he adds, to which reference is made, is the Basuto Mission. We confess our own researches on the subject, like Dr. Grundemann's, have not informed us much. "The Roman Catholics have bishops in Cape Town and Graham's Town, and support large charitable and educational establishments. But their work lies chiefly among the European population, of whom they reckon 8346 among the number of their adherents. The native converts are only 181. They are subsidised by Government to the extent of £1000 annually. The cathedral was completed more than seven years ago at a cost of several thousand

* Allgemeine Missions Zeitschrift, 1874, page 202.

pounds."* In Natal, the Roman Catholic colonists have also a respectable position, and they have of late established some superior schools. As regards Missions, in few parts of the world do they seem to have made less progress. In Basuto land—their Mission is very limited—the Christians of the Book, as the Protestants are called from their use of the Bible, having the entire predominance. I have already referred to a recent Mission sent to Pella, a deserted station of the London Missionary Society and of the Rhenish Mission. When the missionaries arrived, we are informed, " the Rev. Father Pasquerina said holy mass without clerk or congregation within four ruined walls, exposed to every wind, his portmanteau serving him for an altar."† After a little, the prospects of the Mission seem to have grown somewhat brighter. We have no definite statistics to give as to the number of native Roman Catholics in South Africa.

* Silver & Co , South Africa, p. 263.
† Annals of the Propagation, 1875, page 248.

CHAPTER XXVI.

SOUTH AFRICAN EVANGELISATION IN CENTRAL AFRICA.

IT seems to me suitable, in bringing to a close this sketch of South African Missions, to notice those evangelistic efforts which have their basis there, and which are designed and organised to occupy the great Central African field. It has been our aim throughout to show how South African Missions have been all moving northwards in their mission enterprise; and a notice thus of what is being begun by them in Central Africa seems a suitable sequel to what has gone before. It is but a commencement, and yet we may anticipate, with God's blessing on it, great future results. But it is quite beyond our purpose to notice all the mission work now being expended on Central Africa. This would be for us to enter on quite a new field. We cannot thus attempt even an outline of the important and self-denying labours of Bishop Stere of the University Mission. It is true, the deeply regretted Bishop Mackenzie of the same mission was at an earlier time engaged in Natal in the South African field; but we presume the present basis of the Society's operations is Zanzibar, or other Central African stations. For the same reason we cannot notice the mission fields of the Church of England Missionary Society at Uganda and elsewhere —sown already with the blood of martyrs—and our notice can be but casual also of the Mission of the Established Church of Scotland at Blantyre, near the Shiré.

The only two Central African Missions which have their basis properly in South African Evangelism, are those of the Free Church * and the London Missionary Society. The former has taken Lake Nyassa as its field of work, the latter the more distant Lake Tanganyika—both lakes intimately associated with the memory of Dr. Livingstone. I would shortly sketch the Mission plans they have devised for this work, the agencies they have employed, and the measure of success which has accompanied their Mission enterprise.

It is some seventeen years ago since the Rev. James Stewart (now better known as Dr. Stewart of Lovedale) offered his services to commence Missions "somewhere in those internal territories laid open by Lr. Livingstone. He actually joined Dr. Livingstone in his second expedition, and penetrated a considerable way up the Zambesi and Shiré rivers. Dr. Stewart has since been greatly occupied at Lovedale, but he never laid aside the hope of helping to establish a Mission in or near the centre of Africa." It was he who, when the Free Church contemplated a Mission in Central Africa, strongly

* As regards the Free Church, we may notice that the Reformed Presbyterian Church equally shared in the formation of this Mission, but since that time the Free Church and it have been incorporated. May I add that the U.P. Mission, while not formally sharing in the Mission, has given to it good help. I shall have occasion to notice this more fully.

recommended Lake Nyassa, and that the station should be called Livingstonia in commemoration of the illustrious dead.

Engrossed at the time by work at Lovedale and Blythswood, Dr. Stewart could not leave South Africa to pioneer the new Mission. But an admirable agent was found for this in Mr. E. D. Young of the Royal Navy. Mr. Young had been a gunner on board the cruiser Gorgon on the East Coast of Africa; he had spent two years with Livingstone ; he had, as commander of the Livingstone Search Expedition, visited also Lake Nyassa. Confidence could be placed in him "as a man of thoroughly Christian character, great nautical skill, enterprise, spirit, and of pity for down-trodden Africa—amounting to a vehement passion."*

The proposed expedition received liberal support in Scotland. A steam launch was built for the Mission, to be launched on the waters of the Nyassa. It was formed of steel plates in such form that each section could be separated so as to form a load for an individual bearer. This was necessary, as it would need to be transported by native porters past the small cataracts of the Shiré. The small steamer, some 50 feet in length, was called the Ilala, in memory of the place where Dr. Livingstone died. The first Mission Pioneers left England in 1875, consisting of Mr. Young as leader, the Rev. Mr Laws, a Medical Missionary, with others of the Mission staff, such as a seaman, a carpenter, an agriculturist, and 2 engineers. We may say here, that Dr. Laws, who has since been of great service to the Mission, was

* Free Church Report' 1876. Livingstonia, pp. 8, 9.

lent as a missionary generously by the United Presbyterian Church to the Free Church, and they have also continued to pay his salary. Mr Henderson, of the Scottish Established Church, also accompanied the mission party to seek out a locality for their proposed station. We may add here, that the station he selected, Blantyre, has been found excellent.

Passing over the voyage, when the Mission company reached the Zambesi, the Ilala was screwed together, and they ascended in it the Zambesi and the Shiré, as far as the Murchison cataracts. It was here that Mr Young met his old friends, the Makololos; a striking and providential incident to which we have previouly referred. They welcomed him with joy, thousands lining the banks, clapping their hands, dancing and singing, saying their fathers, the English, had come back to them. Their chief also readily promised to aid them in the transport of the Ilala, which had here to be taken to pieces again. It was transported by some 650 carriers, provided by these friendly Makololos to the Upper Shiré, not a piece being lost. The falls extend some 75 miles. For this arduous work of transport, the natives were satisfied with a payment of 6 yards of calico each. The work, Mr Young says, was accomplished "without a grumble or a growl from first to last."* Reconstructing the steamer in the Upper Shiré, they now again steamed along the river for a hundred miles, and then entered the great lake Nyassa. This was on the

* I am indebted in this Mission sketch of Livingstonia, in part to a friendly and genial article entitled "Livingstonia" in the *Gentleman's Magazine*, October, 1877.

morning of the 12th October, "when the rising sun was gilding with his radiance the western mountains; which they all joyfully hailed as a type and emblem of the speedy rising of the Sun of Righteousness on that long benighted region with healing in His wings. While at worship that morning," writes Dr. Laws, "the Hundredth Psalm seemed to have a new beauty and depth of meaning in it as its notes floated over the blue waves." "All those who knew best the vast difficulties of this achievement, have been lost in hearing of it in admiration of the wonderful precision, rapidity, and success, with which the whole had been accomplished, and could only ascribe it to the special help and blessing of the God of providence and grace."* The Ilala was, I believe, the first steamer ever launched on those great Central African inland seas.

The station at Cape Maclear was then selected as forming the best temporary basis of work. It is situated in a beautiful bay at the mouth of a fertile valley, with an anchorage for small vessels, before an island opposite. After being settled, a tour of circumnavigation of the great Lake was made by Mr. Young and some of the party. This was in part to let the tribes know of their arrival, and to prepare them thus for closer intercourse in the future. They found the Lake to be longer than Dr. Livingstone had supposed. Its length is about 370 miles, with a coast-line of about 800 miles. It bends also further to the west than Dr. Livingstone had conjectured. According to the latest observations, the distance from the northern shore of

* Report, Free Church, Livingstonia, p. 15.

Lake Nyassa, to the southern shore of Lake Tanganyika, which lies nearly in the same parallel, may be 190 miles, while to Kilwa, the nearest port in the Indian Ocean, it may be 300 miles.* The voyagers found in their cruise many delightful spots, and pretty islands, and at the N.E. end, a noble mountain-range, from 10,000 to 12,000 feet in height. There, we shall hope may be found in the future a sanatorium for the missionaries, a necessity we should think in Central Africa, as it is in India, for European constitutions. Various tribes occupy the shores, but we can notice only the Maviti who are found at the northern end of the Lake, and also in the west. The Mission, we may say, has, by its information, confirmed the evidence that these tribes are of South African origin.

In this voyage, the Mission party had some opportunity of witnessing the wretched scenes and horrors of slavery. Here walking at one beautiful spot over bleached skeletons, Mr. Young could not help exclaiming, "Surely the devil has had possession of this land long enough." He writes with the frankness of a sailor, " I have strictly complied with your instructions, and have not interfered with the slave trade, but I hope to do it some day, and I don't think there is one of the gentlemen in the Committees in Scotland, I may say, if he had seen the heart-rending and revolting scenes that I have done, but would like to do the same."† Let us hope that so happy a day for Nyassa is at hand ; yet even for

---

* I gather this from a paper read by Mr. Stevenson of Glasgow, at the last meeting of the British Association, in Dublin.
† Free Church Report, 1876. Livingstonia, p. 41.

the hastening on of this bright issue, it cannot be doubted, that the Free Church acts wisely in enjoining on its missionaries and agents in Central Africa the greatest prudence, the avoidance of all threats, and the duty of shunning conflict with arms, save in self defence. The experience of Livingstone has shown what wonderful results, Christian conciliation can in the end accomplish.

Mr. Young continued his valuable services to the Mission at the Lake for a year. The site he chose for a station, even if it be not permanently occupied, may be useful as a centre, accessible from a great extent of coast, and it is excellently adapted as a place of anchorage for the Ilala. Mr. Young succeeded also in suppressing feuds among the native tribes, and in entering into friendly relations with their chiefs for the suppression of the slave trade. M'Ponda, the chief on whose grounds the Mission is settled, admitted that he dealt largely in slaves; but pleaded that by traffic in ivory and slaves he could alone buy cloth and other necessaries from the coast. Mr. Young remarks "that this simple avowal lies at the root of the whole of the East African Coast slave trade." Now, however, his stay was drawing to a close, as the period of leave of absence granted to him by the Admiralty approached its end. But before that time came, Mr. Young was able to meet and to welcome a second mission expedition sent out to strengthen the cause. This consisted of Dr. Black, a medical missionary, with some other Mission labourers. These were met at Delagoa Bay by Dr. Stewart of Lovedale, accompanied by four native Christian agents, who had been carefully trained at Lovedale, and were now on their way as volunteers to aid the Mission work on Lake Nyassa. This last incident may appear one of no great significance—and yet how momentous and happy may be the ultimate consequences of the sons of South Africa carrying the gospel thus to the races of the centre—to tribes akin to them, to countries which their fathers probably passed through, on their southern emigration long centuries ago. I may add that to this missionary party there were united also the agents of the Scottish Established Church. These separated from the Free Church missionaries at the Shiré, to reach their own new station established at Blantyre.

The continued claims of Lovedale on Dr. Stewart did not permit him to remain at Livingstonia except for a limited time. Still, the period was sufficient for the organisation of the Mission—which owes, also, much of its progress to Dr. Laws. The natives have gradually acquired confidence in the Mission and the missionaries. Some 200 have settled down at the station, the population is constantly increasing, and is likely indeed to do so. Direct Mission work is carried on both on Sundays and week-days. The attendance at divine service on four successive Sundays last March, averaged about 240 at three separate services in two localities. The attendance at school is 32, and some of the first scholars were the sons of the Makolo chiefs. The boys, as at Lovedale, take their share in the industrial and out-door work. The agricultural agents also report favourably, although most of the efforts with foreign seed have been necessarily experimental. Still, a fair measure of success has been gained, and the growth of wheat proved possible. Among the various plants tried at Livingstonia, it is interesting to know that the Eucalyptus, which now flourishes so well in South Africa, has succeeded here also. "In the carpentry department a very considerable amount of useful work has been done. All the members of the permanent staff, also, are men earnest, practical, and hard working, and have thoroughly at heart the real and ultimate objects of the Mission."*

We have already remarked that the station at Cape Maclear may probably not remain the permanent centre of the Mission. "Our readers are aware," says Dr. Stewart, "that the original site of 1875 has not been found satisfactory. Its position, though favourable as a harbour, is otherwise unsuitable. It is not high enough in position—its soil is poor and the area small; its capability of sustaining a large population is therefore limited. There is no permanent stream near the station, and therefore no means of irrigation; and, worst of all, there exists the tsetse."† It seems also, that being low, it is unhealthy and feverish, to which cause, we presume must be attributed the deaths of two valuable missionary labourers—Dr. Black and Shadrach Inquinana.

A second exploration of the Lake Nyassa has been made, at the head of which was Dr. Stewart with Dr. Laws. This was partly to select another

---

* For these Mission facts I am mainly indebted to the published statements of Dr. Stewart and Mr. Stevenson.
† Free Church Mission Report, 1878, p. 49.

site, which will probably be on the west of the lake, but the exact spot has not yet been finally decided. The Mission party were accompanied in their voyage so far by Captain Elton, H.M. Consul at Mozambique, Mr. Cotterill, and some other friends who were received as guests. They wished to make an overland journey from the head of the Lake, and were landed with this object at Rombashi.* During this circumnavigation of the Lake, intercourse was commenced with the natives of this northern region, especially at the embouchure of the Kambwe and of the Rombashi. As might be expected the excitement at the first appearance of white men dropping so suddenly upon them was very great. Following Livingstone's plan they thought it better to pave the way for future visits which they can make at any time, than to push on while the people were in this state.

They specially cultivated friendly relations with the natives who command the first part of the

* This expedition was in its land journey unfortunate. They found themselves plunged speedily into the midst of a fierce native conflict in which a good many lives were lost. Mr. Cotterill states that although they fired to intimidate the assailing savages, it was over their heads into the air. Captain Elton unhappily died on the journey, subsequent to this, we presume, from the effects of great fatigue and a broiling sun. In him the cause of East African exploration has suffered a serious loss. We may say that this unhappy conflict with the natives has given rise to some discussion in the Press: the friends of the Mission fearing that this affray in which white men took a part, who had voyaged with them, would paralyse for a time their efforts to approach this part of the Lake. It may also, they fear, interfere with Mr. Keith Johnston's Geographical Expedition. The truth is, there will need to be some careful adjustment in such instances, so that those who are permanently engaged in promoting civilizing and christianising objects, may not be endangered in their efforts by those making passing visits for scientific objects or other ends.

route to Lake Tanganyika. With the co-operation of the natives a good route might be established through the valley which leads to it; and by a third steamer placed on that Lake there might be communications opened for a distance of 1200 miles, and a nearer approach might be made to the centre of the habitable region of Africa. On the other side of the Lake Nyassa, they understood "that a valley apparently separating the Livingstone and Konde mountains stretches in a south-westerly direction." If this is confirmed, it may prove the most convenient line for reaching the coast about Kilwa or Lindy.*

On the departure of Dr. Stewart, the Mission remained under the charge of Dr. Laws, with whom is associated Mr. J. Stewart, C.E. The attention of the latter has been directed to the construction of a route where the navigation of the Shiré is interrupted by the rapids. He has begun a road with good gradients, which will greatly facilitate both commerce and travelling. A steam launch has also been got ready, to sail up the Zambesi to the rapids—intrusted to the care of the Messrs Moir, who are to conduct navigation and trade for an independent Company in Glasgow, called The Livingstonia Central African Company (Limited). "The object in view, it need scarcely be said, is rather co-operation in the civilisation of the country, than

* We quote here again from a Paper read by Mr. Stevenson to the Geographical Section of the British Association. In reference to Kilwa, I may add that Mr. Stevenson has published valuable notes on the country between Kilwa and Tanganyika. James Maclehose, Glasgow, publisher. The Kilwa route may become important as an alternative one, not only to Lake Nyassa but to Lake Tanganyika.

money making." The communications are thus becoming ever easier with South Africa. Dr. Stewart informs us, that in his downward voyage "there was little more than 17 days' actual travel, between Livingstonia and Natal, even including a five days' voyage in a canoe." This is, we may say, not only a marvel in Central Africa; even in South Africa, with slow waggon travelling, it would be quite surprising. But far more interesting to us than all this rapidity of travel—is the fact, that Dr. Stewart took back with him to Lovedale, five boys of Central Africa, to receive there a thoroughly Christian education and training, and thus to be prepared one day to be the Evangelists of the Lake Nyassa. How happy and close a bond of union may thus unite the Centre and the South. At the same time, we must not be too sanguine. "It is not safe," as Dr. Stewart says, "to venture on any prediction, or too confident forecast of what may be the general future history of this Mission; that lies in God's hands, and He can, and will without doubt, order things for the best, though that may not appear to us at the time."*

The expedition of the London Missionary Society has not been so favoured by circumstances as that to the Lake Nyassa—the preparations for which, besides, began at an earlier period. The Lake Tanganyika, being also so much further inland, was necessarily more difficult to reach. There are not, also, those great facilities, which water carriage affords, and the advantages of which, as regards Livingstonia, are increasing. It is to

* Free Church Mission Report, 1878, p. 48.

be hoped that Mr. Keith Johnston, in his expedition to the Lakes, may discover some road to unite the Nyassa and the Tanganyika. An accomplished engineer, such as Mr. J. Stewart, might also surely contribute to this. With a distance of, perhaps, 190 miles, the journey should not be so difficult to accomplish, and it would afford to the London Missionary Society an alternative route, by the Zambesi. More than this, it might ultimately bring Tanganyika very near the South African Missions of the London Missionary Society. Their stations in Matabeleland will, we trust at no distant day, stretch on to Mashonaland, with its rich resources in gold and in fertile lands. From thence, the voyage to the Shiré, to the Nyassa, to the Tanganyika, would occupy but a limited time. How near thus, the southern basis of operations might be brought to those wider mission fields, the Tanganyika must open up!

The directors of the London Missionary Society, to obtain correct information as to the best way of expediting their mission to Tanganyika sent the Rev. R. Price, an experienced South African Missionary, to pioneer the way. He landed at Zanzibar. It naturally occurred to him as a South African, that the system of bearers for transport was a very burdensome one. Could not the South African waggon be introduced? No doubt a waggon Colony is a somewhat slow affair compared with a higher civilisation, yet it is greatly in advance of Central African barbarism. He tried the experiment from Zanzibar, to discover if this method were possible, and having made an experimental excursion to Mpwapwa, which he reached in twenty-six days, he was sanguine as to this means of travelling for the missionaries to the Lake Tanganyika. The mission board at home readily accepted this report, which indeed promised, if successful, to initiate a happy revolution, as regards travelling in Central Africa. They shaped out a plan for the establishment of a Mission with five English Missionaries and a building assistant, to be provided with two years' stores, and to be transported by a waggon train. The Rev. Mr. Thomson, an experienced South African Missionary, was added to Mr. Price with four others, forming a Mission staff of six. Three of them started from England directly for Zanzibar, three again went by the Cape and Natal, and brought with them a number of valuable oxen, with some twelve Kaffir drivers. The expedition having arrived at Zanzibar, proceeded, after careful preparations, on its journey. It did not, however, succeed so well as had been anticipated, either with the waggons or the oxen. The truth is, first expeditions, especially if it be land travelling, rarely do. The carts with their stores were found to be overloaded, the oxen were weak, the drivers became ill, and the expedition had unfortunately thus to retrace its steps. It was evident that the supplies of the Mission were more bulky than had been supposed, and that the carrying power was too limited. Part of the supplies were therefore left behind, and the expedition resumed its way. But still there were many difficulties experienced —troublesome gullies, long, thick, and wiry grass, steep ascents, heavy showers, deep waters. The reception, however, the Missionaries met with on the part of the natives, made in part, sends for these trials. They welcomed them with kindness and hospitality, and were beyond measure astonished at this new mode of travelling—houses on wheels, as the Kaffirs in South Africa call them. Again, however, the Mission party was forced to divide—one, with Mr. Thomson at its head remaining at Kirasa, a station in a healthy position about 40 miles east of Mpwapwa. Mr. Price, with two others, then went back again to the coast to bring up some more supplies. Both parties, we may notice, here began to complain of considerable losses—Mr. Price and his Mission associates, Mr. Thomson also with his staff. One or two of the Kaffirs died; and of the valuable oxen, bought at Natal, and on the coast, out of 115, not 20 survived. The Missionaries were not agreed as to the causes of this, but Mr. Kirk, the British Consul, gave it as his decided opinion that the source of the mischief was the tsetse fly. This is so far discouraging as it would seem to exclude the use of waggons in Central Africa, but the localities may be limited which are plagued with the tsetse, and may yet, with due precaution, be passed in safety. Mr. Price and his colleagues did not linger on the coast, but having engaged some 116 bearers, carried back with them a large amount of stores. There was now a serious consultation on the part of the brethren as to what should be done to carry out the expedition. There was the impracticability of relying on oxen, and the expense, on the other hand, of bearers, if all their stores were to be taken on. It was decided, in these circumstances, that before adopting any new steps, after the rainy season should close they should first consult the Directors, and they authorised Mr. Price, with this view, to return to England. Meanwhile the brethren remaining encamped, benefited by the healthy air of their pleasant camp.

The question which Mr. Price now came to place before the Directors was this: Should there be established a line of stations on the way to Lake Tanganyika as in the Nguru valley, at Usugara, at Mpwapa and the like, to occupy these step by step, and to devote to them a considerable number of men; or would the last mentioned station and Mirambo's town be sufficient as intermediate points before the Lake was reached? The Directors, we think, wisely decided on the latter course. The former, in the judgment of the Committee, was tantamount to an indefinite abandonment of the original purpose for which the funds of their friends were distinctly contributed. They have, accordingly, instructed Mr. Thomson, with three other of the Missionaries, to press on, and they hope that they may be able to complete the journey to Lake Tanganyika during the season, leaving this, however, to their discretion. One of the Missionaries, on account of his health, retired. Mr. Price having been for a time withdrawn for a special purpose from his proper work in South Africa, now returns to it with the cordial expression of the appreciation by the Directors of his zeal and energy in the cause.*

The Missionaries have sent messengers to Mirambo, the powerful chief of the Wanyamwezi, they hope to cross the Ugogo before the end of the rainy

* The statement I have given is an imperfect *résumé* based on the Reports of the London Missionary Society for 1877 and 1878.

U

season. This next stage of their journey exceeds 300 miles in length, and passes on far to the northwest of Unyanyembe. I am sure my readers will say Amen to the prayer closing this part of the Report, "God speed them in their purpose, and grant them a wide and effectual door in carrying the Gospel to the tribes among which it has not yet been preached."*

* London Missionary Society Report for 1878, p. 74.

CHAPTER XXVII.

STATISTICAL RÉSUMÉ.

I HAVE thus attempted to glance round the wide Mission fields of South Africa. There are many thoughts which such a survey may suggest, as for instance, one may ask what has been the numerical success of all these Mission operations. This is a poor criterion indeed of the higher value of Mission work. Still it may have its place. We may ask thus how many Missionary labourers are engaged in the field? what native agencies are co-operating? how many native pastors have been raised up? how many communicants are there in the churches, and how many baptized members? how many children in the schools? and how many higher educational and industrial institutions have been established? I have attempted to answer these inquiries so far as my information enabled me in connection with the individual Missions, and I had contemplated giving a summary also of the general results—drawn from the reports of the various Mission Societies. I have, on mature reflection, decided, however, not to venture on anything farther than a very general résumé, and my reasons for this are the following. First, the statistics given by the Societies differ so much as to details. Some of the Societies afford the most scanty information in their reports as to such Mission statistics as the number of labourers in the field, the native agencies employed, the number of native children in the schools, etc., etc. Others again afford very copious details, as the Wesleyan Society, the Basuto, German, Presbyterian, and American Missions, etc., but it is somewhat tantalizing to find that where one Mission is very full in its details, the statistics of another are quite scanty, and *vice versa*. There is a still more formidable difficulty than this in giving detailed results. Neither the S.P.G., nor the Wesleyans, nor the South African Dutch Church, so far as I have been able to ascertain, separate distinctly in their reports their Colonial from their Mission adherents. It is only, in fact, by a careful comparison of the statistics, furnished by the Cape Blue Book on religious denominations, etc., that an approximation can be reached on the subject. I must confine myself, therefore, to a very general summary, even after having prepared a somewhat elaborate table of details, which I had intended to offer.

May I suggest that it may well form a part of the business of the approaching general conference on Missions, in London, to draw up a carefully prepared schedule of mission inquiries, on some such system as that of Dr. Mullens in connection with Indian Mission statistics. He has admirably led the way, and his elaborate reports go, I may say, much further than mere mission statistics. They give information and insight, into the progress of native society, educationally, socially, and morally.*

It will have been noticed, from the preface to this volume, that my more special commission was to report on the Mission and Colonial Churches, represented at the Presbyterian Council. But to limit myself to these would have given no adequate idea of South African mission work. Besides the interests of the various Evangelical societies are so gathered up into the one bundle of life, that we must deeply feel for each and all. At the same time, the duty was definitely imposed on me, of reporting on the Churches and Missions represented at the Presbyterian Council. This will explain the classification I now give.

The native adherents of the Churches and Missions, represented at the Presbyterian Council, including the Dutch Church, the Free and United Presbyterian Churches, the Berlin and Rhenish Missions, with the Basuto and French Missions, may be estimated at 78,000, and the communicants of these Churches, at a number approaching 16,000.

The other Evangelical Societies, in which we include the United Brethren, the London Missionary Society, the Wesleyan Missions, the American Board, the Hermannsburg and Norwegian Missions have proximately 82,000 adherents, with 15,000 communicants.

* Why, may I venture here to suggest, should we not have a Mission Year Book, as we have a Statesman's Year Book, giving a condensed but suggestive summary of the Mission statistics of the world? I am told it has been tried, but has failed; but all depends on the way in which such an idea is carried out. Might I suggest, that to furnish such a volume to the Christian world would be an attempt worthy of the Religious Tract Society? Brought out under their auspices, the greatest fairness and impartiality would be secured.

The Anglican South African Church has, probably, 20,000 native adherents, with some 4000 communicants.*

The total for South Africa based on these statistics, is the following—180,000 native adherents, of whom 35,000 are communicants. The baptized members are probably at least the double of the latter. If we look at the native population, generally reached by the Missions in their kraal and village preaching, the amount may be safely calculated at a quarter of a million. Beyond these, the Christian Missions have a wide and growing influence over the native population, even where these do not come so directly or continuously into mission contact.

Christianity, it will be thus seen, has made very considerable progress in South Africa, and this great extension dates, we may add, from little more than half a century ago. South Africa ranks second only in numbers to India, although the agencies employed have been far less numerous. But the reason of this is readily seen. In India Christianity has to contend with an ancient compacted civilisation, with which its gigantic superstitions are so intertwined, that to separate them seems almost to rend life away. It is only indeed because Christianity is mighty to the pulling down of strongholds, that it has made those conquests it has won in India. In South Africa, on the other hand, Christianity and

---

* As to the Roman Catholic Church, there are no reliable statistics. In South Africa its missions are limited. The Cape Blue Book gives the native converts as 181; adding other Missions, such as that in Basutoland it is to be presumed the total will scarcely exceed 2000.

civilisation are one, and the attractions of both are combined. The thinking native readily appreciates this double advantage, especially when he sees Christian men like the Missionaries approaching him in so kindly, generous, and loving a spirit, and when he witnesses the quiet, peace, order and sanctities of a Christian home. Insensibly his deeper sympathies are thus won, and he is more open to the divine influences of the Gospel. These successes of half a century are full of promise for the future. We may anticipate that with God's blessing and the Spirit's grace, the Gospel will advance at an ever augmenting ratio, until the mighty millions of Central, as well as of Southern Africa, rally to the Cross.

The information, as I have already stated, that I was requested to furnish, related to South Africa, not only in its Mission, but also in its Colonial aspects. I do not regret this extension, I have already noticed how Colonial Christianity and Missions go hand in hand.

The Statistics which I have been able to gather regarding this, are the following—The number of Colonial adherents belonging to the Churches, represented at the Presbyterian Council, amount to 252,000. This arises from the greatly preponderating numbers of the Dutch South African Churches,—the adherents of which may amount to 240,000. The Wesleyan Society again, in South Africa, may embrace some 50,000 Colonial adherents, and if to these we add the other Evangelical Churches, not included already in our enumeration, the number may be 60,000. The South

African Anglican Church may be estimated at 35,000, and the Roman Catholic Church at 11,000. This would give a total of 358,000 Christian Colonial adherents. Were we to add to them again, the native Mission adherents, the total would be 538,000, in South Africa, making some Christian profession. This is probably a sixth of the whole population of South Africa up to the Zambesi.

Before passing from these statistical details, I wish to notice the valuable co-operative agencies which have so much helped the Mission cause in South Africa as everywhere else. I refer especially to two great Societies, the British and Foreign Bible Society, and the Religious Tract Society. The British and Foreign Bible Society has contributed with its usual large liberality to the work of Bible translation and publication in South Africa. Translations of the Scriptures have been made in the Bechuana, Herero, Namaqua, Basuto, Kaffir and Zulu languages. The entire Bible has been translated into three languages, the Basuto, Bechuana, Kaffir. The total number of copies of the Scriptures issued in these languages amounts to 75,000. Besides these, large numbers of copies of the Dutch Bible have been circulated among the Boers and the Hottentots of the Cape. Bibles in English and other languages have been sent to the Diamond and the Gold Fields. The British and Foreign Society has an efficient auxiliary in South Africa at Capetown, but the Colonists generally might be justly asked to increase their contributions to this valuable Institution.

The Religious Tract Society also gives very liberally to the cause both of Colonial and Mission Christianity in South Africa. A very large number of useful Christian publications have been issued by its aid in the Bechuana, Kaffir, Basuto and Dutch languages. The Pilgrim's Progress, to take an example, has been translated into Kaffir, Basuto, and Bechuana. Large grants of paper have also been made, and Missionaries and Sunday Schools supplied with English Libraries. The Society has aided, in their translation work, the London Missionary Society, the Presbyterian Missions, and the Paris Evangelical Society. Other Societies have also been probably aided, but I do not find any statement regarding these in the return kindly furnished to me. *

* The American Bible Society has also contributed, I believe, to the good work in South Africa by aiding the American Missionaries in their Zulu Translation of the Sacred Scriptures.

CHAPTER XXVIII.

CONCLUSION.

BESIDES the brief statistical résumé which we have given, there are many higher aspects in which, had our limits allowed, we might have glanced over the annals of South African Missions. These afford many interesting and striking displays of Christian character, some of which, indeed, we have already noticed, but there are many other instances which might be narrated. There is, for instance, the deep martyr-like cross-bearing of a Georg Schmidt, the lofty Christian chivalry of a Van Der Kemp; there is the bold championship, by Dr Philip, of the cause of the oppressed Hottentots; there is the courageous defence of the Gospel by a Merensky against all the cruel threats and persecutions of the Bapedi chief Sekukuni. There is Coillard, even now bravely encountering all the perils of the wilderness, and the threats of savage chiefs, with the same high intrepidity which has so marked, in the past, many of the Missionaries. And among the native converts too, many fine instances of Christian character might be found. There is Africaner, once wild as the savage beasts that prowled around his kraal, yet entirely in the end subdued to the Gospel. There is the great chief Moshesh feeling humbly and deeply in his dying days that he is but a little child. There is the cultivated, refined Tyo Soga, dying in Christian peace, while his father the hoary Kaffir chief perishes in his blood. There is the fine courage and zeal of such native Christian Evangelists as Aser and Bethuel, and there is the holy loving activity of a Wilhelmina Stompjes, and these are, after all, but a few representative names of so many. We have already given some higher instances even, as in a Livingstone or a Moffat. In no sphere of work, does more perhaps hinge on the individual, than in the field of the Missionary, his firm faith, his sagacity and tact, his holy decision and courageous resolve. While we are no admirers of hero-worship, yet the triumphs of the Gospel in Mission Fields have often been won by a heroism as lofty as was ever displayed in the battle field. Of some of the great Missionaries it may be almost literally said, "They subdued kingdoms, obtained promises, wrought righteousness, escaped the edge of the sword." When we recall a fierce Moselikatze, so tamed in the presence of the Missionary, or of others, quiet, subdued, and submissive to the Gospel, may we not say, that in a higher almost than even a literal sense, "They have stopped the mouths of lions." The story of these Missions furnishes, too, had we time to tell it, a wonderful history of trials and sufferings, borne with noble Christian magnanimity, not only by the Missionaries themselves, but by their more delicate wives, and their young children. All those extremities the hundred and seventh Psalm so pathetically depicts have befallen them. "Hungry and thirsty, their souls fainting in them; wandering in the desert in a solitary way, finding no city to dwell in." But theirs have also been brighter experiences. Their toils in the heat and burthen of the day have been civilising and christianising. We may say of the happy results, " He turneth the wilderness into a standing water, and dry ground into water springs. And there maketh He the hungry to dwell, that they may prepare a city for habitation, and sow the fields, and plant vineyards, which may yield fruits of increase."

Leaving these memories of the past behind us, we would say something, before closing, as to the future of South Africa. And we shall venture to go here somewhat beyond Mission questions, feeling that all the higher interests in South Africa are so closely bound together. We would look, as it were, at the complex of South African problems, which are pressing for solution, and which indeed, but for the great Eastern Question, would have attracted far greater attention on the part of the British public, than they have received.

The position of South Africa is one which we think may be regarded without alarm, as to the ultimate future, but it is still full of anxiety for the present. It is a period of remarkable suspense, the immediate issues of which it is difficult to anticipate. The tribes in British Kaffraria, and in Kaffraria itself, have been subdued, but the state of the Pondas, and our relations to Umquikela, can scarcely be regarded as yet without anxiety. There is again the conflict, not yet settled, to the north of the

Diamond Fields, there is the undoubted discontent of many of the Boers of the Transvaal, and there is the open conflict with Sekukuni. All these are indeed lesser sources of alarm. Beyond these, there is the thunder cloud which seems gathering in Zululand to the north of Natal, threatening a fiercer storm, more destructive, it may be, than any we have yet witnessed. We may hope that, by wise and vigorous policy, a war with the Zulus may be averted; but this is a great uncertainty. It hangs on the will of an arbitrary and savage ruler. The question with Cetywayo is one ostensibly of frontiers, and this may possibly be solved. But if so, without a more definite understanding as to the future, there will still remain anxiety and perturbation. To allow this would mean simply a continuous chronic state of disquietude. We fear that an end can be put to this only by Cetywayo accepting in good faith the British Protectorate, or by the decision of war. Bishop Colenso writes in a recent letter to the Natal Press: "An annexation of Zululand, if unjust, and therefore wicked, would assuredly bring down on us a divine retribution." For our own part we should expect such a retribution to befall us, if we allowed a barbarous chief on our frontier, against his most solemn pledges given to us, to murder his people, to put to death Christian converts, only because they are Christian, to pursue poor fugitives, who had escaped from his territory, and to seize them and shoot them in cold blood. Cetywayo has been guilty of atrocities far worse than the Bulgarian. A civilised and paramount power cannot escape, either in India or in Africa, from the assertion of its supremacy. The princes of the one, and the chiefs of the other, as they enjoy the security our power affords, must so far accept civilised control. This need not and ought not to end in the crushing of their nationality, but only in the suppression of violent excesses, and bloodthirsty cruelties. I think that in this general statement I express the mind of many, at least, of the South African Missionaries. They are warmly attached to the natives, earnestly desirous of their deliverance from the dangerous evils which threaten them, most wishful for their progress and advancement, but deeply conscious, at the same time, that to commit the native population of South Africa to the savageness of native tyranny, is to endanger their existence, and is utterly inconsistent with their advancement.

But passing from these general considerations, even if tranquillity be again re-established, as we are assured it will, it is a question which must occupy the attention of all interested in South Africa, what remedial measures are to be adopted ?

One of these, it seems to me, must be better arrangements for maintaining the peace of the Colonies in future. There have been six Kaffir risings now, and each of them has found us unprepared. Either there were not British forces enough, or the Colonial contingent was not well organised, and the result was the invasion of savages ravaging with fire and sword, the sacrifice of valuable lives, the destruction of many Colonial homes, and the loss of valuable property to the extent of millions. Surely all this indicates that if Colonial life in the future is to be safe and property to be secure, more energetic measures are needed. In India it is proposed to have a system of insurance to secure against famine,—in South Africa there ought to be, if possible, a Colonial insurance against savage raids. It is a plain necessity to meet this peril, that there be larger and more disciplined forces. Great Britain will no longer afford this aid; the South African Colonies, if they are wise, must therefore make provision for it. We submit our view with all deference. It seems to us to be required that if the Colonies would guard from violence all that is most precious to them, every Colonist must be trained to arms. In the Cape Colony a movement has been wisely made in this direction, but it ought to include all the Colonies. An elaborate military system, such as that of Germany or France, is plainly not required against savage tribes. Perhaps the militia law of Switzerland would be more suitable. It will not be gathered from this opinion that we favour offensive war, but defensive war for our homes and hearths we still hold to be an imperative Christian duty.

Another measure ought certainly to be the disarmament of the natives. This has been so far secured in Natal and the Free State; but it has not been the same in the Cape Colony. To allow arms to savages liable to such frenzies of passion as the Galekas in 1857, is as dangerous as to place them in the hands of a madman. It will be no very easy thing, indeed, to effect this disarmament. A gun is to a native the pride and passion of his life. If his cattle are his real estate, his gun is the great embellishment of his wealth. The possession of guns, too, inspires the natives, who know nothing of the art of war, with the idea that they are the equals of the Colonial and European forces. And this often precipitates conflict. It may possibly lead Cetywayo to brave the European forces.

Another vast amelioration will be that suggested by Sir Bartle Frere in his opening speech to the late Cape Parliament, "the abolishing what remains of the tribal system within the Colony, by refusal to recognise any power of native chiefs, which is not derived from the Colonial Government." This does not mean that native chiefs may not retain a certain place, but that their authority is to be held as based on British Sovereignty. This is a measure needed, not so much, we may say, even in the Cape, as in Natal. In the former the European magistrates have long held the power of the chiefs in restraint and in subordination. In Natal, from the fact of the European magistrates not being established in the locations, it has been, to a considerable extent, in abeyance. But in Natal also, now, the native locations are being opened up, and justice is being administered directly by a colonial magistracy. We would add to this, that if the paramount power of civilisation is to be maintained, the tribes adjacent to the Colonies, but not incorporated with them, must be placed, as we have already said, under a British Protectorate, with a resident located in each, just as we have in India at the courts of the native princes, to see that native law is administered in harmony with the principles of civilisation and justice.

But I think the most important measure to be now adopted, is a speedy enactment giving to the natives personal rights to land. The tribal system of land-tenure is miserable. It gives no support to that great law, teaching us the sacredness of toil,— "In the sweat of thy face thou shalt eat thy bread." The lands under tribal tenure are merely squatted on, not properly and carefully cultivated, and hence, too, when under our peaceful rule, there being no devastating wars, native tribes rapidly grow in numbers, there is, as the Basutos expressed it at their Pitso, to which we have referred, a great hunger for land. When Christian missions have obtained grants of land, and when these have been allocated to Christian families, the same amount of acres, by careful industry, produces far more. Even when the heathen obtain such individual rights, they become vastly more industrious and civilised than in the native locations. In Natal, thus, a native will pay in his location, to government for the ground he occupies, only 14s.; for land he rents from a colonist, he will pay £2.

As regards personal land tenure, a rent system would seem to me to be better for the natives than to give them the fee-simple of land. Even in reference to Colonists there are political economists of high ability in favour of this principle, but, as regards the natives, the reasons are still more decided. It would be a great evil if the natives of South Africa learned merely to squat on the lands, as they do too often in Jamaica and other West Indian Colonies. Probably something like the ryot-warry system of Bombay, one of the best, we venture to say, in the world, would be the most suitable for them, but in the case of South Africa it would need to be adapted to the habits of a people at once agricultural and pastoral. The Swiss land tenure system might be in many things a model. Such a system, if approved, could not be entrusted to better hands to carry it out than to Sir Bartle Frere, from the intimate knowledge he possesses of the Bombay and other Indian systems of land tenure. Might I here suggest, that were such a change of land tenure made, it would be but just, not to overlook the claims of the tribal chief. We would certainly not make him, as we did the chiefs of the Highland clans, the absolute proprietor of the land, nor would we regard him as the Bengal Zemindar, a great blunder in our Indian policy; but it would only be just to grant him a liberal allotment of land to maintain his rank. It may be said, better abolish chieftainship altogether; but we question if this is just, and we cannot but think that among the Kaffirs, attached as they have been for ages to the tribal system, chieftainship may be used as a means to contribute to the elevation of the people.*

On the subject of education I have already said so much that I do not dwell on it here. In the Cape Colony an elaborate system has been formed, of schools of a higher class for secondary education. There are also mission schools, including industrial, which are liberally supported, and farm schools to meet the outlying population. The total number

* As regards personal tenure of land, Dean Green of Maritzburg, Natal, has published in the Natal Press some valuable suggestions on the subject of a Kaffir village sys'em. I think these worthy of consideration in connection with the future of the Zulu tribes.

thus educated in the Cape exceeds 40,000. In Natal Sir H. Bulwer has devoted much thought to the educational question, and the measures which have been adopted will do much, we trust, to elevate education. There is a want in Natal still of a great industrial school, like Lovedale.

While appreciating the efforts that have been made, much yet remains to be done. An extended vernacular system of education in South Africa will greatly contribute to native civilisation, especially if in the higher native schools there be industrial training and English be also taught. There is a growing desire among the natives of the better class, and their number is continually growing, to know the English language.

The encouragement of medical knowledge among the natives is greatly to be desired. The degraded witch doctors exercise a most unhappy influence on the natives. Hence the great advantage which has followed the labours of medical missionaries. Apart from these, the presence of an ordinary European medical practitioner, as one of the government staff in each of the larger native locations, would be of much value in counteracting native superstitions.

I have suggested these various remedial measures, but Christianity, with its living power, is still deeply needed in South Africa. It has a penetrative and pervasive influence, which neither secular education nor civilisation can possess. Take, for instance, the family, even if polygamy were suppressed, its abolition would do but little unless higher and purer influences were at work. If the native races of South Africa have attained to the conception of a higher ideal, they have been taught it by Christianity, especially in many instances by the mission home. It is incalculable, in fact, the happy hallowing results that have accrued to the native tribes from the presence in their midst of the mission family, with its purity, intelligence, holiness, sympathy, beneficence, and peace. Or take the Missionary himself. An African journalist has justly observed that a resident European magistracy, while valuable, will not extinguish the attachment to the hereditary chief. To exercise such an influence there is needed, not a cold intangible abstraction, but one who lives among his people, and attaches them to his person. Now this is just mission life among the native tribes. The natives know that the Missionary is their friend and their advocate for justice; that he is able by his intelligence to direct them; that he seeks not theirs, but them; and thus he has often a deeper hold on the heart of the heathen than their debased, arrogant chief, and obtains a wonderful power to mould their nature and lift them to higher aims. Then, again, as regards that dark cloud of superstition which we have described brooding over the Kaffir mind, nothing can so dissipate and scatter it as the benign light which Christianity sheds on the character of God, on the spirit world, on Providence, Redemption, and eternity. Dr. Moffat has described somewhere, with great power, the change in Africaner soon after his conversion to Christianity; how he would sit the livelong night on a great stone beneath the bright starry skies of South Africa, meditating on God and His works, and on the wonders of His providence and grace. It is this thought of Him who gives rain from heaven and fruitful seasons that raises the native Christian above the wretched juggles of the rainmaker. It is this knowledge of God and the holy agencies which surround Him, who compasses our path and our lying down, and is acquainted with all our ways, which delivers him, too, from the dread of witchcraft and its spells, and from the ghostly terror of the spirits of his ancestry. It is this divine force of Christianity which can alone grapple with the long contracted habits of debasing vice in which the savage has lived, can break the shackles of his slavery, and restore him to his right mind. It is this penetrative power that emancipates a nature trained to deceit and falsehood, and inspires it with the love of truth in the inward parts. It is thus, also, that where the God of Christianity is known as Love, and in His mission of Love the idol of selfishness is dethroned; and in place of it there comes the spirit of self-consecration and self-sacrifice, the noble impellents to a higher life. We cannot, indeed, anticipate that these higher Christian influences will be felt in all their power among Christian Kaffirs any more than among Christian colonists. Still we cannot doubt that the highest assimilating influence—that which can best bind Colonial South Africa into one—will be the extension and the power of Christianity among the native tribes.

S. COWAN AND CO., PRINTERS, PERTH.

www.ingramcontent.com/pod-product-compliance
Lightning Source LLC
Chambersburg PA
CBHW021157230426
43667CB00006B/442